THE QUEST FOR MEANING

THE QUEST FOR MEANING

OSWALD HANFLING

Basil Blackwell
in association with the
Open University

First published 1987
First published in USA 1988

Basil Blackwell Ltd
108 Cowley Road, Oxford, OX4 1JF, UK

Basil Blackwell Inc.
432 Park Avenue South, Suite 1503
New York, NY 10016, USA

British Library Cataloguing in Publication Data
Hanfling, Oswald
   The quest for meaning.
   1. Life
   I. Title   II. Open University
   128'.5   BD431

   ISBN 0–631–15332–2
   ISBN 0–631–15333–0 Pbk

Library of Congress Cataloging in Publication Data
Hanfling, Oswald
   The quest for meaning.

   Includes index.
   1. Life. 2. Self-realization. I. Title.
   BD431.H257 1988   128   87–30000
   ISBN 0–631–15332–2
   ISBN 0–631–15333–0 (pbk.)

This book forms part of an Open University course, A310 *Life and Death*. For further information about this course, please write to the Student Enquiries Office, The Open University, PO Box 71, Walton Hall, Milton Keynes, MK7 6AG, UK.

Typeset by Photo·graphics, Honiton, Devon
Printed in Great Britain by Billing & Sons Ltd, Worcester

Contents

Acknowledgements

I am grateful to Anthony O'Hear, Godfrey Vesey and members of the A310 *Life and Death* course team for helpful comments in the course of writing this book.

The author and publishers are grateful to the following for permission to reproduce material previously published elsewhere:

Chatto and Windus and the Hogarth Press and the Rilke Estate for an extract from *Duino Elegies* by Rainer Maria Rilke, trans. J.B. Leishman and Stephen Spender; Faber and Faber Ltd for an extract from 'Aubade' by Philip Larkin; David Higham Associates Ltd and New Directions Publishing Corporation for an extract from 'Do not go gentle into that good night' from *Poems of Dylan Thomas* © 1952 Dylan Thomas.

Introduction

We're not at one. We've no instinctive knowledge,
like migratory birds. Outstript and late,
we force ourselves on winds and find no welcome
from ponds where we alight. We comprehend
flowering and fading simultaneously.
(Rainer Maria Rilke, *Duino Elegies*)[1]

What is the meaning of life? The question is apt to provoke
different reactions. Some regard it as the most important
question of all, and one to which philosophers must address
themselves if they are to be worthy of their profession.
Others smile indulgently, suspecting that little good can
come out of such questions. There is something to be said
for the second view. We must not assume that a question
which sounds important admits of an answer or is even
meaningful. There is a story about the composer Sibelius
listening with a friend to a recording of his symphony.
When, finally, the friend asked, 'What does it mean?', the
composer could think of no better answer than 'Play the
record again.'

Wittgenstein remarked that what is needed in philosophy
is 'to bring words back from their metaphysical to their
everyday use';[2] and this need is as important for the present
topic as for any other. Now 'meaning' is a word with an
everyday use. What is the meaning (if any) of such and such
a word? What did she mean by her remark? What does it
mean if interest rates come down, or if the soil in the garden
is acidic? These questions may be hard to answer, but there

is no problem about the kind of answer that is being sought. But this is not so with the question about the meaning of life. The difficulty that faces us here is as if we were asked about the meaning of grass, or of the Atlantic Ocean. A similar difficulty arises about 'purpose', when it is asked what is the purpose of life. An everyday use of this word is in connection with human actions or artefacts. We ask what is the purpose of such and such an action or artefact, and expect to be told that they serve some human need or desire. But life is not an action or artefact; and it is not clear how the question about life's purpose is to be approached, or what, if anything, it means.

There are, however, other ways in which questions about meaning and purpose arise in connection with life, and in which these words have a familiar enough application. This is especially clear in the case of particular lives as opposed to life in general. For example, someone in a depressed state of mind may describe his or her life as meaningless. 'When we ask whether a *particular* person's life has or had any meaning', writes Paul Edwards, 'we are usually concerned not with cosmic issues but with the question whether certain purposes are to be found *in* his life'.[3] We may also speak of a 'sense of purpose' in one's life, as when a person complains that his or her life lacks such a sense, or tells us, with satisfaction, that such a sense is now present. Again, someone who has fallen in love may say that life is now 'full of meaning' – though he may not be prepared to say *what* that meaning is.

There are also questions about 'cosmic issues', and about the human condition in general, for which the vocabulary of 'meaning' and 'purpose' is appropriate. If we can get nowhere with 'What is the meaning of life?', we may still pursue such questions as 'Is life meaningless?' And as we shall see, various arguments have been brought forward to show that human life is, indeed, meaningless. We must also be prepared to find that when people ask or argue about the meaning of life they are giving expression to a worry that there is, to put it vaguely, 'something wrong' with human life, something unsatisfactory or inadequate about the human condition, for which the word 'meaningless' or the question

'What does it mean?' may seem appropriate. Such worries may result, for example, from a scientific contemplation of man's place in the universe, or from reflections on the inevitable decay of human works. Again, someone who accepts that a word like 'purpose' is properly applicable to activities within life, but not to life as such, may still wish that it *were* applicable to life as such – that some definite answer could be given to 'What is the purpose of life?', just as we can answer 'What is the purpose of a spade?' In this respect the religious point of view may seem to offer an advantage, for according to, for example, Christianity, human life takes place within the larger plan of a purposive God.

Someone whose life is meaningful in the 'particular' sense may still be assailed by worries about meaning in the over-all sense, and these may undermine his satisfaction with life. Tolstoy narrates that there came a time when he was plagued with questions like 'Why? Well, and then?' He concluded that these questions were unanswerable, and that his life was therefore meaningless.[4] Tolstoy's questions were not directed at particular problems. He was not asking 'Why is there serfdom in Russia?' or 'What shall I do after my next book is finished?' His questions were about life, or his life, as a whole. After the ordinary questions were answered, he still wished for a deeper purpose that would give meaning to the whole.

The first part of this book (Chapters One to Four) is about aspects of life which may seem to render it meaningless – suffering, death and difficulties about human purpose. This leads to questions about the value or 'sanctity' of life, discussed in Chapters Four and Five. One way of finding meaning in life is that of 'self-realization' – living in accordance with one's essential nature; and this is the main topic of the second part of the book (Chapters Six to Ten). It deals with recipes for 'the good life', drawn from such concepts as nature, society, happiness, reason and freedom, and reviews the claims of such thinkers as Aristotle, Rousseau, Kant, Mill and Sartre.

In this part of the book I also discuss the issue of feminism, including the question of 'gender-neutral' language (replacing 'he' by 'he or she', avoiding the use of 'man' to stand for human beings in general, and so on).

Readers of this book may reasonably hope to find in it some definite answers to the questions I have mentioned. They may wish to find out whether life is or is not meaningless, what, in general, is the best way to live, and so on. Such readers are likely to be disappointed. Much of my argument is negative, and consists in rejecting the arguments of others. It seems to me that there is no general prescription for 'the good life', though it can be shown that certain prescriptions are wrong or self-defeating. Again, some values which seem 'self-evident' can be countered by others which seem no less self-evident. (This does not necessarily mean that either is wrong.) On the question whether life is meaningless, I can find no conclusive argument to show that it is, but neither can I show that the worries behind the question are unfounded. Finally, I can offer only a sceptical answer to the question about the value of life – what this value consists in, and whether we are right to regard human life as 'sacred'.

Given these limitations, was there any point in writing the book? And why should anyone be interested in reading it? A question may be worth pursuing even without the hope of a definite or clear-cut answer. This, after all, is often the case with the great, perennial questions with which philosophers are concerned. Take, for example, the question whether there is life after death. There cannot be many people for whom this matter is of no concern. There is, therefore, a motive for studying the arguments of those who have written about it. Now, it would be satisfying if a clear 'yes' or 'no' answer could be given (though most people would be suspicious if the answer were too simple). But what if no such answers were available? This would not eliminate our interest in the question, or take away the motive for thinking about the arguments that have been put forward on one side or the other. Again, the conclusion that there is no conclusion would itself be an important one, and to have reached it would be an important step forward.

Similarly, the motive for asking questions about the meaning and purpose of life would not disappear if it turned out that no clear-cut answers could be given. We would still want to know why this is so, what kinds of arguments may be put forward, and what exactly the issues are about. I hope at least that the book will provide insights in these directions.

NOTES

1 Rilke, R. M. (1968) *Duino Elegies*, J. B. Leishman and S. Spender (trans), Hogarth Press.
2 Wittgenstein, L. (1967, 3rd edn) *Philosophical Investigations*, Blackwell, section 116, p. 48.
3 Edwards, Paul (1972) 'The Meaning and Value of Life', in *The Encyclopedia of Philosophy*, vol. 4, Ed.-in-Chief, Paul Edwards, Macmillan; reprinted in Klemke, E. D. (ed.) (1981) *The Meaning of Life*, Oxford University Press, p. 130 (page references are to Klemke).
4 Tolstoy, L. (1905 edn) *My Confession*, Leo Wiener (trans.), Dent.

CHAPTER ONE

Suffering

> Besides, why prevent people dying if death was the normal and legitimate end of us all? Did it really matter if some huckster or government clerk lived an extra five or six years? And if the aim of the medical profession was to alleviate suffering by the administration of medicine, the question inevitably arose: why alleviate suffering? For in the first place it was argued that man could only achieve perfection through suffering, and secondly, if mankind really learnt to alleviate suffering by pills and drops it would give up religion and philosophy, in which it had hitherto found not only protection from all misfortunes but even happiness. Pushkin suffered terribly before he died, and poor Heine lay paralysed for several years; why then should some Andrey Yefimych or Matryona Savishna not be ill, particularly if but for suffering their lives would be as meaningless and insipid as the life of an amoeba?
>
> Crushed by such arguments, Dr Ragin lost heart and stopped going to the hospital every day.
>
> (Chekhov, 'Ward Six')[1]

Of all the objects of human value, one is regarded as having a special importance. Human life, it is said, is the most valuable thing of all. Why should this be so? One answer is that without it there would be no human happiness. But is life more happy than unhappy? To many it has seemed obvious it is – that, for most people at least, the balance is on the positive side. Yet the opposite view has also been regarded as obvious. Hume, in the eighteenth century, could assume that the negative view would be taken for granted.

The miseries of life, the unhappiness of man, the general corruption of our nature, the unsatisfactory enjoyment of our pleasures, riches, honours – these phrases have become almost proverbial in all languages. And who can doubt of what all men declare from their own immediate experience?[2]

If this is so, what is the point of living? According to the nineteenth-century philosopher Schopenhauer, there is none, except the fear of death. In the concluding pages of his chapter 'On the Vanity and Suffering of Life', he appealed to a number of the great thinkers of the world, from Homer and Heraclitus onwards, to support his negative view. Swift, he tells us, 'early adopted the custom of celebrating his birthday, not as a time of joy, but of sadness, and of reading on that day the passage from the Bible where Job laments and curses' the day of his conception. Schopenhauer concludes, with Byron, that '"Tis something better not to be'.[3]

What are Schopenhauer's reasons for this view? Human life, he claims, is a series of disappointments. Man 'strives his whole life long after a supposed happiness which he seldom attains, and even if he does it is only to be disappointed with it.'[4] He reminds us that after the 'toil-filled years of manhood' there comes 'infirm and often wretched old age, the torment of the last illness and finally the throes of death'.[5] These negative aspects of the human condition have often been lamented; and it is easy to exaggerate their importance, forgetting what may be said on the other side. However, there is more than that to the negative view, and to Schopenhauer's arguments in particular. He draws attention to certain features of life, human life and life in general, which seem to entail that the balance really is on the negative side.

1 'WE FEEL PAIN, NOT PAINLESSNESS'

There are certain disparities between painful and pleasant experiences, from which it follows, according to Schopenhauer, that the former must be experienced to a greater extent. One of these concerns our sense of duration. 'The hours pass the more quickly the more pleasantly they are spent, and the more slowly the more painfully they are spent'.[6] It might be said that what should count is the real and not the apparent duration. But in this context the appearance is more important. If I am having a painful experience that seems to go on for hours, I shall get no comfort from the information that the duration is really, by the clock, much shorter than I took it to be. So it remains true that the balance between painful and pleasant times is adversely affected by the difference in apparent durations.

Another disparity to which Schopenhauer draws attention concerns our attitude to *absent* pains and pleasures. Here again, he claims, the balance falls on the painful side. 'We painfully feel the loss of pleasures and enjoyments, as soon as they fail to appear; but when pains cease even after being present for a long time, their absence is not directly felt, but at most they are thought of intentionally by means of reflection'.[7] Now there is such a feeling as a sense of relief after a painful experience, which Schopenhauer seems to overlook. But this compensation is of limited extent. (The story about the man who banged his head against a wall for the sake of the pleasure of stopping is, after all, only a joke.) The pleasure of relief is a short-lived reaction; and though we may later, as Schopenhauer says, think reflectively about painful experiences that we have had, we do not go on enjoying a sense of relief. By contrast, regrets about lost pleasures and enjoyments may be with us, waxing and waning, for the rest of our lives. In some people, indeed, these regrets are so intense that they find themselves wishing they had never known the happiness that they can no longer enjoy.

There are also regrets about happiness never attained as opposed to happiness lost. And here again the balance seems to be on the painful side. 'I sigh the lack of many a thing I sought.' Such regrets may be intense and permanent. But there is no corresponding positive emotion in the case of painful experiences that we never had (though obviously we would be glad not to have had them).

Schopenhauer believes that the painful side of experience predominates because painful and not pleasant experience is fundamental. 'Pain, not pleasure, is the positive thing, whose presence makes itself felt.'[8] (This, he thinks, explains why the pleasant hours pass more quickly.) He gives a number of illustrations. 'We feel pain, but not painlessness; care, but not freedom from care; fear, but not safety and security.'[9] Health, youth and freedom are 'the three greatest blessings of life', but we are not conscious of them 'as long as we possess them, but only after we have lost them; for they too are negations'.[10] Again, someone who enjoys complete health except for some minor exception will be conscious of that exception – of 'the little place where his shoe pinches' – rather than of his general health.[11]

However, these examples are not sufficient to prove that 'pain, not pleasure, is the positive thing'; for there are positive experiences which are not merely the negations of negative counterparts. The pleasure of looking at flowers, for example, does not exist merely as the contrary of *not* looking at flowers. Nevertheless, it is true that many of the things we most value (health, freedom, security) are negative. A person is healthy if there is nothing wrong with him; free, if he is not constrained, etc. Health does not obtrude itself into consciousness as pain and disability do. Looking back at good times in the past, we sometimes remark, perhaps with regret, that we did not then realize how well off we were; but pain and unhappiness could not escape notice in this way. Again, no news is good news. A day of peace in the world might be one on which nothing worth reporting had happened.

That pain and fear make themselves felt more prominently can also be understood in the light of the struggle for survival. We need these 'alarm bells' to motivate us to take urgent action. But when nothing is wrong, no urgent signals are needed.

Schopenhauer's conclusions extended also to the animal world; but he claimed that human beings are worse affected because their thought is not limited to what is present. Their predicament is 'powerfully intensified by thinking about absent and future things'. An animal, by contrast, is confined to 'present pleasures and sufferings'; its 'joys and sorrows cannot accumulate . . . as they do in man through memory and anticipation'.[12] He referred to a work by the 'philosophical painter' Tischbein, the upper part of which depicted some women whose children had been stolen from them, while in the lower part were shown sheep whose lambs had been taken away. The women displayed 'deep maternal pain, anguish and despair', but the sheep did not; their 'dull animal consciousness' did not equip them for grief of this order.[13] The suffering of man is also enhanced by the constant knowledge that death awaits him; whereas 'the animal only instinctively feels it without actually knowing of it'.[14]

Schopenhauer admitted that man's greater intellect results in gains as well as losses. Just as the human capacity for suffering was greater, so it was with the human capacity for enjoying 'intellectual pleasures' of all kinds – from 'jesting and conversation up to the highest achievements of the mind'.[15] Against this, however, must be set an affliction that is characteristic of human beings and unknown among animals in the natural state, namely, boredom.[16] This affliction played an important role in Schopenhauer's account of human life.

2 THE 'PENDULUM BETWEEN PAIN AND BOREDOM'

Happiness, according to Schopenhauer, 'is really and essentially always *negative*'.[17] As we have seen, he equated happiness (or pleasure) with such negative states as painlessness and absence of fear. But he also argued that happiness always consists in the satisfaction of desire; and that desire is itself a painful condition. Happiness, he maintained, is not something that 'comes to us originally and of itself'; it must always consist in the satisfaction of a desire;[18] and the basis of all desire is 'need, lack and hence pain'.[19] If I desire X, I may be happy when I get it. But prior to that I must have felt a need for X, and this is a painful condition. Thus, if I desire food, I may be happy when I get it; but the prior condition of hunger is a painful one.

This schema of happiness, desire, need and pain is, however, too simple to cover all cases. It is true that hunger may be a painful condition, but it is not always so. Someone

who looks forward to a meal may do so with pleasure and
without any sense of pain or unpleasantness. This may
indeed appear if he is kept waiting too long, but it need not
do so otherwise. Again, many desires have no painful
sensation (such as hunger) connected with them. Someone
who desires to go for a walk or read a certain book will not
be affected by painful sensations if his desires remain
unfulfilled.

Is it true that happiness never comes 'originally and of
itself' but only by way of satisfied desire? We are sometimes
made happy by some quite unexpected event; and there is
such a thing as feeling happy for no particular reason. It is
not clear how this kind of happiness (which admittedly has
its negative counterpart) can be fitted into Schopenhauer's
schema of happiness and desire.

Where there is desire, does this entail a need or lack? It
makes sense to speak of a desire to keep what one already
has. However, if the desire is for something one does not
have, then obviously there may be a need or lack. If I desire
X, then X is needed to fulfil my desire, and the lack of X
would prevent this fulfilment. Yet in another sense (the
sense connected with pain, as required by the argument)
there may not be any need or lack. What is needed to fulfil
my desire is not necessarily something that I need or lack
(and the absence of which must be painful for me). For
example, if I desire to go to the cinema, it does not follow
that I need to do so or would be deficient without it. (The
two senses of 'need' – what I need, and what is needed to
fulfil my desire – are reflected in the two senses of 'want',
one being equivalent to desire, and the other indicating some
lack or deficiency, as when a person is said to be wanting
in good manners or in the necessary things of life.)

The painful aspects of desire and happiness, as Schopenhauer sees them, are, however, only half the story. He holds
that one is in a bad position after, and not only before, the
satisfaction of desire. The satisfaction brings a momentary
happiness, but what then? Deprived of the spur of desire,
there comes over us 'a fearful emptiness and boredom' –
until the emergence of a new desire returns us to a phase of
pre-fulfilment pain. Thus our life 'swings like a pendulum

to and fro between pain and boredom'.[20] 'The wish is pain; attainment quickly begets satiety ... possession takes away the charm'.[21] From the intolerable burden of boredom we try to escape by 'killing time'.[22] The evil of boredom, he says, 'like its opposite extreme, famine, can drive people to the greatest excesses and anarchy'; hence '*panem et circenses* ['bread and circuses'] are equally necessary'.[23]

Here again, it is not difficult to produce objections to Schopenhauer's account. Of course it is not always true that the pleasure of a desire fulfilled is only momentary, and that 'possession takes away the charm'. Someone who acquires a beautiful object, for example, may continue to get pleasure from it all his life. Again, the pleasure of having children does not evaporate as soon as one has them (with or without previous desire). Finally, life does not contain only one desire at a time. If it did, then we might indeed feel bored between the satisfaction of one desire and the emergence of the next. The truth is, however, that we have, at any time, a variety of desires, plans, hopes, idle wishes and so on, which wax and wane from day to day, interacting in various ways with each other and with external realities.

There is, according to Schopenhauer, one way out of the weary round of pain and boredom that he describes. This is the way of 'pure knowledge, which remains foreign to all willing, pleasure in the beautiful, genuine delight in art'. But this, he says, requires rare intellectual talents, and is granted only to a few.[24] Now this may be so if we think of the higher flights of knowledge and of aesthetic pleasures of the more exclusive kind. But many aesthetic and intellectual pleasures are not of this kind. No great intellectual talents are needed to enjoy a beautiful garden or to be entertained by an interesting programme on television. There are in ordinary life many passive ways of avoiding boredom, which do not presuppose the striving to fulfil a need or desire.

Schopenhauer's account of human life is a caricature, but, like many caricatures, it contains a certain amount of truth. In some people's lives, especially, there is an important plan or project to which they devote themselves for many years; and when this is attained, the pleasure of fulfilment is soon replaced by a sense of anticlimax – as if life had 'lost its meaning'.

Again, Schopenhauer is right in regarding boredom as an important and remarkable feature of human life. Here we have a kind of gratuitous suffering, which arises just when we might have thought that a person should be content and in harmony with the world, having fulfilled his needs and desires. According to Schopenhauer, the phenomenon of boredom is proof that human life is of no value in itself. 'For if life . . . possessed in itself a positive value and real content, there would be no such thing as boredom: mere existence would fulfil and satisfy us.'[25] Boredom is a peculiarly human affliction (though, as Schopenhauer observed, it may occur in domesticated animals).[26] Human beings experience a need for 'diversion' and 'killing time'. But is time, unoccupied time, such an ogre that we must try to kill it?

Here again it must be admitted that boredom is not as widespread an affliction as Schopenhauer seems to think. Some people are quite happy to sit and do nothing, for a while at least. And as we have seen, not every satisfaction of desire is succeeded by boredom. But that boredom is an important source of human suffering, as well as of social disruption, can hardly be denied.

3   ARE SOME LIVES WORSE THAN OTHERS?

Into the bleak picture that he paints of the human condition, Schopenhauer introduces certain 'consolations'. One may, he says, derive a 'stoical indifference' to one's own ills from the reflection that the badness of human existence is unpreventable and universal.[27] This may seem small comfort to those whose ills are greater than average. But Schopenhauer argues that such differences are largely illusory, drawing attention to features of life which tend to even them out. Great suffering, he reminds us, makes us insensitive to lesser ills; and when the former is absent, the latter are magnified: then 'even the smallest vexations and annoyances torment us'.[28] The twin evils, as he sees them, of pain and boredom, are obviously not distributed equally among people of different classes; but there is a rough justice. 'Just as need and want are the constant scourge of the people, so is boredom that of the world of fashion.'[29] (In between, he adds, is the middle class, for whom 'boredom is represented by the Sunday, [and] want by the six weekdays'.)[30] Finally, the advantage of the intellectual person in being able to escape to the delights of aesthetic contemplation and 'pure knowledge' are balanced by his greater capacity for suffering; for Schopenhauer holds that, just as the greater intellect of human beings makes them able to suffer more than animals, so it is with people of greater intellect. They are 'susceptible to much greater sufferings than duller men can ever feel'; so that here again 'matters are made even'.[31]

There is also, according to Schopenhauer, a kind of internal regulator or thermostat, which prevents our 'cheerfulness or dejection' from being determined by external circumstances, such as wealth or position; 'for we come across at least as many cheerful faces among the poor as among the rich'.[32] He describes how joyfulness and its opposite may appear in us 'without any external occasion', and then attach themselves to suitable objects. This is an important observation about the emotional life of human beings. Some of our feelings are firmly based on reasons: one feels proud or angry because such and such a thing has happened, and these feelings are unintelligible unless a suitable reason can be given. Joyfulness and its opposite may also be justified by reasons. But there is such a thing as feeling joyful or dejected for no particular reason. It is indeed typical of those who *suffer* from depression that they tend to feel depressed, not when there is a good reason for it, but when reasons are lacking or insufficient. Such people will, however, see the world in a negative way, and this may lead them to find or magnify external circumstances, so as to provide a focus for their depression. And the same is true of the joyful person, who perceives the world accordingly.

In this matter, as in others, Schopenhauer's claims contain exaggeration as well as truth. That 'human cheerfulness or dejection are obviously not determined by external circumstances'[33] is an exaggeration. We sometimes have good reason to say that such and such a person has not had a happy life, has suffered more than most people, etc. We can also say this of whole communities, for example people living under oppressive regimes. It might be claimed (in accordance with the 'thermostat' theory) that such judgements are merely an outsider's view, and that compensations would always be found if we knew more about the case in question. But there is no reason to think that these compensations, whatever they are, must be such as to restore the balance. Moreover, in some cases we already know what they are, already have an inside knowledge of the life of that person, and form our judgements on this basis. Reading the diaries of Tolstoy's wife,[34] for example, we may well conclude that, all things considered, she had a very unhappy life – this being evident both from the external circumstances (her treatment by others, etc.) and her emotional condition as described in the diaries.

Again, the 'thermostat' theory is not really supported by the fact that emotional states may be independent of external circumstances. For it does not follow from this that 'matters are made even'. What we find, on the contrary, is that even in the *same* circumstances people differ in their emotional states. One person is happy by nature, another the reverse. One is disposed to 'look on the cheerful side', another is not. 'He is not a happy person' is a remark that may describe a person's inner condition as distinct from external circumstances. And there is no reason to think that inner conditions have a greater uniformity than external circumstances.

The point about inner conditions is important in evaluating Schopenhauer's argument as a whole. His main arguments are about universal aspects of human experience (such as the positive and negative sides of experience, and the relation of desire and satisfaction). But even if these arguments are accepted, they could not show that life is, on the whole and for everyone, bad. To some extent, at least, this will depend on a person's inner condition, and on whether he is disposed to see things in a good or bad light. As Wittgenstein said, 'The world of the happy man is a different one from that

of the unhappy man'.[35] Someone who has heard arguments
to show that life is, on the whole, bad (or good), may still
be inclined to feel happy (or depressed); and these feelings
must themselves be taken into account in the evaluation of
human life.

4   THE VALUE OF SUFFERING

Schopenhauer's evaluation, as we have seen, is in terms of
pain and suffering *versus* their opposites. But is suffering
necessarily bad? Great suffering has at least the advantage of
making us insensitive to lesser ills. Again, suffering may
serve to enhance, or even make possible, some of the pleasant
experiences of life. There is, after all, an important truth in
the story of the man who banged his head against a wall;
the pleasure of *not* having one's head banged simply does
not exist for those who do not follow his example. And
similar points may be made about such goods as health and
liberty. These things, as Schopenhauer observed, do not
usually enter our consciousness as vividly as their negative
(or as he would say, positive) counterparts. However,
someone who has suffered severe illness or imprisonment is
likely to experience health and liberty in a more positive
way. Moreover, these experiences would be different in *kind*
from those that are available to the person who has not
suffered. Thus suffering brings to life an enrichment which
is not merely one of quantity.

This may also be said about suffering itself as distinct
from instrumental benefits such as those just described. 'I
will drink life to the lees.' This may express a desire to
experience all that life can offer – including painful as well
as pleasant experiences. It may be said that a person who
had never suffered (supposing this were possible) would not
have had a full life.

> For in the first place it was argued that man could only
> achieve perfection through suffering ... Pushkin suffered
> terribly before he died, and poor Heine lay paralysed for
> several years; why then should some Andrey Yefimych or
> Matryona Savishna not be ill, particularly if but for suffering

their lives would be as meaningless and insipid as the life of an amoeba?[36]

Chekhov's Dr Ragin, given more and more to reflections of this kind, concluded that his own life and work, in a remote corner of Russia, were meaningless. What was the point of his working to prevent the sufferings of some peasant or other, when suffering was an essential ingredient of a meaningful life?

Now the fact that Pushkin and Heine suffered as terribly as they did does not entail that others should suffer likewise. If it is true that without suffering life would be 'meaningless and insipid', this does not mean that any amount of suffering is acceptable, or that life gains in meaning in proportion to the amount of suffering. And in general, one may agree with Dr Ragin's point and yet believe that there is far too much suffering in the world, so that the prevention and mitigation of it, in hospitals and other spheres of life, remains a worthy and meaningful activity for people to engage in. Nevertheless, the point remains that suffering is not wholly negative; and to put it only on one side of the balance-sheet would be a distortion of human values.

5 CONCLUSION

The point just made brings us to a general difficulty about the 'balance-sheet' approach to the value and meaning of life. Is there any point in living? As we have seen, Schopenhauer's arguments for the negative answer are open to various objections, and he cannot be said to have proved his case. However, this conclusion does not amount to a satisfactory resolution of the question; for it has not been shown that, contrary to Schopenhauer, life contains more happy than painful experiences. Moreover, to show this is likely to be no less difficult than Schopenhauer's negative enterprise.

But to discuss the value of life in terms of happy and painful experiences is in any case inadequate. There is more to human life than experiences, and more to an evaluation of it than the balancing of experiences. People have wishes, aims and ideals concerning things other than happy experiences; and these other things may be thought to give value and meaning to their lives. As we shall see in later chapters, various prescriptions have been given for 'the good life', and only one of them, the utilitarian, is in terms of pain and pleasure; and even here, the greatest advocate of that doctrine, J. S. Mill, found the mere balance-sheet approach to be inadequate.

NOTES

1 Chekhov, A. (1969) 'Ward Six', in *Lady with the Lapdog and Other Stories*, Penguin, p. 145.
2 Hume, David (1779) *Dialogues Concerning Natural Religion*, Bobbs-Merrill, 1970 edn, p. 82.
3 Schopenhauer, A. (1859) *The World as Will and Representation*, vol. II, Dover, 1969 edn, pp. 586–8.
4 Schopenhauer, A. (1851) 'On the Vanity of Existence', in *Essays and Aphorisms*, Penguin, 1970 edn, p. 52.
5 *Ibid.*, p. 54.
6 *The World as Will and Representation*, vol. II, p. 575.
7 *Ibid.*
8 *Ibid.*
9 *Ibid.*
10 *Ibid.*
11 *Essays and Aphorisms*, p. 41.
12 *Ibid.*, p. 44.
13 *The World as Will and Representation*, vol. I, p. 310.
14 *Essays and Aphorisms*, p. 45.
15 *Ibid.*, p. 44.
16 *Ibid.*
17 *The World as Will and Representation*, vol. I, p. 319.
18 *Ibid.*
19 *Ibid.*, p. 312.
20 *Ibid.*
21 *Ibid.*, pp. 313–14.
22 *Ibid.*, p. 313.
23 *Ibid.*
24 *Ibid.*, p. 314.
25 *Essays and Aphorisms*, pp. 53–4.
26 *Ibid.*, pp. 44–5.

27   *The World as Will and Representation*, vol. I, p. 315.
28   *Ibid.*, p. 316.
29   *Ibid.*, p. 313.
30   *Ibid.*
31   *Ibid.*, p. 314.
32   *Ibid.*, p. 316.
33   *Ibid.*
34   Tolstoya, Sofia (1985) *The Diaries of Sofia Tolstoya*, Cape.
35   Wittgenstein, Ludwig (1961 edn) *Tractatus Logico-Philosophicus*,
     D. F. Pears and B. F. McGuinness (trans), Routledge & Kegan
     Paul, section 6.43, p. 72.
36   Chekhov, *op. cit.*

CHAPTER TWO

Purpose

What is the purpose of life? Does this question make sense? Not everything can be said to have a purpose. One could not properly ask, for example, what is the purpose of the sky, of magnetism, or of dandelions. A piece of equipment can be said to have a purpose, and an action may be done *for* a purpose. But life is not an action or a piece of equipment. Again, such things as magnetism and dandelions can be *put* to a purpose; but does it make sense to speak of putting life to a purpose? We may say of some people that their lives are devoted to a purpose, and this would mean that their activities are largely directed to a single purpose. But when it is asked what is the purpose of life, this usually means something more general, and goes beyond any activities within a person's life. What is sought is a purpose that can be ascribed to life as such – something outside human life, for the sake of which it exists and is carried on. A purpose of this transcendent kind is offered by religion. But leaving aside the religious approach for the moment, it is not clear what can be meant by asking for the purpose of life.

But why should a need for such a purpose be felt? Purpose plays an ambiguous role in our lives. Human life is full of purpose: man is a purposive animal. Purpose is also an important ingredient in a happy, 'meaningful' life, and we complain if someone's life (our own or another's) is lacking in purpose. Yet, as we shall see, purpose cannot, so to speak, fulfil the expectations that it raises. In certain ways we must be left unsatisfied; and that is why we may want to push the quest for purpose beyond its normal scope, reaching out towards something beyond life which would allay our dissatisfaction.

1 THE QUESTION 'WHY?': MEANS AND ENDS

Man is a purposive animal; a life without purpose would not be a human life at all. Most of our activities, important and trivial, are infused with purpose. We buy food in order to eat, put clothes on in order to be warm, sow in order to reap, and so on. There is a purpose in human language. I use words to let you know that p, to find out whether q, or for various other purposes. Again, human actions are identified by their purpose. 'What are you doing?' 'Going to the lecture.' In one sense, what I am doing can be described in physical terms. But this would be only a partial description. What is needed for a full description is a reference to my *purpose* in performing these movements, i.e. to attend the lecture.

We can also ascribe purpose to animals and even plants. The blackbird builds a nest in order to rear its young, and the purpose of bright flowers is to attract insects which will pollinate them. But these phenomena can be described in a mechanical way or by reference to instinct. The blackbird does not *justify* its behaviour as a means to an end; it simply performs these actions automatically, and then other activities (rearing the young, etc.) become possible. Such behaviour (as nest-building) will also be carried on, instinctively, in circumstances in which it will be useless. In the human case, by contrast, we can distinguish between instinctive and purposive behaviour in terms of justification and responsibility. An example of instinctive behaviour is when we fall over and instinctively put our hands out before striking the ground. This is useful behaviour and it serves a purpose. But we are not responsible for it as in the case of actions that we *choose* to do. My purpose in sowing seeds, for example, is one that I would state in *justifying* this action, in explaining why I have chosen to do this rather than something else or nothing at all.

This aspect of human life depends on the ability to represent to ourselves alternative purposes and courses of action; and this we do by means of language. In this sense we live, unlike other animals, in the future as well as in the present. Other animals have an instinct (or 'drive') to do something, and they do it. The action has consequences (which may be beneficial), but these are not present to the animal. Human beings, by contrast, have the capacity to bring the future, so to speak, into the present, by means of language. (This is true, moreover, not only of *the* future, but of alternative futures, hypothetical possibilities, that we take into account in deciding how to act.)

The word 'why' is one of the most important in our language. From an early age we are trained to conceive our activities and attitudes in terms of this word. Why are you doing that? How does your action lead to fulfilment of that purpose? Soon we learn to join in the game of asking 'Why?' ourselves; and then our parents must put up with receiving this question as well as issuing it.

We are taught to organize our activities in accordance with the schema of means and ends, as opposed to acting (or refraining) in accordance with our present inclinations. Here we encounter the conflict between inclination and reason (reason versus the passions, etc.) which is characteristic of human life. We are taught that the superior course of action is that which accords with reason, and the reasonable action that which serves our ends rather than our present inclinations. An action that is done without any end may be criticized as 'pointless' or 'a waste of time'.

But which are the right ends? If we cannot confidently answer this question, then the value of our activities will be in doubt. It may be replied that ends are given by desires: if *X* is my end, that is because I happen to desire *X*. But the question may still be asked whether *X* is a suitable thing to desire; whether I am *right* to desire *X* rather than *Y*.

To act for an end is to act for a reason; and this is satisfying because the reason gives point and meaning to the activity. But what if the end cannot itself be endorsed by reason? Sometimes the end is desired because it serves some further end. I may do *A* for the sake of *B*, and desire *B* for the sake of *C*. But what if I can give no reason for the final desire in the series? According to Hume, this is always our situation.

> It appears evident that the ultimate ends of human actions can never, in any case, be accounted for by *reason* ... Ask a man *why he uses exercise*; he will answer, *because he desires to keep his health*. If you then enquire, *why he desires health*, he will readily reply, *because sickness is painful*. If you push your enquiries farther, and desire a reason *why he hates pain*, it is impossible he can ever give any. This is an ultimate end, and is never referred to any other object.
> Perhaps to your second question, *why he desires health*, he may also reply, that *it is necessary for the exercise of his calling*. If you ask, *why he is anxious on that head*, he will answer *because he desires to get money*. If you demand *Why? It is the instrument of pleasure*, says he. And beyond this it is an absurdity to ask for a reason. It is impossible there can be a progress *in infinitum*; and that one thing can always be a reason why another is desired. Something must be desirable on its own account.[1]

Hume concluded that the 'ultimate ends of human actions' must be treated as facts of nature, to be accounted for, not by reason, but by 'the sentiments and affections of mankind'.[2] But if this is so, may we not question their validity? To describe a given desire as a fact of human nature is not to justify it. And if this cannot be done, what meaning is left in our purposive activities? We began by noting that purpose can endow our activities with meaning. Purpose, and a sense of purpose, are important ingredients of what we regard and experience as a meaningful life. Yet we have to face the fact that all our purposes are based on facts of human nature; and these (like other facts of nature) are not there for reasons of ours, and are not meaningful in the way that satisfies us.

Hume says that something must be 'desirable on its own account'. Now the word 'desirable' is often used to mean 'worthy to be desired'. Thus, if we say it is desirable that children should learn how to add up, we mean that this is a worthy aim (and we could give reasons for this). But Hume is not claiming that pleasure is a worthy aim. In this case 'desirable' does not mean that we *ought* to aim at pleasure, but merely that pleasure *can* be an object of desire.

Again, expressions like 'on its own account' and 'for its own sake' may be misleading. The expression 'for the sake of' is normally used to link two distinct terms, as when we say that A is done for the sake of B. It may be thought that 'for its own sake' expresses a similar relation. But to say that A is done for the sake of A would be nonsense. The expression 'for its own sake' may give the impression that A is done for the sake of *something*, but this is not really so. This way of talking merely serves to soften the transition from reason-based terms to the final term for which there is no reason.

2   'THE END HAD CEASED TO CHARM'

Hume's account is misleading in another way. One of his ultimate reasons for action, as we have seen, is the avoidance of pain, and another is the pursuit of pleasure. But pleasure is a less satisfactory terminus than pain. If all our purposes are in the end based on facts of human nature, then the reason 'Because it is painful' is satisfactory at least in the sense that we have here a single imperative about which we have no choice. But this is not so in the case of pleasure. Hume's 'It is the instrument of pleasure' would not necessarily put an end to discussion as would the response 'Because sickness is painful'. In the case of pain, nature speaks to us with an unequivocal voice. Pleasure, by contrast, can mean a great variety of things. Again, our aversion to pain is fixed, whereas desires for particular pleasures come and go. We may also question whether pleasure as such is what we desire in a given case (as we cannot question whether we desire to avoid pain). Thus we are left, on the positive side, without a clear prescription for action. The sequence of reasoning described by Hume on the side of pleasure may still leave us asking whether pleasure is what we want and, if so, which pleasures are to be preferred.

Thus we may be led to a general scepticism about grounds for action, as we realize that the ends for which we have been working have nothing to sustain them. J. S. Mill tells how he fell into a condition in which all the ends for which he had striven had 'ceased to charm'.

> [I]t occurred to me to put the question directly to myself,
> 'Suppose that all your objects in life were realized; that all
> the changes in institutions and opinions which you are
> looking forward to, could be completely effected at this very
> instant: would this be a great joy and happiness to you?' And
> an irrepressible self-consciousness distinctly answered 'No!'
> ... The end had ceased to charm, and how could there ever
> again be any interest in the means? I seemed to have nothing
> left to live for.[3]

A similar condition afflicted Tolstoy. There came a time
when he found himself asking 'Why?' and 'What of it?'
about all the aims he had previously taken for granted.

> Before attending to my Samára estate, to my son's education,
> or to the writing of a book, I ought to know why I should
> do them. So long as I did not know why, I could not do
> anything ... Reflecting on the manner in which the masses
> might obtain their welfare, I suddenly said to myself: 'What
> is that to me?' Or, thinking of the fame which my works
> would get me, I said to myself: 'All right ... what of it?'
> And I was absolutely unable to make any reply.[4]

It is worth noting that Tolstoy made an explicit distinction
between these ends, and activities (of the same sort as the
avoidance of pain) about which we have no choice. Although,
as he puts it, his life 'came to a standstill', he could still
'breathe, eat, drink and sleep, and could not help breathing,
eating, drinking and sleeping'; but, he adds, 'there was no
life'.[5]

Some people are more inclined than others to be afflicted
by such thoughts. Mill tells us that it happened to him when
he was in a depressed state of mind. But the essential point
is one of logic and not psychology. Afflicted or not, we
have to accept that 'the ultimate ends of human actions' are
not 'accounted for by reason', and that the satisfying,
meaningful relation whereby means are supported by ends
does not exist for the ends themselves.

The scepticism about ends, about the ultimate justification
of action, may be compared with scepticism about the
ultimate justification of knowledge. Asked how I know that

there is a tree in front of me, I may reply that I can see it. But what if I am asked how I know that I can see it? May not my 'seeing' be merely an illusion? Again, to the question how we know that the sun will rise tomorrow, one might perhaps reply by referring to past experience. But what reason can be given for believing that past experience is any guide for the future? Faced with such difficulties, some philosophers have concluded that the common use of the word 'know' is mistaken. To have real knowledge, they argue, we would need to go beyond the ordinary criteria for using this word; to find some further guarantee, perhaps beyond human capacities, that what we take to be knowledge is really knowledge. Similarly, it may be said, the sceptic about ends is not satisfied with ordinary conceptions of worthwhile activity, but pushes the demand for reasons beyond its normal limits, to a point at which it cannot be satisfied. The activities and ends mentioned by Tolstoy, for example, would normally be regarded as worth while, and of this he was well aware. But he still asks, 'What is that to me?' *Why* is it worth while doing things that are, by ordinary standards, worth while?

However, these cases are not really so similar. The scepticism about knowledge may be described as 'academic', in the derogatory sense, for it has little effect on the conduct of life outside the philosopher's study. It has often been noted that, despite their alarming conclusions, sceptics behave just like the rest of us, and go on using the word 'know' just like the rest of us.[6] But this is not so in the case of scepticism about ends. When people are afflicted by this, their doubts are real enough, and their sense of purpose may be seriously undermined. Again, we may say that the philosophical sceptic is merely misusing, or re-defining, the word 'know'; placing artificial conditions on it which are not part of its normal meaning.[7] But this is not so in the case of ends. When Mill tells us that 'the end had ceased to charm', he is not using words in an abnormal way.

3 THE OZYMANDIAS PERSPECTIVE

A human being is able to conceive himself and the world

in a variety of ways and from a variety of perspectives. Near and far, past and future, myself and others – all are brought together in a single conceptual system and available to a single mind. Viewing things this way and that, we experience tensions such as could not occur in an animal. For this reason some thinkers have looked with envy on the condition of animals. We do not feel secure, wrote Rilke, in 'this interpreted world'. 'We're not at one. We've no instinctive knowledge,/like migratory birds ... We comprehend/ flowering and fading simultaneously.'[8]

The ability to comprehend flowering and fading simultaneously is more prominent in some people than in others. There are some who tend to 'live for the present', and others for whom the long-term prospect is more important. But every human being, other than the feeble-minded, must be concerned about the long-term prospect to some extent. From an early age we are taught to provide for the future. To conduct our lives rationally and properly, it is, we are taught, necessary to overcome the initial preference for what is near and immediate. (To do otherwise is reprehensible as 'weakness of will'.) The salesman of endowment policies appeals to our rationality, putting it to us that our later lives should be no less important to us than present advantages. We project ourselves mentally to a time when we shall be glad that we acted prudently now, and this may determine our behaviour now. These abilities and tendencies are an essential part of the survival kit whereby the human species maintains its place in the natural world. However, having this ability, we can also project ourselves to a more ultimate point of view from which all our efforts, present and future, will seem ephemeral and insignificant.

A life in which there is purpose is a meaningful life. But not any kind of purpose will do. I need to be able to hope that my activity will result in something. Pushing a boulder to the top of a hill may be a satisfactory purpose if I can hope to see it lying there as a result of what I have done. But if (like Sisyphus in the ancient myth) I know that it will roll down again immediately, then I shall get no satisfaction, and see no meaning, in the work of pushing it up (unless, indeed, I am doing it for some other result, for example to keep fit). The factory worker who spends all day on a repetitive operation on an assembly-line may find the work boring; but it would not be meaningless, for he would be aware that there is more to it than the activity itself. His activity, together with that of others, will result in something that outlasts the activity, and for the sake of which it is done. It would make a big difference if he knew that, further along the line, there is someone who regularly dismantles what he has done.

But how enduring must the result be? Here we come to another difficulty about purpose. Essential to the schema of activity and result is our concern about the future. But this concern also makes us look towards a further time, when the fruits of all our work will have vanished away. What then was the point of it all?

> Then I considered all that my hands had done and the toil I had spent in doing it, and behold, all was vanity ... For of the wise man as of the fool there is no enduring remembrance, seeing that in the days to come all will have been long forgotten.[9]

There are some whose achievements are described as 'immortal', but they too are doomed to oblivion; and among the 'immortal' works of poets are those which celebrate the inevitable decay of the works of man. In Shelley's famous sonnet 'Ozymandias', the inscription

> My name is Ozymandias, king of kings:
> Look on my works, ye Mighty, and despair!

appears on a fragment found in the desert. It and a few other pieces are all that remain of the colossal monument erected by this 'king of kings' to immortalize his fame. The words of poets are themselves more durable than that – as Shakespeare frequently pointed out in the *Sonnets*.[10] But they too will be forgotten one day. Again, those of us who would lay no claim to immortal works may still feel that we and our activities are part of some lasting institution or, in the last resort, of something as large and lasting as Western civilization or 'human progress'. But these things also are of finite duration, as we well know.

To experience our activities as meaningful, and to carry them out successfully, we must hold them to be serious and important; and this means that what we do, or the recognizable effects of what we do, must have a certain permanence. But what degree of permanence is needed? In ordinary life we generally feel that what we do has enough permanence to make it worth while. Yet we also have available to us that other, long-term perspective from which our activities and our lives appear insignificant. That is why the words of Ecclesiastes, and of many other writers in a similar vein, can strike us as forcefully as they do.

4   THE ENDLESS CYCLE OF GENERATION

Suppose that one of the migratory birds of whom Rilke speaks were to ask itself 'What is it all for?' The preparations for the start; the desperate journey over vast distances with no food; the feverish activity, for those who survive the journey, of mating, nest-building, etc.: what is it all for? So that another generation is produced which will do these things all over again? Then why not stay in Africa and take things easy? Such questions cannot occur to a bird, but they can and do occur to human beings.

Much pain, effort and sacrifice are involved in having children and bringing them up. What is it all for? The human situation, in this respect, has been compared with that of Sisyphus, condemned by the gods to the everlasting task of pushing a boulder to the top of a hill, from which it would invariably roll down, so that the task would have to be started again and again. We may suppose that if Sisyphus had asked himself what it was all for, he would have had to give a negative answer. His punishment consisted precisely in the pointlessness of the task that filled his life. But according to Richard Taylor, we are all in essentially the same position. 'Each man's life', he writes, 'resembles one of Sisyphus' climbs to the summit of his hill'.[11] The difference is merely that 'whereas Sisyphus himself returns to push the stone up again, we leave this to our children'. According to Taylor, most of our effort in going to work, etc., is 'directed only to the establishment and perpetuation of home and family; that is, to the begetting of others who will follow in our steps to do more of the same'.

It seems obvious that this description of human activity is far too narrow. But let us consider that part of it which is concerned with the begetting and raising of children. Why do we have children, and take so much trouble to bring them to a mature age? To this question various answers might be given. One person would say that children are fun; another would speak of affection or companionship; a third of the pleasure of watching children develop; and a fourth of the economic contribution that they may make in the future. There are also those who see in their children a mitigation of their own mortality, taking the view that we 'live on' in our children. Finally, there are those who attach importance to the continuation of the family name. Most people, no doubt, would subscribe to a combination of these and other answers. But none of these reasons, even in isolation, is merely about begetting others who will 'do more of the same'. That may be the *outcome* of our activities, but it is not how we see them or need to see them. Taylor confuses our reasons for having and raising children with what may be called 'nature's reason'. *We* do not have children in order that they may have children who will have further children, and so forth; but it is true that our activities, and the desires and emotions that motivate them, serve this purpose. That is why we are endowed by nature with these desires and emotions – just as the birds are endowed with suitable desires and instincts which lead to perpetuation of their species.

This does not make our position equivalent to that of Sisyphus. Nevertheless, it does leave us with one point of view from which all our efforts and satisfactions with regard to children appear pointless and meaningless. From that point of view they are all subservient to a larger, and to us meaningless, purpose – the endless cycle of generation; and our function on earth is nothing more than to pass on certain molecules of genetic matter ('the selfish gene'[12]) to the next generation, so that they may pass them on to their offspring, and so on indefinitely.

5   TO TRAVEL AND TO ARRIVE

Achievement is one of the ingredients of a purposeful and in that sense meaningful life. Yet, in another sense, achievement is destructive of meaning. 'To travel hopefully is better than to arrive.' In travelling there is purpose and meaning. We know why we are exerting ourselves, and we are inspired by the thought of the goal. But what is the culmination of this happy state of affairs? A goal attained is a goal eliminated. The sense of purpose is eliminated by the achievement of purpose.

This difficulty is illustrated by Taylor in an adaptation of the Sisyphus story. He supposes that the pushing up of boulders is done for the purpose of constructing 'a beautiful and enduring temple'. In that case Sisyphus' labours, though equally hard, would no longer be meaningless. Now we might think this would be a great improvement as far as Sisyphus was concerned. But according to Taylor, that would be a mistake. For what would happen when the temple is at last completed? Then Sisyphus would be reduced to a state of 'infinite boredom'; for nothing would be left for him to do but to 'contemplate for an eternity' what he had wrought. He would, after all, have been better off, his life would have had 'a meaning incomparably better', in the original version of the story, in which no result was achieved.

Taylor's argument illustrates the pitfalls of arguing from analogies. He invites us to see the human condition as analogous to that of Sisyphus. But while the simplicity of the Sisyphus myth makes it useful for highlighting certain aspects of the human condition, it also constitutes an important difference between myth and reality. And one way in which real life differs from the myth is that in real life we do not have only one aim. Someone who has built a beautiful and enduring temple would not be reduced to contemplating it for evermore, but could proceed to other work and pursue other objectives. Life is a texture of purposes, large and small, short-term and long-term, which overlap and interact in various ways; so that the achievement of one purpose leaves us with others yet to be achieved. In building my shed I am filled with a sense of purpose, and this makes the work satisfying and meaningful. I also note, perhaps with some regret, that when the work is completed I shall no longer have that satisfaction. But what, after all, is the shed for? It will enable me to do other work, in pursuit of other aims, which will be satisfying in their turn.

Nevertheless, there remains a difficulty about purpose and achievement, and Taylor's analogy (like Schopenhauer's claims about 'boredom') is true to some extent. Sometimes we do experience boredom and a sense of anticlimax after an achievement. This is especially so where the work has been long and difficult. We look back with regret to the time when we were engaged, perhaps with the comradeship of others, in a long and difficult task. There are some who 'go to pieces' after the achievement of such a task. Someone who is aware of these aspects of achievement may even be motivated to spin out the work when achievement appears to be drawing near.

There is obviously much variation here. Some people will feel the anticlimax more than others, depending on circumstances and individual psychology. Many people, again, have no such dominant objectives in their lives. But behind these variations there is an inevitable logical truth: the sense of purpose cannot survive the achievement of purpose. If my life has meaning because of some long-term aim, then that meaning is eliminated when the aim is achieved.

Another negative aspect of the life of purpose is the pain and difficulty of the struggle prior to achievement. Now obviously not every case of doing something for a purpose will be one in which there is pain and struggle. Whether this is so, and to what extent, will depend very much on the nature of the case and the individuals involved in it. Nevertheless the satisfaction of working for an important goal is often connected with sacrifices to be made for the sake of it. These enhance the value of the goal and the satisfaction of working for it. An achievement that is so easy as not to need any pain or effort will not give us the positive feelings, the sense of being 'buoyed up', that are such important ingredients of the life of purpose.

This interplay of negative and positive also appears at the general level of human progress. Throughout history human beings have worked at making things easier for themselves, finding and inventing ways of getting what they want more and more easily. Especially since the industrial revolution, human progress can be seen largely in these terms. The ingenuity of man, and the genius of particular individuals, have been put to the service of this general aim, and the results have been dramatic. But as is well known, those who reap the benefits, the consumers of the 'affluent society', are not necessarily more contented with life. This is also observable when people of primitive cultures take up the advantages of European know-how, and find the easing of life to be a mixed blessing.

But what is the answer? Should they have refused these advantages? Here is the absurdity of the life of purpose. I want or need X, and it costs me much pain and effort to get it. Someone comes along and offers to make me a present of X, or show me how to get it with no effort. To refuse would be absurd, for, after all, what I want *is* X, and not the pain and effort of getting X. The latter only make sense as the means of getting X. But here, as John Wisdom observed, 'appears that exasperating feature of so much success'.

> Surely when a man sets out on a journey his goal is to reach that journey's end as fast as possible . . . And yet, just as we have it all laid out so that we have only to press a button to be where we want to be, just then the whole thing is apt to seem absurd. Just then we are apt to realize that what we needed was not merely to be at our destination.[13]

We want, and do not want, to remove the difficulties in our lives. To try to do so is our natural response, and one that endows our lives with meaning. Yet this motivation is self-defeating. And a paradigm of the meaningless life is that in which (as in Huxley's *Brave New World*) man has finally succeeded in eliminating all the difficulties that stand in his way.

6 IS LIFE ABSURD?

As we have seen, the life of purpose is unsatisfactory in a number of ways. The schema of means and ends, though satisfying in one way, is marred by the ungrounded status of ends; and for the person for whom 'the end has ceased to charm', reason can provide no remedy. We take our purposes seriously, and yet we must be aware that, sooner or later, all our works must vanish without trace. We devote much effort to the raising of children, though conscious of a point of view from which we and they are merely links in the cycle of generation. Finally, there is the paradox about struggle and achievement. What are we to conclude from these reflections?

Prospero, in his famous speech in *The Tempest*, concluded that 'we are such stuff as dreams are made on'. The spirits whom he had conjured up to perform an entertainment will, he announces, shortly dissolve into 'thin air'; and like that 'insubstantial pageant', all the works of man – 'the cloud-capp'd towers, the gorgeous palaces', etc., even 'the great globe itself' – all will vanish, leaving 'not a rack behind'. The conclusion is that we are such stuff as dreams are made on.

Prospero's argument is easily refuted. While it is true that man and his works will one day vanish, no less than those spirits or the stuff of dreams, they are more substantial than the latter. They will not be dissolved by a wave of the hand, as are the spirits in the play; and whereas we regularly wake up from dreams to the realization that 'it was only a dream', there are no such wakings-up from real life. Prospero, it may be said, makes too much of what the cases have in common – ultimate dissolution – and ignores the differences between them. He would deprive us of distinctions we normally make, between reality and dream, substantial and insubstantial.

However, it would be absurd to dismiss Prospero's

argument in this way, as a mere mistake of logic. If there were no more to it than that, it would not command our attention as it does. We may safely assume that Prospero was well aware of the normal distinctions; his aim was to present, and emphasize, a perspective from which these distinctions will seem less important than they are usually taken to be.

The shifting of perspectives is an important feature of our conception of the world. Consider the question whether such apparently solid objects as tables and rocks are really solid. In his book *The Nature of the Physical World*, Sir Arthur Eddington claimed that they are not. Modern physics had shown, he said, that the table on which he wrote was 'mostly emptiness', with 'numerous electric charges rushing about'.[14] Philosophers have pointed out that Eddington's conclusion must be false, since the word 'solid' is *defined* by such objects as tables (tables that are solid as opposed to being rotten or rickety, etc.), and not by reference to micro-structures.[15] What Eddington did was not to prove that tables are not solid, but to draw attention to a point of view from which they appear not to be so (and from which nothing would appear to be so). It is true, after all, that behind the solidity of the table there is a structure that we would not describe as solid. This is a striking discovery, and one that must affect our conception of the world of solid things. But it does not follow that nothing is really solid, or that the distinction between solid and not solid can no longer be made. Similarly, the argument presented by Taylor, and the comparison of human life with the meaningless labour of Sisyphus, show that life can be regarded from that perspective rather than proving that it is equally meaningless.

Another recent writer, Thomas Nagel, speaks in this connection of a 'point of view'. Having pointed out that we take certain things seriously, he observes that 'we always have available a point of view . . . from which the seriousness appears gratuitous'.[16] His conclusion (like that of Albert Camus) is that life is 'absurd'. But, again, the existence of that point of view does not prove that life *is* absurd, but only that it can appear so. However, Nagel's argument is more subtle. 'What makes life absurd', he says, is that the two viewpoints, the 'serious' and the 'gratuitous', 'collide in us'.

But it still does not follow that life is absurd. To make a mountain out of a molehill is absurd. But to make a mountain out of what can be regarded from one point of view as a molehill is not necessarily absurd. Nor is it so if one is aware of both viewpoints (if they 'collide in us'). Nagel thinks that the absurdity of our life results from the mere awareness of that other, 'gratuitous' point of view, alongside the serious one. The life of a mouse, he says, is not absurd because it lacks the self-awareness whereby it would 'see that it is only a mouse'. 'If that *did* happen, his life would become absurd.'[17] But no reason has been given by Nagel for accepting such a view. If the life of a human being or a mouse is absurd, then this will be so whether the absurdity is perceived by them or not. We might indeed say that the efforts of a mouse are, from one point of view, absurd (futile, meaningless), because they lead to nothing more than the endless cycle of generation; and the fact that the mouse cannot make such judgements would not prevent *us* from making them.

However, while we might say that certain aspects of life (whether human or animal) are absurd from certain points of view, it does not follow that *life* is absurd. Indeed, it is not clear what this statement would mean. The word 'absurd', like others, gets its meaning from certain contexts in which it is at home – situations *within* life, in which, as Nagel puts it, there is 'a conspicuous discrepancy between pretension or aspiration and reality'.[18] But is the word applicable to life itself?

Nagel provides four examples of its use for situations within life.

> Someone gives a complicated speech in support of a motion that has already been passed; a notorious criminal is made president of a major philanthropic foundation; you declare your love over the telephone to a recorded announcement; as you are being knighted, your pants fall down.[19]

These are good examples, but how well do they compare with the case of life itself? In the second and fourth, something exceptional has happened, out of keeping with our moral standards or sense of occasion. But nothing exceptional has happened in the case of life itself; here we are dealing with permanent conditions. In the first and third examples, we need to ask whether the person concerned is aware of the facts. If so, his behaviour can only be understood as a joke, unlike the serious concerns of normal life. If not, then the cases are different from that of life in another way. For what is alleged to make *life* absurd are facts of which we are well aware (the other 'point of view'). Hence we are left without any clear meaning for the claim that life itself is absurd.

7   NATURE'S REMEDY

It needs no subtle philosopher to make us aware of the problems about the life of purpose. They are likely to occur, more or less explicitly, to anyone capable of purposive reasoning – 'even', as Tolstoy puts it, to 'the simplest kind of men'. More than once Tolstoy expressed astonishment at the fact that, in spite of the problems, these people were able to carry on with their lives, unlike himself. The answer to his predicament, he finally concluded, must lie in the religious faith of simple people, which he must try to emulate.[20] The shortcomings of reason must be made up by faith. (The religious approach will be discussed in the following chapter.) According to Hume, however, we must look to nature for the remedy. 'Since reason is incapable of dispelling these clouds, nature herself suffices to that purpose, and cures me of this philosophical melancholy . . .'[21]

Now it is no accident that nature cures us (most of us, most of the time) of these 'melancholies'. Without that, our species might not be viable. Human success depends on such features as intelligence and language; but it also depends on our fondness for activities that involve purpose and planning. This is implanted in us by nature – as is the desire to live rather than to die. These desires are neither reasonable nor unreasonable; we have them, whatever we may think about religion or the meaning of life.

Such is our addiction to the purposive life, that we even

devise ends artificially. Not only do we take life seriously even though we cannot prove it to be so; but we take seriously activities which we know are not so. We play games, collect stamps, repair old machinery. Why? What is the point of it? The players are engrossed, their expressions are serious. They plan every move with great care, and hope for a favourable result. And yet – it is only a game! Have they forgotten this? No; if we asked what they are doing, they would reply: 'Playing a game'. Human beings are compulsive players of games, and this is also true of the 'game' of life – the human life of purpose and achievement. Our reason may tell us that there is, in the last resort, no justification for what we do; no answer to the question 'What is that to me?' And this may actually lead us, as it led Tolstoy, to withdraw from purposeful activity. But this will not last. Sooner or later we shall find ourselves returning to it – pretending to ourselves, if necessary, that it is serious; just as those who are addicted to chess or stamp collecting pretend to themselves that their efforts are directed to a serious and meaningful end.

There is also another way in which nature comes to the rescue. As we saw in Section 2, the problem about means and ends does not arise equally about all activities. Questions like 'Should I be a writer?' or 'Why should I go on being a writer?' are troublesome because these are matters that call for deliberation and choice. But this is not so with activities like breathing and the avoidance of pain. Tolstoy, as we saw, observed that he 'could not help' going on breathing, eating and sleeping, even when, as he put it, his 'life came to a standstill'. Now there are ways in which activities of the deliberative kind are propelled forward by those of the other kind; and in this way the danger of a permanent arrest of purpose is reduced.

An important fact here is our involvement with other people. Someone asks a question; it requires an answer. Someone is counting on me to do something, and will be surprised or upset if I do not do it. These responses are spontaneous (even if not in the same way as breathing or the avoidance of pain); and they counteract the withdrawal from life that may be produced by sceptical reflections about

long-term ends. Yet the long-term ends may be served by
the spontaneous kind of activity.

The raising of children is a good example of this. One
may have long-term purposes or aspirations for one's
children, and here the sceptical questions may present
themselves. What is it all for? Moreover, we must face the
fact that our children 'grow away' from us. We want them
to become mature and independent; and yet we know that
through this they will be *ours* no longer, or only in a
diminished sense. But, in the meantime, 'life goes on'. The
children demand attention – they need physical support,
complain, ask questions; and these demands call forth an
·immediate response from us. These responses are part of the
long-term purpose, but we make them spontaneously and
would find it hard to do otherwise.

Again, consider the case of a lonely scholar who for
twenty years devotes his life to a piece of work that no one
knows anything about. We would not be surprised if, from
time to time, he loses faith, asks himself what the point of
it is, and perhaps gives up altogether. (His doubts may be
of the general kind discussed above, or about his work in
particular.) However, most people engaged in long-term
projects are not isolated from others in this way. The project
may be a collaborative one, in which people meet from time
to time, make demands on one another, give promises, and
interact in various emotional ways. But even the lone writer
of a book may be under pressure from others. Perhaps he
is chased by a publisher to whom he has given a promise;
his friends may enquire how the work is going; and members
of his family, noticing how much time he gives to the work
(perhaps neglecting other commitments), will want to know
what he is up to. Thus, in various ways, we are propelled
forward in our long-term aims and projects by pressures of
an immediate kind, calling forth spontaneous responses on
our part.

8   THE LIFE OF PURPOSE AND ITS ALTERNATIVES

To some people the difficulties about purpose will seem less important than to others. In this matter there is a good deal of variation, depending on circumstances and individual psychology. One person is ambitious to achieve some long-term and important end, and his life is given direction and purpose by this. But others have no such ambitions. Their lives proceed from day to day in a more or less satisfactory manner, but are not shaped by any overall purpose; nor do they think very much in these terms.

Is the second kind of life inferior, or less meaningful, than the first? The man of ambition will probably be able to *say* what the meaning of his life is, when asked; the other may not know what to answer. But it does not follow that he would be less happy or that his life would be meaningless, if this means that there is something wrong with it. Nor would it follow that it is lacking in purpose, in the sense that would make one unhappy. For this life may contain a sufficient quantity of short-term purposes of various kinds. Again, if we consider the matter from a moral point of view, we cannot say that the person who devotes his life to an overall purpose is necessarily superior to the other. This would depend on what his purpose is.

There are also differences between societies in this matter. The emphasis on purpose is characteristic of modern Western society, with its interest in 'progress'. But if we consider (say) the lives of South Sea Islanders before the arrival of Europeans, or the 'simple' people portrayed in some of Tolstoy's writings, we find a different attitude. Here purpose and achievement are less prominent than in our culture.

Is the increased prominence of purpose a change for the better? According to Moritz Schlick, it is a disaster. He spoke of 'the curse of purposes' – a curse that has befallen modern man with his obsession for goal-directed work.[22] 'The entry of goal-seeking into life, and involvement in the network of purposes, betokens ... the true fall of man'.[23] The modern worker, he held, is caught in a futile circle. 'The content of [his] existence consists in the work that is needed in order to exist.'[24] And what of the products of this work? The greater part of them, he claimed, were 'again subservient to work of some kind', while the remainder consisted largely of 'meaningless trash'.

These are, by now, familiar complaints about the mass-production society, and they contain both truth and exaggeration. It is true to a large extent that people identify themselves ('the content of their existence') with their jobs – the work they do 'in order to exist'. (Here is one way in which unemployment may undermine self-respect.) It is also true that much of this work is done for the sake of other work, and that much of what is finally produced is trash. But obviously not all of it is. If Schlick's argument depended on such claims, then it would not go very far. He would also have to face disagreements about what is, and what is not, trash.

However, Schlick's more fundamental point is about the life of purpose as such. It is, he holds, unsatisfactory, because the meaning or value of what we do is never in what we actually do, but always in something else (for the sake of which we do what we do). It would be better, he thinks, if the meaning always lay in the activity itself.

> The last liberation of man would be reached if in all his doings he could give himself up entirely to the act itself . . . The end, then, would never justify the means; he might then exalt into the highest rule of action the principle: 'What is not worth doing for its own sake, don't do for anything else's sake!' All life would then be truly meaningful . . .[25]

Now as I have said (p. 19), the expression 'for its own sake' is not as straightforward as it may seem. To someone caught in the state of mind of Mill or Tolstoy, where 'the end had ceased to charm', it would be no use saying that the end is worth achieving 'for its *own* sake' in the sense in which *A* may be worth doing for the sake of *B*. However, Schlick's recommendation is relevant for those who are *not* caught in that situation; and to them he would say that activities that are not, or not primarily, done for the sake of something else, are more satisfying, more meaningful, than those that are.

This is not to say that the activities would necessarily be different; it may be more a matter of how we regard them. Consider, for example, the activity of 'Do-it-yourself', which has become so popular in recent times. Why does the DIY enthusiast paint his house? One answer, obviously, is in terms of a purpose that is served. The house needs a coat of paint, and the work is done to bring this about. But why is he doing it, as opposed to a professional? Again, the answer may be: in order to save money. But another answer would be that he enjoys painting the house. The sheer satisfaction of covering a surface with paint is familiar to many (and was beautifully illustrated in the episode of painting the fence in *Tom Sawyer*). However, this satisfaction is not incompatible with the other answers. And the same is true of the person who is working 'in order to exist'. The fact that he is working for an end (which may be more or less remote, and more or less valuable) does not exclude the possibility of enjoying the work in itself, of 'giving himself up entirely to the act itself'. People are often led to believe, both by workers' organizations and by managers, that there is no sense in work except as a means to an end: the earning of money by workers, the production of goods for profit. On this view, work is a burden that must be borne, a necessary evil that must be accepted, for the sake of the end. But this is a false view, for an activity may be both satisfying in itself, and done for the sake of an end. As Schlick pointed out, the cobbler, the weaver and the tiller of fields, though working in order to earn a living, can each

> ... experience in his own case this transformation of the means into an end-in-itself, which can take place with almost any activity, and which makes the product into a work of art. It is the joy in sheer creation, the dedication to the activity, the absorption in the movement, which transform the work into play.[26]

Schlick believed that the quality of the product would depend on the spirit in which the work is done. From work done in the right spirit, we would get 'a work of art'; otherwise there would be 'only trash and empty luxury'.[27] But this view, though attractive, is hardly plausible. He also held (as the quotation shows) that work done in the right spirit is a kind of play. The 'liberation of man' was to be found in play, and this meant going back to the time of youth, a time when 'the curse of purposes' had not yet taken over. It was a mistake, he said, to regard youth as a time of 'incompleteness', 'a mere introduction and prelude to real life'; youth is 'primarily a time of play, of doing for its own sake, and hence a true bearer of the meaning of life'.[28] Education, he believed, should be designed to preserve the playful side of man; it should 'take care that nothing of the child in man is lost as he matures'.[29]

Schlick is right in drawing attention to valuable qualities of youth, which are liable to be killed off by an educational system that is largely geared to the schema of means and ends. At school we are taught not to 'play about', but to work hard, and often with painful effort, to get good marks and pass exams, these being themselves regarded as means to further ends. Such a regime often has detrimental effects on such qualities as originality and spontaneity, and, more generally, the capacity to enjoy life. The concentration on purpose may lead us to 'take life too seriously', to lose sight of other ways of living and being happy.

The case of school also highlights a general defect of the life of purpose. Purpose is directed to success; but success is correlative with failure. Where there is no possibility of failure, it makes no sense to speak of success. And the *satisfaction* of success is correlative with the *dissatisfaction* of failure. Hence, in mortgaging our happiness to the achievement of success, we run a corresponding risk in the case of failure. Some people, inevitably, will fail rather more often; and this may cause them to feel that *they* are failures, or even that life is meaningless as far as they are concerned. Such people may benefit from the perspectives, discussed in previous sections, from which human purposes and achievements seem less important or unimportant. But they may also be reminded of the importance of those non-purposive aspects of life to which Schlick drew attention.

These are matters of judgement and detailed policy. But it would be a mistake to think that 'the entry of goal-seeking into life', lamented by Schlick, could be reversed altogether. For as I pointed out at the beginning of this chapter, the question 'Why?' and the schema of means and ends are built into our very language. It is indeed largely this that makes human language different from other types of communication. A being that always 'gave himself up to the act itself', that did not have the notion of acting *for* something, would not be part of this language-community. Pre-verbal infants fall into this category; but the development away from it is an essential part of growing up, and of becoming a full member of the community. Does Schlick think we should try to reverse this process? Would not such a reversal 'represent a relapse to a lower level, to the status of plants and animals'?

> For the latter assuredly live for the moment, their consciousness is confined to a brief present ... Man, on the contrary, has the privilege of embracing long periods, whole lifetimes, in the span of his consciousness ...[30]

This relapse to a lower level is not what Schlick is advocating. His claim is that man 'can shake off the curse of purpose' without losing the concept of purpose or the capacity for surveying the past and the future. It is a matter of giving the right importance to purpose, rather than of trying to rid ourselves of the concept (as if that were possible). The road on which we travel leads somewhere, but the important thing to realize is that every part 'has its own intrinsic meaning, like a mountain path that offers sublime views at every step ... whether it may lead to a summit or not'.[31] Our enjoyment of the journey should not be conditional on whether we achieve the summit or not.

As already remarked, there is such a thing as an excessive concern about purpose, to the detriment of spontaneous and playful aspects of life. But the advantages of the Western preoccupation with purposive activity are no less obvious, for example in the fields of science and technology. Perhaps Schlick would have dismissed these activities and their products as unimportant (or 'trash'); but would he have said the same about the works of Beethoven or Kant? Yet we may be sure that their works could not have been created without a strong sense of purpose on the part of their authors, and a whole context and tradition of purposeful activity. The life of purpose, as I have shown, has various difficulties and disadvantages; but when we contemplate alternatives, other difficulties make their appearance.

NOTES

1 Hume, David (1777) *Enquiries concerning Human Understanding and the Principles of Morals*, L. A. Selby-Bigge (ed.) and revised by P. H. Nidditch, Clarendon Press, 1975 edn, p. 293.
2 *Ibid.*
3 Mill, J. S. (1873) *Autobiography*, Oxford University Press, 1969 edn, p. 81.
4 Tolstoy, *op. cit.*, pp. 17–18.
5 *Ibid.*, p. 19.
6 Hume tells us that while in his study he was reduced by his sceptical (and other) reflections to a state of 'melancholy and delirium'; from which, however, he was able to cure himself by going out to dine and play games with his friends (*ibid.*, p. 269). Presumably he *knew*, even while in his study, that he could get his dinner and encounter his friends at such and such a place.
7 See Hanfling, O. (1987) 'How is Scepticism Possible?', *Philosophy*.
8 Rilke, R. M. (1923) *The Duino Elegies*, I and IV, J. B. Leishman (trans.), Hogarth Press, 1968 edn, pp. 24 and 48.
9 *Old Testament*, Ecclesiastes, 2:11.
10 'Not marble, nor the gilded monuments/Of princes, shall outlive this powerful rhyme ...' A long-standing question about the *Sonnets* concerns their object: whom were they addressed to? But it may be said, in the case of many of them, that the object of the poem is the poem itself.
11 Taylor, R., 'The Meaning of Life', in his (1970) *Good and Evil*, Macmillan; reprinted in Klemke, *op. cit.*, pp. 141–50.
12 Dawkins, R. (1976) *The Selfish Gene*, Oxford University Press.
13 Wisdom, John (1954), 'What is there in Horse Racing?', *The Listener*, pp. 1015–16.
14 Eddington, Sir Arthur (19??) *The Nature of the Physical World*, Dent, Everyman edn, pp. 6–8.
15 The issue is discussed by Wittgenstein, L. (1958) *The Blue and Brown Books*, Blackwell, p. 45.
16 Nagel, T. (1971) 'The Absurd', *Journal of Philosophy*, LXVIII, 20.

17   *Ibid.*, p. 160.
18   *Ibid.*, p. 153.
19   *Ibid.*
20   Tolstoy, *op cit.*, p. 59.
21   Hume, David (1739) *A Treatise of Human Nature*, L. A. Selby-Bigge (ed.), Oxford University Press, p. 269. The 'clouds' in this passage are not about means and ends, but Hume would have said the same about them.
22   Schlick, M. (1927) 'On the Meaning of Life', in *Philosophical Papers*, vol. II, Reidel, pp. 122 and 133.
23   *Ibid.*, p. 126.
24   *Ibid.*, p.114
25   *Ibid.*, p. 118.
26   *Ibid.*, p. 117.
27   *Ibid.*
28   *Ibid.*, p. 121.
29   *Ibid.*, p. 128.
30   *Ibid.*, p. 118.
31   *Ibid.*

CHAPTER THREE

God

The sea of faith
Was once, too, at the full, and round earth's shore
Lay like the folds of a bright girdle furl'd;
But now I only hear
Its melancholy, long, withdrawing roar,
Retreating to the breath
Of the night-wind down the vast edges drear
And naked shingles of the world.

(Matthew Arnold, *Dover Beach*)

1 INSIGNIFICANT MAN

Questions of meaning and purpose have not always troubled
people as they do today. In a religious age these questions
were referred to the care of a wise Creator. This Creator,
it was believed, had made the world and all things in it for
a purpose. Man, and each individual man, were part of a
grand design. Moreover, man occupied a place of special
importance in this design, being made 'in the image of God'
by a special, separate act of creation. He was given the
power of reason, setting him above the animals; and, unlike
them, had an immortal soul. This meant that death was not
the end of a person's life, but only a passage to another and
higher form of existence, in accordance with God's purpose.
The earth and all its creatures were given to man; they

existed for humans' purposes, as part of the grand design. Man's habitation, the earth, occupied a central place in the cosmos, with the sun and other heavenly bodies being provided for its benefit.

What is left of these beliefs today? Today we believe that the earth is a minor planet circling the sun, which itself is an undistinguished star, one of a vast number of stars in a galaxy which in its turn is one of an innumerable, perhaps infinite, number of galaxies. This minor planet came into being through some casual splash of cosmic materials, went through various chemical processes, and will continue to exist and be fit for habitation until such time as conditions change again, perhaps through a relatively minor change in the sun's temperature. We are told that life probably arose through an accidental combination of certain chemicals, and that there is no reason to think that such conditions cannot arise, and have not arisen, elsewhere in the universe. The theory of natural selection tells us that the human species, so far from being brought into existence by a special act of God, is the outcome of a blind process of selection by survival, having developed by imperceptible degrees from an ape-like creature, with the modern chimpanzee as a close cousin. Psychologists tell us that to a large extent human thought and action are determined by dark unconscious processes rather than by the light of reason. Again, while it remains true that man has special powers of speech and reasoning, it is not clear why these should be regarded as more special than the remarkable powers, of one kind or another, that distinguish other animals. There is no reason to think that man is better or 'higher' than they; and in view of his destructive activities, it would not be unreasonable to give an opposite judgement.

What of the belief in God's purpose and the life after death? This is still held by many people, but they are in a minority, at least in the Western world. And even religious believers, surrounded as they are by secular culture, cannot be as comfortable with religious accounts of meaning and purpose as was once the case.

Modern views of man and the world do not merely result from the replacement of one explanation or theory by another; there has been a change in the very concept of explanation, of what an explanation should be like. It was previously thought that the only real or really satisfactory kind of explanation was by reference to purpose. One would explain a phenomenon by saying what it was for, what purpose it served for man or beast or God. There was also causal explanation, by reference to what preceded the phenomenon; but this kind of explanation was thought to be incomplete and inferior. It was only with the other kind that we could have real understanding. In modern times, however, and especially since the time of Hume, causal explanation has largely supplanted the other, teleological, kind. Modern scientific theories are not couched in teleological terms; and modern laws of nature are not about ends and purposes, but about observed regularities in the world. We explain why something happened, not by looking forward towards an end or goal, but by looking backward to an antecedent cause.

Such explanations are in a certain sense less satisfying than those of teleology. The explanation by reference to laws of nature says, in effect, that an event, or sequence of events, occurred because things always happen like that. But this is merely to refer one brute fact (a particular one) to another (a general regularity). Hence it is sometimes said that modern science is in the end only descriptive; it tells us *how* things happen, but not *why*. A teleological explanation, by contrast, gives sense or meaning to the event. This is especially clear in the case of conscious human actions, where the sense of meaning of the action can be given by the agent in terms of his or her purpose. If this kind of explanation could be applied to natural phenomena at large, they too would have this kind of meaning. But, as I have said, this way of explaining has been largely given up in favour of the other, 'meaningless', kind of explanation, which has proved more fruitful in other respects.

What is the bearing of these changes on our conception of ourselves? 'It might be argued', writes Kurt Baier, 'that the more clearly we understand the explanations given by science, the more we are driven to the conclusion that human life has no purpose and therefore no meaning'.[1] Baier rejects this conclusion. He points out that in an ordinary sense of purpose, human lives are no less purposeful than they were before. We still conduct our lives largely by pursuing goals of one kind or another. The question 'Why are you doing that?', i.e. 'What is your purpose?', is asked no less than it was before, and in many cases a satisfactory answer can be given. It is true that some people conduct their lives in a less purposeful way than others; but, again, this has always been so and has nothing to do with scientific developments and the modern conception of man's place in the world. According to Baier, indeed, 'Science has not only not robbed us of any purpose which we had before, but it has furnished us with enormously greater power to achieve these purposes'.[2]

Baier also distinguishes a secondary use of 'purpose', as applied to things rather than persons, as when we ask 'What is the purpose of that gadget you installed in the workshop?'[3] In this case we are not saying that the thing is motivated by a purpose; the point is, rather, that it is meant to *serve* a purpose, the purpose of the person who made or installed it. Is purpose in this secondary sense diminished by the scientific view? No; we continue to make all sorts of things which are designed to serve a purpose and which are said, in this sense, to 'have a purpose'.

But what of man himself? Man himself could be said, on the religious view, to *serve* a purpose, as distinct from having purposes of his own; and *this* ascription of purpose, this answer to the question about the purpose of life, is no longer available if the religious view is given up. But according to Baier, this answer was never worth having. 'To attribute to a human being a purpose in that sense . . . is offensive. It is degrading for a man to be regarded as merely serving a purpose.'[4] In treating a man in this way, says Baier, we would 'reduce him to the level of a gadget, a domestic animal, or perhaps a slave'; would be 'treating him, in Kant's phrase, merely as a means to our ends, not as an end in himself'.[5]

These observations are true and important, but are they relevant? If *we* treated human beings in that way, as 'serving a purpose', then we would not be giving them their due respect, and our treatment would be morally offensive. But it does not follow that human beings would be degraded in serving *God's* purpose, that *He* degrades them by treating them in such a way, or by creating them for His purpose. A similar point may be made about the relation between men and animals. Most people would say that it is not degrading for an animal to be used for a purpose. For example, if someone keeps a dog for the purpose of discouraging burglars, this would not be degrading or morally offensive.

Religious believers are not, and do not need to be, offended by the idea that they are there to serve the purpose of a higher being. They can also claim that this gives their lives a kind of purpose and meaning that they could not have on the scientific view alone.

Again, Baier's observations about the continuing, and indeed inevitable, role of purpose in our lives do not help us with the feeling of insignificance that results from the scientific revolution. It *is* a shock when we learn these facts about the human situation in space and time; and it *was* a profound shock when these ideas were first introduced. Does it follow from them that our lives really are meaningless? Of course there is no syllogism which proceeds from premises about cosmology or natural selection to the conclusion that our lives are meaningless. And it is appropriate to point out, as Baier does, that there are criteria for describing a human life as meaningful or meaningless, which have nothing to do with questions of cosmology or natural history.

The scientific picture does, however, deprive us of meaning in another sense. There is a connection between meaning and *importance*; and if the scientific picture is correct, we do not have the importance that we thought we had. This connection between meaning and importance is reflected in the use of the word 'insignificant'. Something that lacks importance may be described as insignificant or (in that sense) meaningless. This is one way of understanding Macbeth's verdict that 'life's but a walking shadow ...,' signifying nothing'.[6]

2   GOD'S PURPOSE AND THE PROBLEM OF EVIL

A religious believer, even if he has to come to terms with the 'insignificance' of man in the modern scientific picture of the world, can still adhere to the belief that human life is given meaning by God's purpose. This may help us to deal with yet another way in which the meaning of life may be undermined. Consider a person who is overwhelmed by some unexpected personal disaster. Such a person may ask: 'Why me? What have I done to deserve this? What is the sense of it? All I have wanted and worked for (all that has given meaning to my life, in that sense) has been destroyed, or seems utterly trivial compared to what has now happened. A meaningless, fortuitous evil has taken my life over.'

In one way the problem is a personal one, affecting those unfortunate people who have been struck down in this way. But the problem also concerns life in general. The point is that such disasters are liable to strike each and every one of us, out of the blue, and without rhyme or reason. We must recognize that such meaning and happiness as we find in our lives are contingent on the non-occurrence of random events over which we have no control and in which we can see no sense.

When it is asked why such a thing has happened, we sometimes reply 'God knows'; and this is usually taken to mean that nobody knows – or perhaps that there *is* no answer to the question. But of course the reply may be taken literally. Someone who reflects on the problem, whether as a personal sufferer or from the general point of view, may hope to find meaning in something permanent that is not exposed to the fluctuations and contingencies of ordinary human life.[7]

If God exists, and if we are here to serve His purpose, then life has a meaning in spite of the difficulties noted above. But this answer is not without problems of its own. What, we may ask, *is* God's purpose? What is He using me for? And can I be sure that His purpose is a good one?

In answer to the first question it is sometimes held that

man was created in order to serve God, by praising Him or doing His work. A difficulty about this is that it makes God seem deficient – as if He had need of our work. This problem was addressed by Milton in the sonnet 'On His Blindness':

> ... God doth not need
> Either man's work, or His own gifts; who best
> Bear His mild yoke, they serve Him best ...

Such was the poet's answer to the problem of how he could serve God after the loss of his sight. What could God require of him with this disability? Would he not be excused from further labours? But 'Patience, to prevent/That murmur, soon replies' that God has no need of the labours of Milton or anyone else; the essence of the service that God requires from us is to 'Bear His mild yoke'. Although 'thousands at His bidding speed', we can serve Him by merely being part of His creation, accepting our allotted space with patience. The poem concludes with the famous words 'They also serve who only stand and wait'.

This is a suitable answer to someone who thinks that God must need our services in the gross sense of not being able to manage without them. But the modesty of this view, which prevents the imputation of deficiency to God, also makes it less suitable to endow our lives with a sense of purpose. If I believe, like Cromwell for example, that God wants me to perform certain mighty deeds, then this will give my life a sense of purpose (but with the implication that God has need of my services). If, on the other hand, I believe that God wants nothing from me but to 'Bear His mild yoke', then I may complain that this leaves me without any sense of purpose. In this case, the mere belief that I am serving God will not supply that sense of purpose which ordinarily gives meaning to life. (Could it be God's purpose to deprive my life of purpose?)

The belief that I am here merely to serve the purpose of a superior Being is also insufficient in another way. In a *Punch* cartoon which appeared at the start of the shooting season, one grouse was depicted saying to another: 'We're all put on earth for a reason'. This statement was true enough in the case of the grouse; but the reason was not of the right sort to endow the grouse's life with a satisfactory meaning.[8]

The doctrine of patient acceptance of God's creation presupposes that what we are to accept is good, that this creation is worthy of acceptance. In the Book of Genesis we are told that God, having created the world, pronounced it to be 'very good'. But even if it was so before the Fall of Adam, it may not seem to be so after that. This brings us to the notorious 'problem of evil'. We can, it seems, easily imagine a world which, if not totally devoid of evil, is a good deal better than the one we have; and a race of human beings who are a good deal better than those that inhabit this world. It is true that according to some views, our service to God includes repentance and the redemption of sin, and obviously these could not exist if there were no sin. But this returns us to the difficulty of the previous answer. Why should God be in need of a race of sinners who are also capable, occasionally, of repentance? Again, while it is clear enough that repentance is a good thing, it is far from clear that this good thing, when it occurs, outweighs the preceding evil that is done, the suffering of innocent people and so on.

It may be replied that our moral judgements are subject to God's correction; so that if He described the world as 'very good', then it is so, whatever we may think. Here we come to fundamental questions about the nature and source of moral knowledge. If this knowledge has to be taught by God, how are we to account for its existence among people who grow up in a non-religious environment? But is morality taught at all? If someone tells me ('teaches me') that such and such a thing is right or wrong, why should I accept what he says? Perhaps he can show that it follows from moral principles that I recognize and to which, perhaps, I had not paid sufficient attention.

But what if he tells me new principles? I would have to *see* that what I am told is right, and could not merely take his word for it. 'Even the Holy One of the gospel', wrote Kant, 'must first be compared with our ideal of moral perfection before we can recognize him to be such'.[9] If those who encountered Jesus could not have *recognized* his deeds and sayings as morally good (as conforming sufficiently to their ideas of morality), then they would have had no ground for accepting His teachings or following His example. (This is not to deny that someone like Jesus may help us to see that our way of life was not as good as it might be, or as we had taken it to be.)

Here is a responsibility that we have as rational beings and cannot abdicate to a higher authority, whether human or divine. The point was well illustrated by Jean-Paul Sartre with the example of God's command to Abraham to sacrifice his son on an altar. Of course, Abraham must do what is commanded by God. But, asks Sartre, would not Abraham wonder whether this command had really come from God? 'If an angel appears to me, what is the proof that it is an angel; or, if I hear voices, who can prove that they proceed from heaven and not from hell ...?'[10] Similarly, if we are told that God says the world is good, this may not put an end to our questioning.

What began in our discussion as an *advantage* for the religious view, now turns out to be a difficulty. The belief in God was introduced as a *solution* to a problem of evil. (The problem was about personal catastrophes, but also arises about unnecessary evils in general.) It looked as if this belief might serve to restore meaning to our lives in spite of the senselessness of evils (and the relegation of human existence to 'insignificance'). But now we have arrived at the more familiar 'problem of evil', which has long been regarded as a *difficulty* for believers.

When faced with such difficulties, defenders of religion sometimes appeal to the limitations of human intellect. If we cannot make sense of God's purpose, or of other aspects of religious belief, may this not be due to the narrowness of our perspective, as compared with God's? 'Who are you, a man, to answer back to God? Will what is moulded say to its moulder, "Why have you made me thus?"'[11] If only we could see things properly, in the way that God can see them, then we would understand why things are as they are, in accordance with His purpose.

However, this kind of defence must be used with caution. It is only too easy for the religious apologist to resort to it whenever the going becomes difficult – when he finds it hard to explain his beliefs or defend them against a sceptic. But it will then be open to the sceptic to reply that the apologist has withdrawn from the arena of rational discussion, thus, in effect, giving up the argument.

There are also problems about the *meaning* of the believer's statements. For example, if he speaks of God as 'a loving father', then, to understand what he means by this, we shall need to know what he means by words like 'loving' and 'father'. These words, like most others, get their meanings from the way they are used in ordinary human situations. If they are extended outside these contexts, for example in talking about animals, then there must be a sufficient overlap between the conditions existing in the extended context and those in the original one; for example, a sufficient resemblance between loving behaviour in animals and in human beings. It is not obvious that there are such overlaps in the case of descriptions of God, as given by believers and to be found in the scriptures. Here again, the answer is sometimes given that human language (like the human intellect) is not adequate for the purpose, that we cannot expect to be able to describe God adequately in our language. This answer is readily acceptable if it means that we must not expect words in the religious context to have just the same meanings as in ordinary situations. But there must be a sufficient overlap to justify the extension of this language to the religious context. Otherwise we might as well replace the believer's 'loving' and 'father' by terms like 'X' and 'Y', whose meaning is as yet undetermined.

But these difficulties, serious as they are, still leave it open to the believer to believe that God has a purpose that is beyond human understanding. According to Baier, such a belief is not worth very much. It cannot possibly, he says,

> be a satisfactory answer to our question about the purpose of life. It is, rather, a confession of the impossibility of giving one. If anyone thinks that this 'answer' can remove the sting from the impression of meaninglessness and insignificance in our lives, he cannot have been stung very hard.[12]

However, the idea of a purpose that is beyond one's understanding is familiar enough; and it is possible, even in the human world, to have faith in such a purpose, and to be reassured by this faith that one's life is guided by a purpose. A child may have faith of this kind in the purposes of his parents, believing that 'mummy knows best'. He feels reassured by the thought that his activities are under the guidance of a purposive intelligence, although these purposes are beyond his understanding. Similarly, an adult, say an employee in a big organization, may get satisfaction, may feel that his life has meaning, from the belief that his activities are serving an overall purpose, even though his understanding of that purpose may be deficient or non-existent. The same may be true of those who follow a charismatic leader, perhaps with considerable sacrifices.

An obvious advantage of understanding the purpose is that this entails knowing that there *is* a purpose; and this would be so if we could understand God's purpose. In that case we might also be heartened by the recognition that it is a *good* purpose, conforming to our 'ideal of moral perfection', as Kant put it. Failing that, we may wonder whether there is any purpose, and indeed whether God exists at all. But for someone who already has this belief, it is not unreasonable to draw comfort from the idea of a purpose that is beyond his understanding.

3   THE LIFE HEREAFTER

The idea that there is more to human life than we can understand is connected with the view that there is more to it than existence in the physical world. Whether there is survival after death is a question that will be examined in the next chapter. But in religious contexts an affirmative answer is often taken for granted; and the life hereafter has an important role in religious conceptions of the meaning of life. For the non-believer death is a negative event, and the prospect of it casts a negative shadow over his life. The believer, on the other hand, may regard it as something positive, as part of God's purpose for man, the inauguration of a state of being in which the imperfections of our earthly life are, in one way or another, corrected.

One way in which this could happen is by removing the difficulty discussed in the previous section. If our condition in the after-life brings us closer to God, then we may expect to gain a better understanding of His purpose for the world and for ourselves; and we shall no longer be plagued by difficulties such as the problem of evil. These benefits will not, of course, apply to those non-believers who do not see the existence of evil as requiring explanation. But perhaps even a non-believer will benefit from the greater understanding for which he saw no need during his earthly life.

Whether non-believers would receive these and other benefits is a difficult theological question; and a variety of views have been taken concerning the treatment of non-believers, and, indeed, believers, in the after-life. According to some views, the way in which our lives are 'completed' after death is by the meting out of justice. The righteous are rewarded and the wicked punished, thereby straightening out the gross inequities that we find in earthly life. This culmination will presumably be more satisfying to the righteous than to the wicked. But, whether righteous or wicked, we may wonder what purpose is served by meting out punishments which do no good other than to redress an imbalance. Again, how can we make sense of a God who surrounds us with opportunities for evil, and then punishes us for taking these opportunities?

> Oh Thou, who didst with Pitfall and with Gin
> Beset the Road I was to wander in ...
> For all the Sin wherewith the Face of Man
> Is blacken'd, Man's Forgiveness give – and take!

In any case, the conception of God as a judge meting out rewards and punishments cannot 'form the basis of a moral system'.[13] It is, as Kant insisted, essential to our understanding of morality that this motive is independent of such inducements. We are to act 'for the sake of duty' and not for the sake of rewards to be gained or punishments to be avoided.

Sometimes, the life after death is invoked, not by way of moral sanction, but to provide consolation for the bereaved, especially in cases of premature death. Milton's 'Lycidas' is an elegy for a friend lost in shipwreck, and the young man is mourned at length. But in the end all this is revoked; he is, after all, '. . . not dead,/Sunk though he be beneath the watery floor'. Not only is he not dead, but he has passed to a far happier state.

> With nectar pure his oozy locks he laves,
> And hears the unexpressive nuptial song
> In the blest kingdoms meek of joy and love.
> There entertain him all the saints above . . .

But how are we to conceive of a life of eternal bliss? As was said in Chapter Two, an important ingredient of a meaningful life on earth is the sense of purpose and achievement. The life of heavenly bliss, by contrast, would seem to be one of passive enjoyment. Now it is true that passive enjoyments are an important ingredient of a good life on earth; but they would not have the value they have, were it not for other periods of more or less strenuous activity. A life which consisted only of passive enjoyment (like those described in some futuristic novels) would strike us as tedious and not worth living; and an eternity of such life would be far worse. 'After man had placed all pains and torments in hell', wrote Schopenhauer, 'there was nothing left for heaven but boredom'.[14]

Of course we must not take a poetic description of the after-life (such as Milton's) too seriously. Perhaps what is said here poetically could be expressed more satisfactorily (for present purposes) in other terms. However, the difficulty is not merely one of description; for it is not easy to conceive how *any* life of that sort, lacking the challenges and corresponding satisfactions of earthly life, could be satisfying to human beings. Here again the believer must resort to the point about the limits of human understanding, claiming that although the solution of the problem lies beyond our understanding, we can rely on God.

4   MEANING AND THE RELIGIOUS CALENDAR

We have examined some of the ways in which religion may be thought to give meaning to life, or to overcome negative features that may seem to deprive life of meaning. One other connection of religion with meaning, involving yet another sense of 'meaning', ought to be mentioned. This kind of meaning is not about purpose, significance or moral perfection, but about such matters as pattern and rhythm. Consider the difference between a design drawn on a piece of paper and a meaningless scribble; a piece of music and a meaningless cacophany; the structure and rhythm of a poem and the unstructured deliveries of ordinary speech. Here we have another kind of meaning that is satisfying to human beings.

Now this kind of meaning (structure, rhythm) is also to be found in the rhythm of our lives. A Christian or Jewish life, for example, is punctuated by a pattern of feasts, fasts, rituals and seasons, and this gives meaning to such a life. The lives of all of us have this meaning to some extent. That our days are arranged into weeks, for example, makes a difference to the meaning of life. And various other rhythms, timetables, etc., introduced in various ways, give structure (and meaning, in that sense) to our lives. There are also the great natural rhythms of night and day, and the seasons of the year. However, a religious life will usually have a greater richness of meaning, in this sense, than a secular one.

Another meaningful aspect of religious life concerns actions that are done because they are fitting – not in the purposive sense, but in the sense of being suitable to an occasion. Rituals and commemorations are fitting in this sense; and in performing them we have the satisfaction of acting in a meaningful way. The child at the Jewish Passover service asks: 'Why do we eat bitter herbs this evening?' And the answer comes: 'Because the Egyptians embittered the lives of our ancestors with hard labour.' The child does not ask because he does not know; his asking is itself a ritual, to be performed, year after year, on that occasion. Here is a meaningful pattern of action which has nothing to do with purpose or success.

The satisfactions obtained from such activities, and from the religious life in general, are to some extent a matter of individual psychology. What is satisfying to one person may be boring to another. What for one is the charm of regularity, will be a tedium of repetition for another. But however this may be, the advantages of the religious life, such as they are, do not affect the *credibility* of the doctrine. Those who believe must do so on other grounds.

NOTES

1   Baier, K. (1957) 'The Meaning of Life', Inaugural Lecture delivered to Canberra University College; reprinted in Klemke, *op. cit.*, p. 102.
2   *Ibid.*, pp. 103–4.
3   *Ibid.*, p. 103.
4   *Ibid.*, p. 104.
5   *Ibid.*
6   Shakespeare's lines 'Life's but a walking shadow, a poor player/That struts and frets his hour upon the stage' etc. echo the words addressed to Job by one of his friends: 'For we are but of yesterday, and know nothing, for our days on earth are a shadow'. But Job's insignificance was different from that of modern (Shakespearian) man. For in Job's case there was thought to exist a superior Being (relative to which Job was insignificant), which gave meaning to the whole scheme of things.
7   *Cf.* Wohlgenannt, R. (1981) 'Ist die Frage nach dem Sinn des Lebens sinnvoll?', E. Morscher, *et al.* (eds), *Philosophie als Wissenschaft*, Bad Reichenhall.
8   *Cf.* Nozick, R. (1981) *Philosophical Explanations*, Oxford University Press, p. 590.
9   Kant, I. (1948 edn) *The Moral Law*, H. J. Paton (trans.), Hutchinson, p. 73. Kant, a Christian himself, went on to quote from the Gospel to support his point.
10 Sartre, J.-P. (1948) *Existentialism and Humanism*, Methuen, p. 31.
11 *New Testament*, Epistle to the Romans, 9:20.
12 Baier, *op. cit.*, p. 106.
13 *The Moral Law*, p. 104.
14 *The World as Will and Representation*, vol. I, p. 312.

CHAPTER FOUR

Death

This is a special way of being afraid
No trick dispels. Religion used to try,
That vast moth-eaten musical brocade
Created to pretend we never die,
And specious stuff that says *No rational being*
Can fear a thing it will not feel, not seeing
That this is what we fear – no sight, no sound,
No touch or taste or smell, nothing to think with,
Nothing to love or link with,
The anaesthetic from which none come round.

(Philip Larkin, 'Aubade')

One of the great facts of life is death. The day we first become aware that we, and those close to us, must die, is an important one in our development. Here also is something that distinguishes human beings from animals. An animal may suffer pain and fear when threatened with death, but it has no conception of death as such. It cannot be said to fear *death*, as distinct from painful experiences which may lead to death. For us, by contrast, these are separate objects of concern.

For us, also, there is concern about the future, of a kind that cannot be attributed to animals. A dog, remarked Wittgenstein, may 'believe his master is at the door. But can he also believe his master will come the day after tomorrow?'[1] Human beings have a conception of the future because their language enables them to represent future states of affairs in the present. We are concerned about the future;

and much of our life consists of activities directed to future aims, which may be more or less distant. From our earliest days we learn to give importance to these, as opposed to instinctive preferences for the present and very immediate future. But if I consider my future in the long term, what do I see? 'Then I said to myself "What befalls the fool will befall me also; why then have I been so very wise?" And I said to myself that this also is vanity . . . How the wise man dies just like the fool!'[2]

Through the ages human beings have viewed the prospect of death in very different ways. Some have thought that it makes nonsense of our lives, while others have held that life without death would be meaningless. For Shakespeare's Hamlet, it was 'a consummation devoutly to be wished'. Others, like Philip Larkin, have regarded it as an object of fear, while Dylan Thomas wrote that 'Old age should burn and rave at the close of day; /Rage, rage against the dying of the light'. Epicurus and his followers argued that it is a mistake to regard one's extinction as an object of fear or regret. All of these views will be discussed in the present chapter. Another view, to be considered first, has been that death is not the end, but only a passage to another phase of life.

1   IS DEATH THE END?

For most of this chapter I shall assume that there is no personal survival after death. If this is not so, if there is life after death, then obviously our view of death, and its implications for the meaning of life, will be affected accordingly. One such view, connected with religion, has been considered in the previous chapter. But it will be appropriate to begin the present chapter by presenting some of the difficulties about survival after death.

When Socrates, shortly before drinking the poison, was asked by one of his tearful friends how he would like to be buried, he gave a jocular reply: 'Any way you like; that is, if you can catch me and I don't slip through your fingers'.[3] Socrates was sure that he, the essential he, would live on after the death of his body. And many people through the ages have felt, or argued, that death is not the end, or, alternatively, that it *may* not be the end, that this is at least an open possibility. The latter view was taken by Moritz Schlick, who regarded survival as 'an empirical hypothesis', which he would have to verify after his death.[4]

If survival after death is a possibility for human beings, is it so for animals? Do animals have souls, and if so, could these survive the dissolution of the body? It is sometimes thought that here lies the essential difference between animals and ourselves – especially by those who think of the matter in religious terms, as discussed in the previous chapter. Descartes speculated in one of his letters about the existence of souls in animals. He argued that since animals do not, as far as we can tell, think in the way that human beings do, there was no need to ascribe souls to them. But the matter could not be proved, and if they did have thoughts of the relevant kind, then 'they would have an immortal soul like us'.[5] Yet he regarded this as 'unlikely' because, he said,

> there is no reason to believe it of some animals without believing it of all, and many of them such as oysters and sponges are too imperfect for this to be credible.

But what is unlikely is not impossible; and as far as Descartes's argument goes, the survival of oysters and sponges after the death of their bodies remains a possibility.

It may be thought that someone who denies this possibility must be a materialist, holding that only material things exist. But is there not more to a human being, at least, than the body? And if so, may not this something more survive the dissolution of the body? The difficulty about these questions is one of meaning and not credibility. What, we must ask, is the entity whose survival is here postulated? If we could point to some entity that exists during life, and that is independent of the body, then we could suppose that it exists after the decay of the body. But what would be the entity in question? A common view is that it is the soul. But what is meant by 'soul'? Is the soul a kind of entity that can have separate existence? If not, then the survival hypothesis is without meaning, for we do not understand *what* it is that is supposed to survive.

We cannot take it for granted that, corresponding to the noun 'soul', there must be an entity which can be supposed to have a separate existence. One of Lewis Carroll's philosophical jokes, in *Alice in Wonderland*, was that about the Cheshire Cat with a smile on its face. According to the story, the cat disappeared, but the smile remained behind. Now in one sense the cat's smile was something additional to the cat, but not in the sense that would admit of separate existence. A smile is not something that can be supposed to exist separately from the face on which it appears.

Now the word 'soul' is not used, in ordinary discourse, to refer to entities that are independent in the relevant sense. Such expressions as 'heart and soul' and 'he knew in his soul ...' do not mean that we have to regard the soul as an independent entity. The same is true of the more commonly used 'mind', which is sometimes equated with 'soul' in putting forward the survival hypothesis (for example, by Descartes). When we say of a person that he has a good mind, for example, this means that his intellectual abilities are good, and not that he possesses a non-physical organ, the mind. The truth of the remark would depend wholly on the relevant abilities, and not on the existence of a non-physical entity. And similar points may be made about making one's mind up, having something on one's mind, etc. Again, we could not *teach* someone the meanings of 'mind' or 'soul' by indicating a corresponding entity, as we might teach the meanings of 'lung' or 'kidney'.

So far, then, it is not clear *what* is being supposed to survive, when survival is attributed to the mind or soul. There would be similar difficulties about such terms as 'conscience', 'character' or 'wisdom'. We need not hold, with materialists, that conscience (say) is some kind of brain-process, in order to agree that it is not an entity that could exist apart from the person.

We may also consider the matter from the point of view of the word 'exist'. What would the word mean in this case? Other things besides bodies are said to exist, and the word must be understood in a sense suitable to the object. We might say, for example, that there exist two prime numbers between 20 and 30, and this would not be understood in the sense of bodily existence, but in a sense appropriate to numbers. Other ways of existing are those of a poem, a piece of music, a smell, or an opinion (in either the individual or the shared sense). Now we may take it that the hypothesis of personal survival is not meant in any of these senses of 'exist'. In what sense, then, is it meant? The way in which we exist when alive is a *bodily* way. A human body occupies a certain space, which cannot be occupied by others; it forms a physical unity, and so on. But this way of existing cannot be ascribed to the non-bodily entity that is supposed to survive after death.

Now it is essential to the survival hypothesis that the soul or mind be that of the person concerned (thus 'John Brown's body lies a-mouldering in his grave, but his soul goes marching on'). The soul that goes marching on must be that of John Brown, if there is to be personal survival. But sometimes the hypothesis is expressed, more simply, in terms of the name or pronoun alone. Thus it may be said that *John Brown* will, or may, survive the death of his body: or that *I* hope to do so. But do such names and pronouns refer to an entity that is independent of the body in the required sense? Does 'I', for example, mean a non-bodily entity? In 'I am six feet tall' it obviously means a bodily entity. But what about 'I am thinking'? In the first case, 'I' can be replaced by 'my body' (or 'this body'), but not in the second. But neither can it, in the second case, be replaced by a *non-bodily* entity. Thinking is attributed to a *person*, and although 'person' does not mean 'body', a person is a bodily entity – one that is identified by its physical appearance, position in space and so on. Hence we have still not discovered any entity that could be supposed to exist independently of the body.

One way, however, in which we may be tempted in this direction is through an exercise of imagination. It seems so easy to imagine oneself existing apart from one's body; does this not prove that the supposition makes sense? 'I can easily imagine', wrote Schlick, 'witnessing the funeral of my own body and continuing to exist without a body'.[6] Now it is true that I can easily imagine (picture to myself) my body

being put into a coffin, and so on. But to imagine this is
not to imagine *myself* witnessing this scene; it is merely to
imagine the scene. 'Myself witnessing' is not part of what
is being pictured. This distinction can also be made in the
case of other, more usual, imaginings. I can imagine (picture
to myself) a ship sailing down the river; and here again, I
would not be part of the picture. I could, however, imagine
another scene in which I *would* be part of the picture: I
would picture myself standing, for example, on a hill
overlooking the river, with the ship going past in front of
me. But this addition could not be made in the case of
imagining my own funeral. For in this case there is no
bodily, visible observer to be imagined by me. What Schlick
was able to imagine was not *himself* existing and witnessing,
but only a body undergoing certain processes. We must not
let this exercise of the imagination tempt us into thinking
that a separate, observing 'self' is part of what we imagine,
or that there is such an entity which would be capable of
independent existence.

Finally, there are certain other senses in which people
speak of survival. It is said that we 'live on' in our children
or, again, in the memory of those we leave behind; and we
sometimes use the word 'immortal' in speaking of great
poets, for example. These ways of living on are important,
and may do something to mitigate the sense of final
termination that is liable to trouble us when we think about
death. However, they do not tell against the view that when
we die, we exist no longer as persons. These uses of 'live
on' and 'immortal' are, after all, no more than metaphorical
ways of saying that the dead person is remembered, that a
great poet's works are admired long after his death, and so
on. Our discussion has not cast doubt on this kind of
survival, but on the kind of personal survival that people
hope for when they hope, or wish, that they themselves
will not cease to exist.

2   THE CONSOLATION OF NATURE

The meaning of life, and what life means to us, is affected
by the knowledge that death lies in wait. According to

Schopenhauer, death renders human activity 'essentially vain'. If there were any value in it, 'it would not have non-being as its goal'.[7] Others have claimed, on the contrary, that life without death would be meaningless.

An obvious objection against Schopenhauer is that he confuses 'goal' with what comes at the end. The fact that death comes at the end does not mean that it is our goal – unless, indeed, one's goal is suicide. If this *were* the goal of most people, then we might agree that human striving is essentially self-destructive and in that sense vain. But for most of us death is not the goal. We have other goals, of many different kinds, which may be said to give meaning and purpose to our lives, without any tendency to self-destruction.

Nevertheless death casts a negative shadow over our lives. This is connected with the point made earlier about the human orientation towards the future. We come into the world having only instinctive drives and reactions; like animals, we live in the present. But then we are trained to consider ourselves as we shall be in the future. This involves an emotional redirection. We come to identify ourselves with our later phases and to have an emotional engagement with them. But then we must also represent to ourselves that final phase in which we pass into non-being; and then we may exclaim, like the author of Ecclesiastes, 'How the wise man dies just like the fool!'

Through the ages there have been attempts to show that death is not an evil, that to complain about death is a mistake. One argument has been that death is natural. Lucretius, in the first century BC, asks us to imagine 'Nature herself' addressing those who complain about death. 'What is your grievance, mortal, that you give yourself up to this whining and repining? Why do you weep and wail over death?' She ('nature') goes on to suggest that the enjoyment of life must have a natural terminus, in the same way as other enjoyments. 'Why, you silly creature, do you not retire as a guest who has had his fill of life?'[8]

Lucretius' argument would not be applicable to cases in which death comes abnormally early; such a person would not be said to have had his fill of life. But how well does it apply to someone who dies at a normal age? The comparison with the guest is far from perfect. The guest who retires from a banquet no doubt hopes to be ready for another one in due time; and this is not so with the 'retirement' of death. Another metaphor that needs to be treated with caution is that of 'a ripe old age', which is sometimes used by way of consolation. Death at a ripe age is not acceptable in the same way as, say, the picking of fruit when it is of a ripe age; it does not bring the benefits that we enjoy from picking fruit when it is ripe. Nevertheless the metaphor is appropriate in indicating that such a death is more acceptable because it comes at a time when death is normal and to be expected.

This appeal to normality is rejected by Thomas Nagel, who asks us to suppose that 'the normal lifespan were a thousand years'. In that case, he says, 'death at 80 would be a tragedy. As things are, it may just be a more widespread tragedy.'[9] The truth is, however, that whether death at a given age is a tragedy does depend on what the normal lifespan is. To describe an event as tragic, we need to consider not only the event itself, but its place in the context of what is normal. As Nagel admits, 'the death of Keats at 24 is generally regarded as tragic; that of Tolstoy at 82 is not'. This is not to say, of course, that Tolstoy's death must leave us altogether unmoved. But there is good reason for not describing it as tragic.

If a person's death is natural and normal, does it follow that it is not an evil? The word 'natural' has a favourable connotation, but as we shall see in a later chapter, the relation between natural and good is complicated and controversial. It is clear, however, that we do sometimes complain about natural events, and that the reasonableness of such complaints is not, or not necessarily, brought into question when it is pointed out that the events are natural. An example is the expression of grief at a bereavement, where we grieve about our own deprivation, as distinct from feeling sorry for a person who died. It would be absurd to say that such grief is unreasonable merely because bereavement is natural. To be deprived of someone dear to us is a reasonable cause for complaint, if anything is. Another example, again connected with death, is the apprehension that we may feel about old age (as distinct from death), and the complaining of old people about the infirmities and disabilities which are typical of that time of life. Here again, it would be absurd to claim that pain and disability are not proper objects of apprehension and complaint merely because they are natural for that time of life.

Should we conclude that natural suffering is no less bad than unnatural? This appears to be Nagel's view. 'Normality', he writes, 'seems to have nothing to do with it, for the fact that we will all inevitably die in a few score years cannot by itself imply that it would not be good to live longer'.[10] Now it is true that the normality of a thing does not remove it altogether from the sphere of regret. But to claim that it has 'nothing to do with it' is going too far. The sufferings and infirmities of old age – provided they are not of abnormal proportions – are not regarded with the same horror as similar sufferings and infirmities occurring at an earlier age. This would also be so if the sufferings of old age were greater than they are. Nagel asks us to suppose that we were certain of six months of agony prior to death, and he poses the question: 'Would inevitability make *that* prospect any less unpleasant?' But this is a misleading question. What *would* make the prospect less unpleasant would be, not its inevitability, but its normality. If the agony were normal and natural, this would mitigate the prospect of it to some extent. A similar point may be made about the sufferings of women in connection with childbirth and the monthly period. These pains and sufferings are serious enough, but the fact (or belief) that they are natural helps to make them more acceptable. Similarly, if death is an evil, the fact that it is natural should make it more acceptable – though not removing it altogether as an object of complaint, as Lucretius would argue. When the misleading metaphors about the guest at a banquet, and so on, have been stripped away, the argument about nature provides consolation, though it does not show that regrets about death are altogether mistaken.

3   WHEN DEATH IS PRESENT

Death, wrote Epicurus, 'is of no concern to us; for while we exist death is not present, and when death is present, we no longer exist'.[11] Now it is true that, when we no longer exist, death (or anything else) is of no concern to us. But may not something that is not yet present be of concern to us while we do exist? Most of our concerns, indeed, are about what is to come rather than about what is already present. It appears that Epicurus' argument is based on a false premise.

However, the argument is not refuted so easily; for the first part of it must be taken in conjunction with the second. Suppose there is an evil, E, which has this peculiar characteristic: if E occurred at time t_1 it would affect us at t_1; if it occurred at t_2 it would *not* affect us at t_2. Moreover, we know that E cannot occur at t_1. In that case, should E be of concern to us at t_1? We may be inclined to answer 'no'. Similarly, the fact that death will not affect us after we are dead may be held to entail that we ought not to be concerned about it while we exist.

But can nothing affect us after we are dead? According to Lucretius, death redeems us from all suffering. We may 'rest assured, therefore, that we have nothing to fear in death. One who no longer is cannot suffer . . .'[12] But this claim may be disputed. In 1927 a court action was brought against a newspaper for printing a libellous article about the former British Prime Minister, W. E. Gladstone. Gladstone had been dead some thirty years; but it would not be inappropriate to say that he was *harmed* or *injured* by the libel. Nagel has drawn attention to various ways in which one may be harmed without having any knowledge of the harm, for example by being betrayed, deceived or ridiculed behind one's back.[13] Another example is that of people deprived of educational opportunities, who may not know, and may indeed be incapable of understanding, the harm that has been done to them.

We cannot conclude, then, that being dead is not an evil, merely because it lies outside our experience. Moreover, death is not excluded, as are the other examples, from being a possible object of concern or even fear. In the examples of betrayal, lost opportunities, etc., we assumed that the victims would be unaware of what had been done. By contrast, our unawareness of death only begins, so to speak, after we are dead.

But on the other hand, how serious are evils that are not experienced by the person concerned? Nagel takes issue with the saying 'What you don't know can't hurt you',[14] giving his examples of betrayal, etc., in opposition to it. But such sayings are not to be defeated so easily. It is, after all, just in such cases as those cited by Nagel that the saying is used, and regarded as an appropriate move in the moral language-game. And people sometimes say that, for their part, they do not care about (so-called) injuries to themselves of which they will never have any knowledge.

Others, however, would not say this; for them 'What you don't know can't hurt you' would not be the last word. In this matter, as in some others, moral ideas may differ, depending on a person's character and attitude to life, and on the particular case. What may safely be said, however, is that if there are unexperienced evils, they are not *as bad* as those within our experience. We also regard it as morally acceptable to speak less politely (without going as far as betrayal, etc.) behind a person's back, than we would if he or she were present. Our moral concerns are primarily about evils that *are* experienced and only by extension about those of which we are unaware.

There is some truth, then, in the Epicurean arguments. If being dead is an evil, it is one that is at least mitigated by the fact that 'one who no longer is' cannot experience it.

4   DEATH AND OTHER FORMS OF NON-EXISTENCE

On tombstones we sometimes find comforting inscriptions in which death is described as a kind of sleep. In this case 'sleep' may be connected with hopes of a re-awakening; but it need not be so. Many writers have taken comfort from the idea that death is a kind of everlasting sleep. Socrates, on being condemned to death, told the jury that if death is the annihilation of consciousness (this being one possibility that he considered), then it 'must be a marvellous gain'. There was, he said, nothing happier in life than a night of dreamless sleep; and death could be regarded as 'one single night' of such sleep.[15] John Donne, in the sonnet on death, argued that death must be more pleasant than sleep or rest, being the perfect example of which they were mere imitations. 'From rest and sleep, which but thy pictures be,/ Much pleasure, then from thee, much more must flow.' And Lucretius addresses the dead person as follows: 'You are at peace now in the sleep of death, and so you will stay till the end of time.' Turning to the mourners, he asks: 'If something returns to sleep and peace, what reason is that for pining in inconsolable grief?'[16]

How appropriate is the comparison of death with sleep? An obvious difference is that whereas death is the end of life, sleep is merely an interruption of it. When going to sleep, I know that I shall be able to continue tomorrow what I have been doing today, that I shall see again the things and people that concern and interest me, that I can look forward to the further future, and so on. Another difference is that (as Socrates pointed out) we look forward to and enjoy our sleep; whereas one cannot be said to enjoy one's death (even where death is painless). It is true that some unfortunate people look forward to death to end their sufferings; while others, mainly elderly, face death with equanimity. But our attitude to sleep is more positive (and also more general) than this. Sleep is the natural satisfaction of a desire that arises in us. We feel *sleepy*, and in going to bed and falling asleep we experience the satisfaction of fulfilling a natural need, just as, when we feel hungry, we experience satisfaction in fulfilling that need.

It is not *being* asleep that we enjoy. There is no enjoyment when one is unconscious (leaving aside the possible enjoyment of dreams). The enjoyment of sleep is that of *going* to sleep and, perhaps, waking up with the sensation of refreshment that may come after 'a good night's sleep'. It is because of these satisfactions that sleep is, as we may say, one of the pleasures of life.

But these benefits are not enjoyed in the case of death. There is no such sensation as 'deathy', and dying is not a pleasurable experience, as going to sleep is. Nor do we enjoy the refreshment of waking up in the case of death. Again, whereas everyone desires, from time to time, to go to sleep, most of us do not desire to enter the 'sleep' of death. (This fact may be attributed to the machinery of natural selection. A race of beings to whom life and death became indifferent would not survive very long.)

Another comparison is that between non-being after death and non-being before birth. What should be our attitude to the two periods? 'Look back at the eternity that passed before we were born, and mark how utterly it counts to us as nothing.' This, wrote Lucretius, 'is a mirror that Nature holds up to us, in which we may see the time that shall be after we are dead'.[17]

But is it true that time before we were born counts as nothing to us, that we have no regrets about not having been in existence then? We do sometimes express such regrets – not having been alive to hear Caruso sing or have discussions with Socrates (supposing one would have been in a position to do so). But these are regrets about particular experiences and not about the shortness of life. (One might, similarly, regret having missed various experiences *during* one's life.) Such regrets may also exist with regard to the future; there may be some specific event for which one would like to be alive in the future. But one may also wish to live longer, and feel sad at the prospect of death, not because of any particular experiences, but simply for the sake of life itself, whatever it may bring. And there seems to be no corresponding regret in the case of the past. We do not wish to have been alive earlier, merely for the sake of longer life. And in general it may be said that we are, contrary to Epicurus' advice, more deeply affected by the thought of non-existence after death than by the thought of non-existence before birth.

Why should this be so? The answer lies in the natural emotional orientation which propels us in the course of our lives. 'We are', as Montaigne said, 'never present with, but always beyond ourselves', 'fear, desire, hope, still push us toward the future'.[18] It is true that we also have backward-looking emotions: pride, shame and regrets of various kinds. And we sometimes think about the past, going over past experiences in our minds or in conversation. (This is especially true of old people.) But there is a sense in which concern about the future must be overriding. We need this orientation; it is part of the machinery of natural selection.

Every day of our lives we engage in activities directed to the future (even if only trivial ones like shopping); we make plans, discuss them with others, work for some future goal; and experience, more or less intensely, those forward-looking emotions of which Montaigne speaks. Without this concern for the future the human species would not be as successful as it is, and perhaps not viable at all. This is not to deny that we also need our memories of the past in order to deal with the demands of life; we need to learn from experience, remember where we are with a given task, and so on. But these thoughts about the past are necessary because of their relevance for *future* action. The future is what we can affect by our actions. If I wish that something will happen, I may be able to bring it about by suitable action. And even if the future event is outside my control, I can take measures to react to it in suitable ways when it occurs. It also makes sense to consider what *might* happen in the future (with or without my intervention), weighing up alternative courses of events. By contrast, to speculate about what might have happened in the past, and about what we might have done, had we acted differently is, proverbially, an idle pursuit.

Here then is an explanation why we may be more concerned about what lies in the ultimate future, i.e. our non-existence, than about non-existence before birth. However, it may be objected that while this is an explanation, it is not a justification; that, to be consistent, we should have the same attitude in both cases. But if the argument is about consistency, then it will not be adequate for Epicurus' intention. For as far as this argument is concerned, we may as well adjust our unconcern about past non-existence to the concern which we feel about non-existence in the future; thus becoming, contrary to Epicurus' intention, *more* regretful than we were before.

Now one thing that death and pre-natal non-existence have in common is that they are inevitable; and it may be thought that here lies the point of the argument. We can do no more about the one than about the other, so that regret is as unreasonable in the first as in the second.[19] But is it unreasonable to feel regret about what is inevitable? In a utilitarian sense, the answer must be 'yes'; it is (as we sometimes tell ourselves) no *use* worrying about what cannot be helped. Yet such emotions are not based on a mistake. The person concerned is not worrying because he thinks this will help him; but, given a suitable case, worrying is a natural and (in another sense) reasonable reaction. Many of our emotional attitudes are in this sense futile without being unreasonable. We feel grief at a bereavement. Does it do any good? 'Don't be sad, it will not bring the lost person back.' Such advice is misconceived. We do not have these feelings because we think they will make things better; and to point out that they will not, is irrelevant. Another example is that of a person on a ladder, who feels afraid although he knows it is perfectly safe. It would be no use telling this person that he would be better off without his fear. He knows his fear serves no purpose and may even interfere with what he is trying to do. But he is not under any illusion, and his fear is not unreasonable. Similarly, it would be no good Epicurus telling us that we ought not to regret death because such regrets are futile.

There is a similar difficulty about Derek Parfit's claim that a more balanced attitude towards past and future would make us happier. Parfit introduces an imaginary character, 'Timeless', who cares as much about the past as about the future. Reminded about past suffering, he is as much distressed as when he learns that he is going to suffer; and his attitudes to past and future enjoyments are similarly equal. Parfit claims that if we were like Timeless, we would greatly gain 'in our attitude to ageing and death. As our life passes, we should have less and less to look forward to, but more and more to look backward to.'[20] What we have to look backward to would, of course, contain bad as well as good, but, says Parfit, in looking back 'we could afford to be selective ... we could allow ourselves to forget most of the bad things', while preserving the good things in our memories. But we cannot, without disastrous consequences, be selective in this way about the future.

Now it may be questioned whether the supposition of such a person as 'Timeless' is coherent. But even if it is, there remains a difficulty about selection. We may agree, without resorting to that supposition, that we would be happier if we could 'forget most of the bad things' from the past. We do indeed try to reason with people who dwell too much on the bad things (past as well as future), pointing out that they do no good by this and only make themselves and others miserable. But someone may be well aware of this and yet unable to change his outlook. Moreover, he may not want to be selective even if he could; preferring the true perspective to a more cheerful one.

Similarly, regrets about non-existence after death are futile, as are regrets about the past. But it does not follow that these regrets are misconceived. And given our emotional orientation towards the future, it is natural and unavoidable that we should feel more concerned about death and the time after death than about past non-existence.

5   DEATH AND THE GOODNESS OF LIFE

I have considered a number of mitigations and consolations concerning death, coming mainly from the Epicurean philosophers. But is there any reason *for* regarding death as an evil? Death is obviously a negative event. It is also bound to be of concern to us, since it makes a big difference to our prospect of the future. But is death an evil, a suitable object for regret and not merely concern?

One reason for regarding death as an evil has been indicated by Williams. We may wish not to die because death would prevent the fulfilment of our plans and desires for the future. Thus, as Williams says, 'wanting something itself gives one a reason for avoiding death'. He allows that the person who dies would not know what he is missing, but, he concludes, 'from the perspective of the wanting agent it is rational to aim for states of affairs in which his want is satisfied, and hence to regard death . . . as an evil'.[21]

However, this argument is not applicable as widely as might be thought. Not every case of wanting something would count as a reason for avoiding death. I may want to buy a new jacket or plan to make improvements to my garden, but such things could hardly be regarded as 'a reason for avoiding death'. Only very special plans and desires could have this role. For example, one may desire to make a pilgrimage to Mecca before one dies; or there may be an important piece of work to which one has devoted one's life and which one wants to see completed. In such cases we can speak about reasons for avoiding death. But many people have no such plans or desires.

Again, the fact that the dead person will not know what he is missing is an important qualification, and one that does affect 'the perspective of the wanting agent'. Suppose I have some important plan or project, and look forward very much to its completion in due course. How would I like it if someone or something were to prevent this? Probably I would be very upset; and I would do all I can to resist such interference. But what if the prevention were due to death? Here the answer might be: 'Oh well – in that case I wouldn't be in existence to have any regrets.' What I certainly do not want is to *see* my plans frustrated; but if I die, that is another matter. As we saw in Section 3 of this chapter, attitudes about unexperienced evils may differ; and some people would be less concerned than others about the thwarting of their desires by death.

Another reason put forward for regarding death as bad is that life is good. But is life good? In one of Gilbert and Sullivan's operas, we are told that 'life's a pudding full of plums'. Nagel has declared, more guardedly: 'All of us, I believe, are fortunate to have been born';[22] and he concludes from this that death is a misfortune for the one who dies. But are we fortunate to have been born? Schopenhauer, for one, held that life is not worth living.

It is also assumed that whether life is, on the whole, good

or bad, is a question that can be asked about any given life. Thus 'if a certain kind of life is good, it is better than nothing. If it is bad, it is worse than nothing.'[23] R. M. Hare, who says he is glad to have been born, uses a 'golden rule' argument against the abortion of 'any fœtus which will, if not aborted, turn into someone who will be glad to be alive'.[24] And Kurt Baier claims that there are 'criteria and standards' for the 'evaluation of a life', just as there are for the evaluation of 'students, meals, tennis players', etc.[25]

If the badness of death depends on the goodness of life, then the degree of badness should be proportionate to the degree of goodness. If life is very good, then death must be very bad. But since we are aware of death during life, the shadow that it casts over a very good life will be so much worse, thus diminishing the goodness of that life. So the goodness of life would be self-defeating to some extent. A similar point was made by Schopenhauer, on the assumption that life is bad. Who could bear the thought of death, he asked, 'if life were a pleasure?' But life is not a pleasure, it is the opposite. Hence death has 'the good point of being the end of life'.[26]

How are we to decide whether life, in general or in particular, is good or bad? There are extreme cases of suffering and disability in which it may be said that, for the person concerned, life is clearly bad. But what are we to say of people leading more or less normal lives? Is your life, or mine, good or bad? The question seems simple enough, and we may be inclined to give a positive answer without hesitation. But have we reasons for such an answer? To describe something as good is usually to imply that there is some way in which it is good, something we can refer to as a reason for calling it good. We may speak of an *episode* in life in this way, having in mind reasons which are specific to that episode. A stay abroad was good because one met such and such interesting people; a visit to the theatre was bad, because the play was boring. One may also speak of a certain period in one's life as happy or unhappy, for appropriate reasons. But life itself is not an episode or a period; and the description of life as good cannot be meant in that way. Of course, there are plenty of good things in life – human relationships, aesthetic pleasures, the satisfaction of a job completed. But there are also plenty of bad things. That life is a mixture of good and bad is, after all, a truism. It is also worth noting that much of life – the daily round, etc. – is neither particularly good nor particularly bad. (Consider how we answer the question 'How are you?') If we say that life is good, is it because we have weighed the good things and the bad things (including, presumably, those in the future) and found that the good weigh more?

Consider a very simple example. Suppose I feel hungry for an hour and then eat. Which was greater, the pain of hunger or the pleasure of eating? The former, because it lasted longer? Or the latter, because it was more intense? But was it more intense? And if so, was the difference of intensity such as to make up for the longer time? Perhaps we can make such comparisons in extreme cases. Someone who suffers severe hunger over a long period and then gets a small amount of food which still leaves him hungry, may be said to have had more pain than pleasure. But what makes sense in extreme cases need not make sense when we are dealing with commonplace examples; and still less so, when the question is about a person's whole life.

There are similar difficulties about the talk of 'a life worth living', and about being 'fortunate' or 'glad' to have been born, or to be alive. One might properly say that one is fortunate, or glad, to be living in England, for example, and this would be understood to mean that there are certain respects in which England is a better country to be living in than elsewhere. But no such meaning can be attached to the remarks about being alive. Again, when we say that something is worth while, we mean some action that is worth doing, in spite of the effort needed, because of advantages to be gained. 'Is it worth going all the way to London?', 'Is this book worth reading?' are questions of this kind. But life is not an action, and we do not, in normal circumstances, *choose* to remain alive.

Conceding that life contains misery as well as happiness, Nagel has argued for the goodness of life (and consequent badness of death) in another way. He claims that 'perception, desire, activity' are 'benefits in themselves'; the mere availability of experience is good, regardless of its content. Life is 'worth living', he holds, even when 'the bad elements of experience' are not outweighed by the good. 'The additional positive weight is supplied by experience itself, rather than by way of its contents.'[27] Philippa Foot, rejecting Nagel's claim as 'implausible', nevertheless speaks of a person who 'has no doubt that existence is a good to him', though he has 'no idea about the balance of happiness and unhappiness in his life'.[28] But what does it mean to say that existence is 'a good to him'? If we asked someone to name the 'goods' (benefits, advantages) in his or her life, could existence appear among them? When Job cursed the day of his birth because of his great sufferings, his friends put forward various arguments to reconcile him to his fate. Could they have consoled him by pointing out that at least he had the benefit of existence? Similarly, as Mary Mothersill suggested in reply to Nagel, it would be nonsense to regard non-existence (being dead) as a misfortune – as if we could say of someone: 'Poor Smith! First he loses his job; then his wife leaves him and now, to top it all off, he's dead'.[29]

It is true that, given a suitable occasion, the expressions I have criticized ('good', 'worthwhile', etc.) may be applied to life itself. For example, 'It's good to be alive' may be used as an expression of happiness. But the person who says this is not expressing a judgement that life contains more good than bad; nor is he claiming that experience or existence are goods in themselves, regardless of content. He is not talking about life in the abstract, but giving expression to his state of mind there and then. (This may be in reaction to specific events, or because he happens to feel happy for no particular reason.) There are also, of course, occasions for expression on the negative side, as when someone says that life is not worth living. Again, when this person's fortunes are restored, he may express his satisfaction by saying that *now* life is worth living. And this may also provide a context for regarding death as a misfortune. Thus we might pity someone for dying just when his fortunes had begun to turn. But these remarks make no sense in the abstract, and cannot support any general thesis about the goodness of life or the badness of death.

There is also a disparity between positive and negative situations; and misunderstanding may be caused if this is ignored. A person in desperate circumstances (such as Job) *may* have reached the belief that his life, as a whole, is bad rather than good, and he may decide, therefore, to put an end to it. But it does not follow that those who do *not* commit suicide have judged the opposite. To decide on suicide one needs very strong reasons; but no decision is called for, and no reasons are needed, for remaining alive. We do not remain alive *because* we judge that life is good – or for any other reason.

It is true that when our lives are in danger, we have a strong desire to be saved. That is why, as Foot points out, someone who saves my life may be described as 'my benefactor'.[30] But it does not follow from this that life can be described as a 'benefit', a 'good thing', etc. The desire to cling to life is one that exists in us independently of reasons. This point may be illustrated by the 'Eastern tale' that Tolstoy recounted in *My Confession*. A traveller, pursued by a wild beast, escapes by jumping into a dry well, only to find that at the bottom there is a dragon, eager to swallow anyone who falls in. The unfortunate man manages to hold on to a branch which keeps him out of reach of both dangers. But he knows his time is limited. Nevertheless, seeing some drops of honey on the leaves of the bush, he reaches out and licks them. 'Just so,' concludes Tolstoy, 'I hold on to the branch of life, knowing that the dragon of death is waiting inevitably for me ... And I try to lick that honey which used to give me pleasure.' But now 'I clearly see the dragon, and the honey is no longer sweet to me'.[31]

Now there are obviously differences between the 'branch of life' on which we find ourselves and that of the unfortunate traveller. For most of us, remaining alive is not a struggle, and our thoughts are occupied with other things than the avoidance of death. But what if we were in that desperate situation? Was the man *wrong* to reach for the honey? If someone falls overboard a thousand miles from land, and knows he has no chance of being picked up, will he be wrong if he swims? These desires (or 'drives') are not justified by reasons, but that does not make the behaviour unreasonable. The mere desire can count as a reason for behaving in these ways. Similarly, if people have a desire to eat, make conversation, play games or study history, then that is a reason for doing these things. If someone who expects to die tomorrow desires to eat today, then that is a reason for eating today. And the same is true of the desire for life itself. We do not desire it for a reason (because it is 'good'); but *that* we desire it is a reason for holding on to it, even if the struggle is hard.

6 DEATH AND THE DESIRE FOR LIFE

Perhaps it will now be said that death is an evil simply because it goes against the desire for life. If we desire strongly to keep something (for whatever reason or for no reason at all), then we are harmed by being deprived of it. On this view, the conclusion about death would be based on the desire, rather than the desire being based on a view about death. But what is the status of the desire for life? A person in danger, as we have seen, will struggle hard to avoid death. But it does not follow that there is an abiding desire to avoid death whenever it may come. Our discussion has shown, on the contrary, that there is a good deal of indecision about this, so that people are easily influenced by dubious metaphors and comparisons. Most of us would probably not wish to die at an abnormally early age; but for many people the important thing is to avoid suffering rather than to have more of life.

The uncertainty about the desire for life may be illustrated by supposing that we were offered an 'elixir of life', which would make one immune from ageing and fatal illness. If such a preparation came on the market, who would buy it? And how much would we be prepared to pay? It might be thought that the opportunity to defeat death and remove its baleful shadow would be eagerly seized. Yet to many people the prospect would be repugnant. The chances are that we would be swayed (as so often with issues of supreme importance) by slogans, false comparisons and prevailing fashions. It would also depend on the manner in which the issue made its appearance – whether in the fabulous way presented here, or as a question of paying for scientific research into the prevention of ageing. (Such research is already in progress.) It would also make a difference if what occurred were a gradual change – an extension of life further to that which has already taken place, rather than an abrupt elimination of ageing, etc.

Nagel, eloquent in his denunciation of death and belief in the good of life, would, it seems, be among the buyers of an elixir of life. He writes: 'Given a simple choice between living for another week and dying in five minutes, I would always choose to live for another week; and by a version of mathematical induction I conclude that I would be glad to live forever'.[32] But this is curious reasoning! Does Nagel need mathematical induction to find out what he wants? Someone who thinks that the matter can be resolved by such methods shows, rather, that he does not really know what he wants. It is true enough that most of us would resist death when it presents itself, and would be horrified by the threat of 'dying in five minutes'. But it does not follow that we must have the same attitude to death whenever it may come.

It might be thought that in such an important matter we must all know what we want – and know it immediately and not by a roundabout method. But this cannot be taken for granted. Apart from basic desires like the avoidance of pain and a few others, what we desire is largely determined by social and cultural circumstances. (We shall see in a later chapter that this is a major difficulty for a utilitarian philosophy which assumes that existing desires are the fundamental data of morality.) And when it comes to matters of supreme importance, matters of life and death, our desires may be left unclear.

There are well-known differences among cultures in this matter. In a warlike society it may be widely accepted that to die well in battle is more important than to be alive. Again, consider how the romantic poets viewed death. '. . . and, for many a time/I have been half in love with easeful Death,/ . . . Now more than ever seems it rich to die,/ To cease upon the midnight with no pain . . .' Such thoughts were expressed in various ways by Keats, Shelley and others. The early death of Keats, as we noted earlier, may properly be described as tragic (unlike that of Tolstoy, at a ripe old age). But was it tragic *for him*? If Keats's words are to be believed, it was not. Most of us do not share this attitude to death, but we can understand it and sympathize with it when we read the poem. In short, the desire for life is not as universal or well-established as certain other human desires.

Again, consider our attitude to that loss of life which we call sleep. The time we spend sleeping may be described as a subtraction from life. Now it is true (as discussed in Section 4) that the 'death' of sleep is accompanied by satisfactions which are not there in the case of death. (There is also the point about sleep being an interruption and not the end.) But if the regrets about death are about the cancellation of consciousness and experience, then they should apply also to sleep. And here there seems to be an inconsistency in our attitudes. We go to great lengths to prolong life, and much wealth and effort have been devoted to research into ways of enabling people to live longer. An average person today can have *more* of life than an average person in the past, and this is regarded as a great benefit. But we do not have this attitude towards sleep. If a drug were available which would render sleep unnecessary (and take away the desire for sleep), we could have more of life. (Alternatively, we may imagine a drug which would reduce the duration of sleep without abolishing it altogether. In this way we could still enjoy its satisfactions, while keeping the negative aspect to a minimum.) But there seems to be no demand for such drugs. Some people, it is true, complain that 'there are never enough hours in the day' to allow them to do all they would wish; but most of us, most of the time, do not regard sleep, and the withdrawal from life that it entails, as a matter for regret. In this case, we are happy to accept that our conscious lives are curtailed by about one-third.

It is sometimes thought that death is acceptable because the alternative, everlasting life, would be unbearable; and that this is why we should refuse the elixir of life. This idea has been illustrated in a number of myths and stories, including a play by Karel Čapek to which Williams refers. Here we are introduced to the daughter of a sixteenth-century physician with an experimental turn of mind, who had administered a dose of elixir to her. Now aged 342, she is desperately bored with life, refuses a further dose, and so dies at last. Williams claims that death, so far from rendering life meaningless, is a necessary condition of meaning – that 'immortality, or state without death, would be meaningless'.[33]

There is a difference, however, between immortality and the kind of protection that might be provided by an elixir. The latter (we may suppose) would give protection against ageing and fatal illnesses; but could it preserve us from other dangers, such as being run over by a lorry or being blown to pieces by a bomb? To suppose that it could, we would need to assume a miraculous suspension of the laws of nature. The person concerned would have all sorts of miraculous powers of action; and there are other implications which perhaps render the whole supposition incoherent.

Let us therefore consider an elixir of the more modest kind, avoiding these large issues. A person taking this substance might, with reasonable care, expect to live to 342 and perhaps longer. Would this be desirable? It may be thought that such a person would become desperately bored with life. But is someone aged 342 more likely to be bored than someone aged 42? Williams compares the case to that of a sentry 'standing too long at his post'. But this is a poor comparison. In the first place, sentry-duty is anyway a monotonous occupation, unlike many others. But more importantly, life is not an occupation, and cannot be described in the same terms as occupations and activities that take place *within* life. We may ask whether sentry-duty, football, television or philosophy are, or could become, boring occupations; but to speak in this way of the 'occupation' of living would be a category-mistake.

Someone who complains of being 'bored with life' is not bored with life as such, but with the activities, or lack of them, *in* his life. Hence it is not surprising that a person aged 20 is no less liable to be bored than an older one; and such cases are familiar enough. Conversely, there is no reason to think that someone aged 342 would be more likely to be bored with life than a younger person. His or her life may be rich in challenging tasks and new experiences, with obligations to meet, troubles to get into, and pleasures to look forward to. It is true that these experiences would not have the freshness of those of a young person embarking on life. There are first-time experiences (falling in love, 'discovering' a great novel) which have a special charm and intensity through being first-time; and this cannot be repeated. But, after all, this is something that affects all of us in later life. And while it is a cause for regret, it does not mean that later life is unbearably boring; nor does it become more and more so as we get older. The life of the elixir-drinker would be, so to speak, all middle-age; but that is not such a bad prospect. A more serious disadvantage would be the loss of one's friends and relations with only a normal span of life. But again, one would probably become adjusted to this; and one might, in any case, think it a price worth paying. (We might also develop the more complicated supposition of everyone, or perhaps a group of people, taking the elixir.) But however this may be, there seems to be no support for the view that life without death would be meaningless or unbearable; and our hesitations about the elixir remain in conflict with the desire for life, and longer life, that we express in other contexts.

7   CONCLUSION: THE MEANING OF DEATH

That the prospect of death is an important ingredient of human life few would deny. It is also, on the whole, a sombre rather than a cheerful prospect. This may be due to the association of death with suffering (the sufferings of old age, and of bereavement). But it is safe to say that death itself, non-being as such, is viewed with concern. What should be our conclusion about death? Is it a matter for regret? Does it render our lives meaningless?

It might be thought that with such an important matter,

some important conclusions should be forthcoming. But this need not be so. It may be that when we have thought about death in appropriate ways, examining the role it plays in our lives, comparing it with other states of non-being, etc., the conclusion is bound to be mixed.

As we saw, death is in some ways like sleep, and like pre-natal non-being; and when we view it in these ways, we may be comforted. But the analogies are imperfect. (This is hardly surprising, given the peculiar place of death in our lives.) Neither sleep nor the pre-natal state is an elimination of one's future; and the future is bound to be of special concern to us. Does it follow that death is an evil, perhaps the greatest evil that can befall us? No, for as Lucretius pointed out, when we are dead we are released from all experience of evil. Now we may agree (with Nagel) that one may be said to suffer evil even though one is not conscious of the fact; and it may also be admitted that death is an evil if it interferes with important projects that a person has. But, as we saw, this applies less to some people than to others. Again, evils which fall outside the victim's experience are less serious than those which do not; and some people would not care about them.

Another complaint about death, as we saw, is that it renders our lives meaningless. If this were so, then life would not be worth living and therefore death would *not* be an evil. However, there is no reason to think that death renders life meaningless, unless we regard it, like Schopenhauer, as the 'goal' of life. There are all sorts of goals within our lives, but it is not clear that we can speak of a goal of life as such. Some people, admittedly, have an overriding goal to which they devote a large part of their lives; but this goal would not be death. Some people, again, do have death as their goal; they try to bring about their own death, and may succeed. But for them life has become meaningless on other grounds, and not because of the prospect of death that we all share.

Is the conclusion, then, that the prospect of death makes no great difference to our lives? No, of course it makes an enormous difference. We may say that it makes a difference to the 'meaning' of life. But this difference is not one that can be summed up by saying that life with death means one thing (or nothing), while life without death would mean another. Nor is it simply a question of good or bad. Death, like life itself, is not amenable to such conclusions.

NOTES

1 *Philosophical Investigations*, p. 174.
2 *Old Testament*, Ecclesiastes, 2:15–16.
3 Plato, *Phaedo*, 115; in *The Last Days of Socrates*, Penguin, 1969 edn, p. 179.
4 Schlick, *op. cit.*, p. 470.
5 Descartes, R. (1970) *Philosophical Letters*, A. Kenny (trans.), Oxford University Press, p. 208.
6 Schlick, *ibid.*
7 *Essays and Aphorisms*, p. 54.
8 Lucretius, *The Nature of The Universe*, R. E. Latham (trans.), Penguin, 1951 edn, p. 124.
9 Nagel, Thomas (1970) 'Death', *Nous*, IV, 1; reprinted in Nagel (1979) *Mortal Questions*, Cambridge University Press, p. 10.
10 *Ibid.*
11 Epicurus, 'Letter to Memoeceus', in *Letters, Principal Doctrines and Vatican Sayings*.
12 Lucretius, *op. cit.*, p. 122.
13 Nagel, *op. cit.*, p. 4.
14 *Ibid.*
15 Plato, *The Apology*, 40c–d; in *The Last Days of Socrates*, p. 75.
16 Lucretius, *op. cit.*, p. 123.
17 *Ibid.*, p. 125.
18 Montaigne, *Essays* (1508–88).
19 If I had existed at an earlier date, would 'I' have been the person I am? It may be argued that a person is identified by his date, or approximate date, of birth. According to Nagel, 'anyone born substantially earlier than he was would have been born someone else' (*op. cit.*, p. 8). But I agree with Parfit, Derek (1985) *Reasons and Persons*, Oxford University Press, p. 175, that the logical incoherence of a supposition does not necessarily preclude it from being an object of regret. Parfit gives as an example the Pythagoreans' regret when they discovered that the square root of two is not a rational number. Another example is that of personal survival after death, as discussed in Section 1 of this chapter.

20 Parfit, *ibid.*
21 Williams, B. (1973) *Problems of Self*, Cambridge University Press, p. 85.
22 Nagel, *op. cit.*, p. 7.
23 Parfit, *op. cit.*, p. 487.
24 Hare, R. M., 'Abortion and the Golden Rule', in Rachels, J. (ed.) (1979, 3rd edn) *Moral Problems*, Harper & Row, p. 159.
25 Baier, *op. cit.*, p. 113.
26 *The World as Will and Representation*, pp. 578–9.
27 Nagel, *op. cit.*, p. 2.
28 Foot, Philippa (1978) *Virtues and Vices*, Blackwell, p. 37.
29 Mothersill, Mary, 'Death', in Rachels, J. (ed.) (1971, 2nd edn) *Moral Problems*, Harper & Row, p. 372.
30 Foot, *op. cit.*, p. 35.
31 Tolstoy, *op. cit.*, pp. 11–12.
32 Nagel, Thomas (1986) *The View from Nowhere*, Oxford University Press, p. 224.
33 Williams, *op. cit.*, p. 82.

CHAPTER FIVE

The value of life

'You ask how the human race would continue?' he said, settling himself down again opposite me . . .
'Why should it continue, the human race?' he said.
'Why? We wouldn't exist, otherwise.'
'And why should we exist?'
'Why? So we can live.'
'But why should we live? If life has no purpose, if it's been given us for its own sake, we have no reason for living.'
(Tolstoy, *The Kreutzer Sonata*)

1 THE 'SANCTITY' OF LIFE

In the previous chapters we encountered various difficulties about the value and meaning of life. Nevertheless, human life is thought to have a special sanctity. Underlying many of our moral judgements, and disputes about them, is the assumption that human life should not be ended or prevented without weighty reasons – according to some, not for any reasons. This principle is at work in disputes about euthanasia, suicide, abortion and capital punishment. Life, it is said, is the most precious thing we have; and taking a person's life without justification is the most heinous crime of all. The death penalty is supposed to be the most severe punishment of all; and giving one's life the greatest sacrifice of all. 'Greater love hath no man than this, that a man lay down his life for his friend.'

The sanctity of life is often thought to have overriding importance with regard to other moral principles. To prevent the pain and suffering of others is a moral duty; but in spite of this, people afflicted with a painful and incurable illness are kept alive because life is sacred. The prolonging, through scientific research, of human life in general is also thought morally right, whatever the consequences might be. Pneumonia, once 'the old people's friend', is conquered by modern drugs. This means that people can live longer; but it also means that instead of a relatively easy death from this disease, they are likely to suffer a far more painful end from diseases such as cancer.

Why should the sanctity of life have such a high position in our moral code? The fact that we (atheists included) use the words 'sanctity' and 'sacred' in this connection is worth noticing. We hardly use these words in connection with other moral principles, such as promise-keeping or the prevention of suffering. Why are they used in regard to life? Is it to indicate the special, overriding importance of this principle? Or is it because, as with matters of religious faith, we feel that the principle cannot be justified by reason?

Among the propositions commonly put forward to support the principle, some are true but insufficient, while others are doubtful. Among the former is the fact that killing a person often entails suffering on the part of the victim or his family. On this view, the sanctity of life is deprived of its independent status, and becomes subsidiary to the principle that we should not inflict suffering on others. Moreover, since the latter is 'defeasible' (i.e. one *may* inflict suffering for the sake of a greater good or to prevent a greater harm), the sanctity of life could no longer enjoy an 'absolute' status. Finally, there is the fact that killing does not always entail suffering. It may be painless for the victim; and whether he or she would be greatly missed, or missed at all, depends on the case.

Another true, but insufficient point, is that if killing were permitted, life and living would be insecure. This reason against killing was given by G. E. Moore. 'The fact that, if it were a common practice, the feeling of insecurity, thus caused, would absorb much time, which might be spent to better purpose, is perhaps conclusive against it.'[1] This is certainly a reason that *may* be very important, but whether it is so would depend on the circumstances. In a society in which the desire and occasion for killing were not very common, the disruption and insecurity would not be very great; and if other kinds of activities were *more* disruptive, then they would have to be regarded, on Moore's view, as more wicked than killing. Moore's reason suffices to show that there is (or is likely to be) *something* wrong with killing; but it does not explain or justify the special importance that is attached to this prohibition.

More recently, R. E. Ewin has defended the prohibition on 'social contract' grounds, derived from Hobbes. 'We enter the social contract primarily to protect our lives ... The minimum condition that must be met by people if they are to co-operate with each other is that they should not kill each other.'[2] But this reason, again, does not go far enough. Even if the prohibition against killing is a necessary condition of human co-operation, it is not the only one; and other prohibitions may be more important from that point of view, depending on circumstances. Similarly, assuming that we do 'enter a social contract', it is not obvious that the primary objective must be to protect our lives. Whether this is so would depend, again, on the circumstances.

An objection against killing which is less dependent on circumstances concerns the violation of rights. Other things being equal, a person has the right not to be interfered with by others. Killing is a form of interference, therefore it is wrong. This point can also be stated in terms of a right to decide. A person has the right to make his own decisions concerning his life. Ending one's life would be a very important decision, and no one but the person concerned has the right to make it.

This is another reason that does not go far enough. It explains why there is something wrong with killing, but not why this principle should have such a special importance. For it is a familiar fact that the right of non-interference is often overriden by other moral considerations; and the same would be true of the prohibition against killing, if this were the reason for it. Again, violations of the right to decide, though morally objectionable, are not regarded as more seriously wrong than other moral offences, such as causing gratuitous suffering to others. Someone who is upset because another person took the right of decision away from him may be told not to make too much of this, especially if he suffered no harm as a result. 'What does it matter, it turned out all right anyway.' The appeal to rights does not account for the special importance of the 'sanctity of life'.

The rights reason is also ineffective for cases of losing life by causes other than intentional killing, for example through an accident or by natural causes. The special value of life is held to obtain also in these cases; yet there is (or may be) no violation of rights here.

Another, related reason concerns desire. Other things being equal, people have the right to do or have what they desire; and one thing that people normally desire is to remain alive. This reason again has the deficiency of being too easily overridden; for we often judge it right to overrule a person's desire in the interest of more important considerations. It may be said that the desire to live deserves special respect because it is stronger than any other. But is this so? How strong is the desire to live? This is not an easy question to decide. Usually when we speak of desires, and strong desires, there is a question of trying to do or get something, and then the strength of desire can be judged from the amount of trouble to which a person will go to satisfy his desire. But life is not an object of desire in this sense. For most of us, in normal conditions, life and death do not present themselves as options, and no effort is needed to stay alive (but a considerable effort would be needed to end one's life). It is true that in other circumstances we may need to defend our lives, and may go to great lengths to do so. A person whose life is threatened, whether by natural causes or by another person, is likely to defend himself to the utmost. Does this show that life is what we desire above all? The trouble with this kind of evidence is that there are always other factors involved than the mere ending of life. Our resistance to dying may be at the same time a resistance to pain: we desire to avoid pain and not merely death. Similarly, an animal attacked by a predator will struggle with all its might to escape. But this does not prove that the animal desires life, as distinct from desiring to escape from a painful and frightening experience. (Indeed, it makes no sense to ascribe to animals a distinct desire for life.)

Again, the evidence for the human desire for life, and the exceptional strength of that desire, needs to be balanced (as we saw in the last chapter) against evidence to the contrary. Some people, of course, actually decide to end their lives. Others, while not going so far, wish that their lives would end, or perhaps wish this from time to time. Again, there are those who would say that they are not greatly troubled by the possibility of death, feeling, perhaps, that they have seen enough of life, have experienced the best that life can offer, and so on. Then there is the widespread acceptance of *risking* one's life. This may be done for a moral reason (fighting for a noble cause) or for mere sport or amusement (hang-gliding, driving a car). Finally, there is the uncertainty about the 'elixir of life', as discussed in the last chapter.

Sometimes the sanctity of life is thought to depend on the quality of life. If life is on the whole good, then to take it away will be to deprive someone of a lifetime (or the remainder of a lifetime) of goodness. But is life good? Is it good to be alive? Is being alive better than being dead? As we have seen in previous chapters, these questions have not always been answered in a positive way. Some have claimed that life is not good, and others that death is not bad. (We have also seen that there is reason to question the meaning of such questions.)

If we accept that life is good, will this be a suitable reason for regarding it as sacred? If 'good' simply means 'sacred', then obviously it will. But if 'good' refers to the quality of life, the happiness of the person concerned, then the principle will again become relative, contrary to the absoluteness of the sanctity of life; it will depend on the quality of particular lives. Such a view is taken by Jonathan Glover, who speaks of 'a life worth living'. 'One reason', he writes, 'why it is wrong to kill is that it is wrong to destroy a life which is worth living'.[3] Glover does not claim that life is always worth living, but only that particular lives are so. Nor is he prepared to say 'what things do make life worth living'.[4]

On this view, some lives – and it will be hard to say how many – will not be covered by the prohibition against killing. But there would also, it seems, be consequences for those whose lives are only moderately good, or only just worth living. Killing one of these would be wrong, but not as wrong as killing a more fortunate person. Moreover, the wrong would be further mitigated if the killing helped to make other people's lives more happy, more 'worth living'. (Such a view was taken by Raskolnikov in Dostoevsky's *Crime and Punishment*, to be followed by bitter repentance after the killing.)

If the prohibition against killing were based on the goodness of life, then the same reason should impose on us a duty to produce more and longer life. Glover, speaking of life as 'a good thing', argues that a longer life is better because 'more of a good thing is better than less of it'.[5] But this reasoning would again lead to a dilution of what is usually meant by the sanctity of life. For, by this reasoning, killing, say, a middle-aged person (with only part of the 'good thing' to look forward to) would be a less serious crime than killing a younger one.

Another consequence of this view concerns the creation of life as opposed to its termination. In a section entitled 'Extra Happy People', Glover concludes that, 'other things being equal, the more people with worthwhile lives there are the better'.[6] It would follow that if 'other things' *are* equal (and assuming that most lives *are* 'worthwhile'), then we have a duty to produce more people. Now it might be said that this does not affect us, because in the world as we know it other things are not equal; the production of more people would lead to shortages, resulting in a reduction of happiness for those already in the world. But this way out would only apply to certain places and times. Even today, it is likely that many countries could support a larger population without detriment, or undue detriment (should not a moderate detriment be acceptable?) to the existing population. We must also consider the matter by comparing past and present population numbers. Is the world a vastly better place now than it was in the year AD 1000? If so, it will not be because of the vast increase in population that has taken place. Since the beginning of civilization, the human population has risen steadily all over the world, but would anyone claim that it has, in this respect, become a better and better world? Whatever may be said for such views, they are not what is meant by the sanctity of life.

Another reason that is given for the special importance of killing is not dependent on speculations about the likely happiness of a person's life. Killing, it is said, is wrong because it takes away any chance of happiness that a person *might* have had. Moreover, it does so with complete finality. A person who is put into a prison-camp for twenty years might still find some happiness there, or perhaps after he comes out; or the sentence might just possibly be commuted. But this is not so with one who has been killed.

This is an important difference, which helps to account for the special seriousness that we feel about killing. But it does not explain why killing should be regarded as a *worse* punishment than others (or, as the case may be, a worse crime). The finality of an action does not by itself make it either good or bad. And the point about depriving the victim of any possibility of happiness must be balanced against the possible future misery that he would be spared. 'Rest assured', wrote Lucretius, 'that we have nothing to fear in death. One who no longer is cannot suffer ... Pain and sorrow will never touch you again.'[7] What the present argument needs is the claim that the mere possibility of happiness (some possibility of some happiness) is worth more, and should outweigh, any likelihood of suffering and misery. But this is hardly plausible; nor is it a principle that we follow in choosing between courses of action in ordinary life.

It has also been claimed that death is the worst evil because it removes the possibility of all experience, whether good or bad. According to Aristotle, 'the most fearful thing of all is death; for it is the end, and it is assumed that for the dead there is no good or evil any more'.[8] Now this remark again has the virtue of bringing out the seriousness of death. But the fact that death puts an end to both good and bad is not a reason for concluding that it is the most fearful thing of all (or killing the most evil of all crimes). And as we have seen, Lucretius used a similar premise (in his case, drawing attention to the end of suffering) to show that 'we have nothing to fear in death'.

Finally, it is sometimes said that the sanctity of life needs no argument because it is self-evident. Now to claim that a moral principle is self-evident and needs no argument is a precarious move. It is well known that what seems self-evident to one person may not seem so to another. For example, some would regard it as self-evident that the sanctity of life applies to all forms of life, including large and small animals, and even plants and perhaps bacteria; while others would refuse to apply the principle to animals, and might laugh at the idea of applying it to an amoeba or a cabbage.

Nevertheless, we may agree that, in ethics as in epistemology, 'reasons come to an end'. We cannot *prove* that grass is green, but this does not mean that the proposition is open to doubt. If someone were to deny it, he must be using words with a different meaning, so that his 'denial' would not really be a denial. The word 'green' is *defined* by such examples as grass, so that 'grass is not green' would (under present conditions) be self-contradictory.

Now the same may be said of certain moral propositions. There are examples which are definitive of such words as 'right', 'wrong' and 'ought', and by reference to which we learn what these words mean.[9] In the human environment in which we learn our native language we are placed in situations in which we are told, and need to be told, that harming other people is wrong, that we ought to tell the truth, not take away what belongs to others, and so on. It is in such situations that we learn what the words 'wrong', 'ought', etc., mean. In this sense, the relevant principles may be described as self-evident. 'Self-evident' does not mean that the principles are known through some peculiar faculty of cognition or feeling, which might vary from one person to another; the knowledge concerned is, rather, that of the meanings of the words in question, in the language that is shared by all.

But can the same be said about the sanctity of life? We are not likely, in early life, to be in a position to kill other people; and our moral concepts are not acquired from, or defined by, reference to examples of this kind. Nor is this a contingent matter, as if things might have been otherwise. The norms of telling the truth and promise-keeping are acquired in the very process of learning human language. The child who learns to say that *he will* do such and such a thing will learn, at the same time, that he is (in suitable conditions) *obliged* to do it.[10] And the fact that we grow up in a human environment, in the company of other beings with human needs and interests, will ensure that the norms about property and consideration of others will be among the original paradigms by which moral language is learned. This is the basis from which we can go forward to *use* moral language – for example, in asking whether a certain kind of action (one that is *not* among the paradigms) is right or wrong. But the sanctity of life is not among the paradigms; and to question this principle is not nonsensical, as it would be nonsensical to question whether we have a moral obligation to be honest, or whether grass is green.[11]

2   THE VALUE OF HUMAN AND OTHER EXISTENCE

The point is often made, by those who regard life as sacred, that this special value belongs to every single human life. On this view, the taking of two lives must be a greater evil than the taking of one; and the greatest evil that could possibly be imagined would be the annihilation of the human race altogether. Yet to produce arguments for this view is no less difficult than in the case of single lives.

The possibility of suffering must again be set aside. We are not talking about the frightful suffering that would result, for example, from a nuclear holocaust, but about the annihilation – the total annihilation – of the human race, as distinct from any suffering connected with it. We might suppose that this is brought about instantaneously, without any suffering, by God or some super-beings from another planet. But even if there were suffering, we could still ask the question about the evil of annihilation as distinct from that of suffering (and it might be claimed that the former would be greater than that of any amount of suffering).

As for the argument about insecurity, this would have less application to the total than to the particular case, as Moore pointed out. 'The general disutility of murder', he wrote, 'can only be proved provided the majority of the human race will certainly persist in existing'.[12] But if 'universal murder' were to take place, there would be no people left to feel insecure, so that this could not be a reason against it. Hence, according to Moore, the question of universal murder must depend on whether human life is, on the whole, good or bad. But the view that it is bad had never, he maintained, 'been either proved or refuted conclusively'. Hence, 'that universal murder would not be a good thing at this moment can ... not be proved'.

Here again it might be said that what is wrong with 'universal murder' is that it would take away all possibility of human good or bad. Now Moore himself held that 'by far the most valuable things, which we know or can imagine, are certain states of [human] consciousness' (which he proceeded to define).[13] And it might be thought that any quantity of these valuable things, however small, should outweigh any amount of states of consciousness on the negative side – or, as we might prefer to put it, any amount of evil and suffering. Such a view seems to be taken by Glover, who thinks that 'to end the human race would be about the worst thing it would be possible to do'.[14] This opinion, he says, is based on 'a belief in the intrinsic value of there existing in the future at least some people with worthwhile lives'. But would 'some' be enough? Suppose the prospects were that two people's lives would qualify, just about, for this description, while the rest of mankind lived in misery. Would it follow that to end the human race would be the greatest possible evil? If the goodness (or worthwhileness) of life is the criterion, then the question should depend on *how many* people lead worthwhile lives, and how many do not; and on the *degree* of worthwhileness or the contrary. And if the balance is on the negative side, then the answer will likewise have to be negative.

Now Moore, as we have seen, did not think that the

pessimistic view of life had been refuted; and others, as we saw in Chapter Two, have argued in favour of that view. But if we assume that the question cannot be settled one way or the other, is there any sense in preferring the existence of the human race to its extinction (assuming this to be painless)? 'Would it have mattered', asks Glover, 'if the human race had become sterile thousands of years ago?'[15] He confesses that if someone is indifferent to these questions, he has 'no argument to convince them' that the positive answer is right.

It might be thought that with such weighty questions, there must be correspondingly weighty reasons which will produce clear and emphatic answers. But this assumption should be resisted. We cannot take it for granted that moral questions always have answers, or that this is more likely to be so where the question is very important.

If we set aside the question about the quality of life, what other consideration can we appeal to? One consideration is that which was used by God in the *Old Testament* when He decided to destroy the human race (except for one family, that of Noah) because of its wickedness. Now God did not do this by way of *punishment*; His reason was, rather, that He regarded man as a failure – a bad piece of work, and not fit to take His place as one of God's works. 'And the Lord was sorry that he had made man on the earth, and it grieved him to his heart.'[16] Similarly, someone who had it in his power to end the human race today might judge the question, so to speak, from God's point of view, asking himself whether man presents a morally satisfying spectacle, and perhaps judging that the earth would be better off without him. This way of considering the question will not, however, make it any easier to decide; the point is merely that this *is* another way of considering it.

Another consideration, which may at least account for the tendency to give the positive answer (in favour of existence), may also be introduced by reference to God's point of view. A question that has occupied philosophers and theologians has been why God created anything at all. Is something better than nothing? Leibniz, among others, held that existence is good in itself, and this is why God preferred creation to non-creation. Existence is good, and the more of it there is, the better. This does not mean more in quantity, but more in variety; it was desirable that every possible type of existence should be actualized. (This was 'the great chain of Being', later celebrated by Pope in his *Essay on Man*.)

Now these views may strike modern readers as quaint, especially if they do not bring to them the religious presuppositions which could earlier be taken for granted. They may regard it as absurd to ask whether it is good that something should exist – unless it were to be good *for* someone or something. The question whether existence as such is good, or whether more of it (more variety) is better than less, may strike them as meaningless. Such questions do, however, have a place in modern thinking; they have, indeed, had a good deal of exposure in recent years. To appreciate their importance, it will be useful to digress into questions other than that of the human race itself.

Consider the feelings we have, or may have, about the extinction of a language such as Welsh. It is sometimes said that this language is worth preserving because of its poetry and role in Welsh culture. But why should these things matter? It is no good answering that those who read that poetry and live in that culture are better off than they would be otherwise. For who knows? Perhaps they, or some of them, or most of them, would be no less happy reading other poetry and living in another culture. What is valued in this case, however, is the existence of that language and culture in themselves, as distinct from any superior benefits they might bring. We may wish to say that the world would be 'poorer' without them; and, more generally, that the rich diversity of cultures existing in the world is good in itself.

Again, why do we preserve things in museums? One answer, obviously, is that people may get pleasure from looking at them because they are beautiful. But this is only true of some objects – especially those selected for display by the museum authorities. Of others we might say that they are valued because of their instructive role. They help us (whether laymen or specialists) to understand the life of past ages. But this, again, will only be true of some of them.

There is such a thing as valuing these objects simply as objects from the past, without any further reasons. Who would wish to destroy a jug, many centuries old, even if it has neither beauty nor instructive value? Some people might, but others would be horrified by the idea.

We have similar thoughts about the animal world. The naturalists on our television screens tell us, or warn us, of the extinction of this or that species. Why should this matter? Does it matter if one of the three species of rhinoceros goes out of existence? Is it really so bad that the world no longer contains any dodos? What is wrong with draining some wild, unvisited area of Lincolnshire, and putting it under cultivation? The publicity that is given to such questions nowadays is proof enough that people care about them. But is it mere existence that they care about? If we ask ourselves why these things should be preserved, we may give an instrumental answer, referring to adverse consequences of extinction or destruction. One such answer is that of ecology: if one species or habitat goes, it upsets the balance of the rest. But why should that be regarded as bad? If the answer is that it will lead to the extinction of other species, then the same question will arise again.

At this stage we may refer to adverse consequences affecting the human race. If the balance of nature is disturbed, there may be erosion of land and famine for those who live in that region. Some measures may have adverse effects concerning the whole planet, the habitat of man as a whole. However, these matters are debatable and vary with different cases. It can sometimes be claimed that the benefit to man lies on the side of destruction rather than preservation – for example, in getting rid of pests or organisms that are detrimental to our health. Again, it may be pointed out that much of the natural environment that we regard today as beautiful and worth preserving is the result of human interference with nature in earlier times (for example, in the English Lake District).

But whatever may be said about the instrumental arguments, there remains a concern about mere existence; and a sense of loss is experienced when we learn that one of these things has gone out of existence. This concern was forcefully illustrated in the case of a recent Australian election, in which a major issue was the proposal to build a dam on a river in a wild area of Tasmania. The case was cited by Peter Singer, who pointed out that hardly a single one of the electorate would ever penetrate that wilderness or see the area concerned. They wanted it preserved, he said, not 'to further their interests', but *for its own sake* ... they think the wilderness of south-west Tasmania has value in itself'.[17] He pointed out, moreover, that if any sizeable proportion of those who voted in favour of preservation were to visit the area, this would destroy one of the main reasons for preserving it: 'its untouched state ... would be destroyed'.

What is the moral status of this concern? If someone tells us that he is not concerned about the destruction of nature (apart from any adverse effects on man), can we accuse him of moral deficiency? It is sometimes thought that the concern about nature conservation can be defended in terms of acknowledged virtues and vices. Singer uses such terminology in discussing the case of the Tasmanian river. 'The respect for wilderness' shown by the voters in that election, he says, 'is a sign of much needed humility on the part of our species'.[18] And we often hear about the 'arrogance' and 'greediness' of man in such contexts. But are these terms applicable to our dealings with nature? People who have an exaggerated opinion of themselves and ride roughly over the interests of other people would be described as arrogant; and those of opposite tendencies, as humble. But in dealing with nature we are not dealing with people. Admittedly, the word 'arrogant' may be extended, quite naturally, to cover our relations with nature; nor is it absurd for Singer to use the word 'humble' as he does. But to use the word in this way is to *make* a moral judgement rather than to give a reason for it. And someone who disagrees with the moral judgement (that it is wrong to destroy a wild habitat) will also object to the extension of such words as 'humble' and 'arrogant' to discussions about nature.

There is a similar difficulty about the talk of man's 'greediness'. A person is said to be greedy if he takes more than he needs or is entitled to; and it might be said that this is so in the case of man's relations with nature. But there is no such person as 'man'. The contractor who diverts rivers and clears away jungles does it in order to earn his living. He may or may not be a greedy man; but if he is, it will not be because he earns his living in a way that involves the destruction of nature. And the same is true of others (e.g. politicians) who are involved in the destruction. They are not greedy people merely because they decide or approve such actions – though they may be greedy or morally culpable on other grounds. A similar fallacy arises in speaking of the 'foolishness' or 'irrationality' of man in his dealings with nature – or to take another example, in building up vast arsenals of weapons. Of course, these are wasteful, dangerous, and so on; but no one is so foolish as not to realize this. And there is no such person as 'man' to whom the so-called 'foolishness' can be ascribed. The people who make the relevant decisions do so for perfectly intelligible reasons and are not, or not necessarily, fools.

The defender of nature who sees the issue as one of moral relations between nature and man, victim and aggressor, will also have to face a criticism that was put forward by Mill. Nowadays we think of the animal world largely in terms of admiration. But this was not how Mill saw it. He spoke of 'the odious scene of violence and tyranny which is exhibited by the rest of the animal kingdom, except in so far as tamed and disciplined by man';[19] seeing here a negative version of the 'argument from design', whereby the existence of a beneficent God is thought to be proved from the goodness of the world. According to Mill, the evidence could only lead in the opposite direction.

> If there are any marks at all of special design in creation, one of the things most evidently designed is that a large proportion of all animals should pass their existence in tormenting and devouring other animals. They have been lavishly fitted out with the instruments necessary for that purpose.[20]

Now we must be careful not to view the animal kingdom through a distorting prism of anthropomorphic concepts. The word 'tormenting' (used by Mill) suggests a kind of gratuitous cruelty that is more characteristic of man than of animals. Again, human beings can suffer in certain ways in which animals cannot. But it remains true that animals are regularly subjected to fear and pain by other animals, have their young taken away and devoured by predators, and so on. If animals cannot suffer in all the same ways as human beings, their sufferings are real enough to disturb us.

Nowadays there is not as much concern about this aspect of nature as in the time of Mill (and Tennyson, who spoke of the animal world as 'red in tooth and claw'). We are more concerned about saving nature from the inroads of human interference, which are so much greater now. On our television screens we admire the beauties and intricacies of animal life, portrayed more vividly than ever before, and we applaud those who try to conserve it. And yet when the wolf or leopard seize their terrified prey and tear it apart, we feel glad that the camera does not focus too closely on the scene, or perhaps omits it altogether. Yet it would be thought absurd for conservationists to take this kind of suffering into account when deciding, say, how to manage a wild-life area. Suffering that is due to the action of man is deplored and to be minimized. But the suffering imposed by the wolf or the leopard in the course of nature is a different matter. We are horrified when we see it, and yet we regard it as natural and therefore acceptable. It might well be that if the wild-life park were given over to intensive crop-growing, there would be less suffering by animals; but this would not be regarded as a reason for making the change. The suffering of the animals does not come into consideration at all: it is part of nature.

There is a remarkable similarity between this attitude to nature and the view taken by religious people about God's Creation. 'Whatever is, is right.' It must be right, because God made it so. Similarly, and contrary to Mill's view that nature is to be 'tamed and disciplined by man', we feel that 'whatever is natural, is right'. Mill wants us to conclude that nature is bad because of the violence and suffering of animals. But we may reply that since nature is not bad, the latter does not count.

The value that is placed on nature conservation cannot be justified in terms of fundamental moral principles. But the fact that many people feel this concern is itself a moral datum which must be respected. Thus if I do not care about conservation, I still have a duty to respect the wishes of those who do – even if these wishes cannot be justified. It is also relevant to consider the wishes of future generations. It is at least plausible to think that some people in the future will care about the preservation of nature (and likewise, of ancient artefacts, etc.) and would regret today's destruction, as many of us regret what was destroyed in the past.

Finally, returning to the main question, we may regard human existence too as having 'value in itself'. On this view, the preservation of the human species is valued, not because it is morally admirable, nor because human life is on the whole more happy than otherwise, but in the way in which we may value the preservation of wild habitats, ancient artefacts, etc. Human existence is not good *for* the human race, or for anything else; but it may be valued nonetheless. Our concern about protecting what exists against human or other destruction may extend also to the existence of man himself.

Such considerations may also be at work in the case of individual lives. We may hold that a person's life is valuable, not because of its 'quality', in one sense or another, but because it is unlike anything else in the world. No person is quite like any other, and the world is poorer, less rich in variety, when someone is no longer with us. In this sense, in being 'different', all human beings have an equal value – one that is not contingent on their abilities or achievements, or capacity for happiness. Conversely, a common complaint about conditions in the modern world is that the individuality of people (and of places, regions, dialects, etc.) is reduced, so that people become more and more alike – the workers on the production line tending to become as alike to one another as are the products with which they deal.

Here then is a way of defending, or at least accounting for, the value that we place on human life, in general and in particular. However, this 'conservation argument' may not be found very satisfactory. The human species, we say, is unique, and if man and his works were to disappear from the earth, it would be a poorer place in that sense. (Hence, we may suppose, God decided against that option, making sure that annihilation would not be absolute.) But, it may be felt, there must be more to the value of human existence than merely the point about conservation. On this view, the extinction of the human species would be no worse than that of the dodo. It could even be argued, on conservation grounds, that the case for the dodo is stronger, since human beings are more likely than dodos to bring about the extinction of other species.

It may be thought that the human case is stronger, because the human species is more special than any other. But this would be difficult to prove, since there is no way of measuring degrees of difference in the abstract. Every species has features which are unique to it, and there is no way (other than prejudice) of adjudicating between the human species and others in this matter. We could not, so to speak, prove to a dodo (a giraffe, a butterfly) that our species is more special than theirs. It might be said that this is just where the crucial difference lies – in the fact that these creatures could not even have such a discussion or such reflections, these being peculiarly human abilities. But again, though this is certainly a crucial difference with respect to the discussion, it does not follow that it should be given a decisive weight in the calculus of unique features possessed by the human species and others. The most that can be said is that the unique features of our species, and the survival of that species, are bound to be more important for us simply because we are members of it.

NOTES

1 Moore, G. E. (1903) *Principia Ethica*, Cambridge University Press, pp. 156–7.
2 Ewin, R. E. (1972) 'What is Wrong with Killing People', *Philosophical Quarterly*, pp. 137 and 139.
3 Glover, J. (1977) *Causing Death and Saving Lives*, Penguin, p. 54.
4 *Ibid.*, p. 52.
5 *Ibid.*, p. 55.
6 *Ibid.*, p. 70.
7 Lucretius, *op. cit.*, pp. 122–3.

8   Aristotle, *Nicomachean Ethics*, 1115a, Penguin, 1976 edn, p. 127.

9   *Cf.* Bambrough, R. (1979) *Moral Scepticism and Moral Knowledge*, Routledge & Kegan Paul, pp. 137–8.

10   For further argument, see Hanfling, O. (1974–5) 'Promises, Games and Institutions', *Proceedings of the Aristotelian Society*, vol. LXXV.

11   *Cf.* Ewin, *op. cit.*, p. 134.

12   Moore, *op. cit.*, p. 156.

13   *Ibid.*, p. 188.

14   Glover, *op. cit.*, p. 70.

15   *Ibid.*, p. 69.

16   *Old Testament*, Genesis, 6:6.

17   Singer, Peter (1983) *The Listener*, 14 April, p. 11.

18   *Ibid.*, p. 14.

19   Mill, J. S. (1962 edn) *Utilitarianism*, M. Warnock (ed.), Fontana, pp. 57–8.

20   Mill, J. S. (1875) *Three Essays on Religion*, London, p. 58.

CHAPTER SIX

Self-realization

The chapter-headings in this book represent aspects of the human condition – perspectives from which to consider questions about the meaning and value of life. As we have seen, a number of different questions are involved. One is about whether life has meaning or is meaningless; another about how we should conduct our lives. The second kind of question was not very much in evidence in the discussions of death and suffering or in the comparison of man with Sisyphus. To a large extent these discussions were concerned with negative features, which might be thought to show that life has no meaning and no value (or perhaps, not as much as we may have thought). This is also true of the 'scientific' perspective, according to which man does not occupy the central place in the cosmos that had once been attributed to him. But when we turned to the religious approach, we were dealing not only with a type of answer to these questions, but also with a way of conducting our lives. Someone who accepts that life is given a meaning by God's purpose will also (at least in the Christian and some other religions) take this as entailing a certain prescription of how to conduct his life. Again, Schlick's observations about 'the curse of purposes' in human affairs entail that we ought, as far as possible, to choose the alternative life of 'play'.

In the chapters that follow we shall be concerned with the second kind of question – how to conduct our lives. One of the main ideas here is that of 'self-realization', or living in accordance with one's nature. <u>What does this mean? Is it</u> <u>a matter of doing what I am naturally inclined to do? But</u> <u>perhaps this is contrary to what, on moral or other grounds,</u> <u>I think I *ought* to do.</u> Again my inclinations and moral views are largely the result of the influence of others. Can I then regard them as truly mine? We are all shaped by the society in which we live and, more fundamentally, by being part of a human society at all. But we commonly contrast society with nature, and the social (or civilized) state of man with the world of nature. According to some thinkers, this state of man is a distortion or corruption of his nature. What then must I do to follow the path of self-realization, of living according to my nature?

Again, does self-realization mean that one is to live according to how one is, or according to how one could be? We are sometimes told, in connection with educational and other policies, that the objective is to enable people 'to realize their potential'. This may be thought to provide an answer to a well-known objection to the ideal of *equality*, namely, that people are obviously unequal in their natural abilities and dispositions. What equality demands, it is said in answer to this, is not that everyone be given the *same* education, but that all should have the same opportunity to realize their potential, such as it is. But which is the relevant potential? Of any child at school we might say that here is a potential doctor, refuse collector, engine-driver or drug-peddler. Some of these options might be ruled out on moral grounds, and others, perhaps, on grounds of innate inability. But this will still leave an infinity of options. Does each child have a 'true' potential – a way of life for which he is fitted, more than for any other? To answer 'yes' would be to suppose that there is some universal standard by which the true potential, the true self-realization, could be identified. We sometimes speak in this connection of happiness and of achievement, perhaps noting that these two standards may lead in different directions. They are, in any case, in need of further definition if they are to serve as guides. (What kind of happiness, achievement of what?)

When a person or child is said to have a potential for X, it means that he could achieve X, given a suitable input of effort by himself and others. But how much effort is acceptable? J. S. Mill began to learn Greek at the age of three, and was brought up on an intensive programme of education devised by his father. It may well be that without this he would not have become a great philosopher. But was the effort worth while? It may have been so if we take into account the benefit to others. But was it worth while as far as he was concerned? Mill himself had doubts on the matter. His case is particularly vivid, but the same problem arises quite generally. Just how much effort may be put into the realization of a child's potential? Are we doing him an injustice if we push too hard, or if we do not push hard enough?

If a person has a potential for such achievement, is it a deprivation if circumstances do not allow him to realize it? 'Let not Ambition mock their useful toil,/Their homely joys, and destiny obscure.' In his *Elegy*, Thomas Gray speculated how, with suitable education, one villager might have become a hero like John Hampden, another a 'glorious Milton', and a third an Oliver Cromwell, shedding 'his country's blood'. He makes the point that a life of distinction may be notable for negative as well as for positive reasons. However, the essential question that he puts before us is whether a life of distinction, even without any shedding of blood or other evil, is preferable to the obscure life – given that the person concerned would have been capable of both.

Are there some activities or qualities that are good for human beings in general? Is there a general recipe for the good life? Such a recipe would tell us which of our potentials we should try to realize. A number of thinkers have offered such recipes. One view has been that the way to realize our true nature is to go *back* to nature, to the 'natural' or 'original' human state in which we lived prior to the formation of societies. Others would say, on the contrary, that the nature of man is to transcend his nature; that his true realization lies in pursuing those activities and forms of organization in which we differ from the world of nature. Another view has been that a person's identity is defined by his or her station in society, so that true fulfilment lies in living in accordance with that station. Finally, it has been held that the ultimate self-realization is that which is not determined by our nature, or any particular person's nature, or any other principle or prescription; and that what matters is a choice that is free from any such considerations. These and other views about the good life will be discussed in the following chapters.

CHAPTER SEVEN

Nature

1 THE GARDEN OF EDEN

> And the Lord God commanded the man, saying, 'You may
> freely eat of every tree in the garden; of the tree of the
> knowledge of good and evil you shall not eat, for in the day
> that you eat of it you shall die.' ... But the serpent said to
> the woman, 'You will not die. For God knows that when
> you eat of it your eyes will be opened, and you will be like
> God, knowing good and evil.'
>
> (Genesis, 2:16–17 and 3:4–5)

The serpent was right. They did not die, and their eyes were
opened to the knowledge of good and evil. But did they do
well to follow the serpent's advice? Was it wise to eat of the
forbidden tree? In the biblical story the man and the woman
were punished for their disobedience: he would henceforth
eat his bread 'in the sweat of his brow', and she would bring
forth her children in pain.

The new condition of man may be described as unnatural,
in more than one way. Animals do not bring forth their
young in pain, or pain of the same order, as human mothers;
nor do they sweat and toil to obtain their food. Animals do
not have knowledge of good and evil, in the sense in which
human beings have it; they do not have our moral concepts.
This, again, is strikingly illustrated in the Bible, where we

are told that 'the eyes of both were opened, and they knew that they were naked'; a knowledge which caused them to sew fig-leaves together, with which to cover their nakedness. Such knowledge, and such behaviour, is peculiar to unnatural man.

The term 'unnatural' has a derogatory connotation. We speak of natural behaviour, natural food, and a natural environment, with approval, and of their unnatural counterparts with disapproval. Nudism, renunciation of the archetypal fig-leaf, is defended as being natural ('naturism'); and there is a general presumption that what is natural is good.

The Bible story, leaving aside colourful details, is the true story of man emerging from a previous state. Man was once like the animals, and his knowledge of good and evil was of the same order as theirs. He did not have such concepts as shame, nor was he endowed with the host of complicated and often negative emotions which are characteristic of human relations and the cause of much tension and misery.

Man changed from being just another animal to being an animal with very special powers, and very special capacities both for suffering and for enjoyment. Was this a change for the better? When Rousseau investigated the question, he concluded that it was not; that the human condition had been flawed and distorted by these developments. Man, he claimed, was 'naturally good'; but that men in their present state are wicked, is proved by 'a sad and continual experience of them'.[1] He surveyed the enormous labours and achievements of man, and concluded that he would have done better to remain in the 'state of nature'.

> When we consider, on the one hand, the immense labours of mankind, the many sciences brought to perfection, the arts invented [etc.] and the teeming vessels that cover the sea; and, on the other hand, estimate ... the real advantages that have accrued from all of these works to mankind, we cannot help being amazed at the vast disproportion there is between these things, and deploring the infatuation of man, which, to gratify his silly pride and vain self-admiration, induces him eagerly to pursue all the miseries he is capable of feeling, though beneficent nature had kindly placed them out of his way.[2]

2 'ARTIFICIAL MEN AND FACTITIOUS PASSIONS'

The silly pride and vanity of which Rousseau speaks were not part of the constitution of original man. 'Original man having vanished by degrees', he writes, we find in society 'only an assembly of artificial men and factitious passions ... without any real foundation in nature'.[3] He describes in detail how these factitious and largely negative passions would have come into being. Original man, according to Rousseau, is endowed with only two emotions, these being sufficient for his condition. The two are self-love (*amour de soi*), an interest in his own preservation and welfare; and compassion, an unreflective feeling for the suffering of others.[4] On the other hand, there is what he calls *amour-propre*, a 'factitious feeling, which arises in the state of society, [and which] leads each individual to make more of himself than of any other, causes all the mutual damage men inflict one on another, and is the real source of the "sense of honour"'.[5] Original man, says Rousseau, might feel joy at seizing the prey of a weaker man, or grief at losing his own to a stronger man or animal, but he would not be insolent or spiteful; 'he could know neither hatred nor the desire for revenge'.[6]

It is sometimes thought that human beings are morally superior to the animals in virtue of their power of reason. Through this power, it is held, we can know what is right and wrong, and are able to behave in a 'humane' rather than in a 'brutal' way. But Rousseau draws attention to ways in which reason can interfere with natural goodness. We have a natural propensity to feel compassion, but this can be thwarted by the power of reason, for reason may tell us to turn away from 'the misfortunes of others' when to attend to them would not be in our interest. 'Perish if you will, I am secure.'[7] The thinking man 'has only to put his hands to his ears and argue a little with himself, to prevent nature' from arousing his compassion. 'Uncivilized man', by contrast, 'has not this admirable talent'; he is 'ready to obey the first promptings of humanity'.[8]

The institution of property opens up new possibilities of usurpation, inequality and the enslavement of man by man. It is true that in the state of nature 'one man . . . might seize the fruits which another had gathered . . . or the cave he had chosen for shelter'.[9] But these violations would be of limited extent; they would be dictated by 'real want' and not by the 'desire to surpass others'. And the usurper would be able to retain only such goods as he could defend by his personal presence.

What is the origin of the emotions and attitudes comprised under *amour-propre* – vanity, pride, honour, hatred, spitefulness, revenge and the rest? Rousseau ascribes a crucial importance to man's propensity to see himself as others see him, and to be concerned about how others see him. He describes how, in the early days, after men had begun to live in settled communities, they might have assembled for singing and dancing. And then

> each one began to consider the rest, and to wish to be considered in turn; and thus a value came to be attached to public esteem. Whoever sang or danced best, whoever was the handsomest . . . came to be of most consideration . . . From these first distinctions arose on the one side vanity and contempt and on the other shame and envy . . . producing combinations fatal to innocence and happiness.[10]

People acquired a sense of ambition, 'the thirst of raising their respective fortunes, not so much from real want as from the desire to surpass others'.[11] By contrast, to a person in the original human condition a word like 'reputation' would have no meaning.

> He would have to know that there are men who set a value on the opinion of the rest of the world; who can be made happy and satisfied with themselves rather on the testimony of other people than on their own . . . The savage lives within himself, while social man lives constantly outside himself, and only knows how to live in the opinion of others.[12]

Endowed with the natural emotions of self-love and compassion, man lives in harmony with himself and his environment. These emotions contribute to his welfare like other natural processes; we may regard them as part of the legacy of natural selection. The artificial emotions, by contrast, arise through our ability to reason and reflect, especially in comparing ourselves with others of our kind. Artificial man is also blessed with finer emotions of love and friendship. But, says Rousseau, we cannot have these without their negative concomitants.

> As we prefer, so we want to be preferred; love must be reciprocal. To be loved, we must be worthy of love; to be preferred we must be more worthy than the rest, at least in the eyes of the beloved. Hence we begin to look around among our fellows; we begin to compare ourselves with them; there is emulation, rivalry and jealousy ... He who feels how sweet it is to be loved desires to be loved by everybody; and there could be no preference if there were not many that fail to find satisfaction. With love and friendship there are born dissension, enmity and hatred. Among all these diverse passions, I see enthroned deference to opinion; and foolish mortals, enslaved by its power, base their very existence on what other people think.[13]

As in the case of Schopenhauer, it is easy to accuse Rousseau of exaggeration and rhetoric and thus to underestimate the importance of his claims. The institution of property, he claims, 'irretrievably destroyed natural liberty ... and, for the advantage of a few ambitious individuals, subjected all mankind to perpetual labour, slavery and wretchedness'.[14] But while it is true that many people live, and lived in Rousseau's time, in wretchedness and perhaps slavery, it cannot be said that this is the universal condition of social man (leaving aside the 'few ambitious individuals'). It is also a mistake to think that inequality, even very great inequality, necessarily entails enslavement or extreme poverty for some. The existence of a number of very rich people in a society is not incompatible with a reasonable degree of independence and affluence for the majority.

Again, Rousseau's characterization of love and friendship ignores an important feature of these emotions. Friendship, and especially love, may exist *without* the friend or beloved being regarded as 'more worthy than the rest'. This point was well made by Montaigne in his essay 'On Friendship': 'If I were pressed to say why I love him, I feel that my only reply could be: "Because it was he, because it was I'".[15]

Again, the point about living in the opinion of others does not apply to everyone to the same extent. We sometimes criticize a person for being concerned too much about what others think of him, thus having 'no character of his own'. On the other hand, there are those who are not concerned enough about the opinions that others have about them, and they may be criticized as inconsiderate.

But when these qualifications have been made, we are still left with an important truth about the human condition. Once endowed with the factitious passions and the concepts that go with them, we are able to regard and evaluate our lives 'from the outside'. This perspective leads us to feel proud or ashamed of what we have done or are doing. It matters to us, to a greater or lesser extent, whether others think well or badly of us. In some contexts at least, this will depend on whether we appear better or worse than others; and as Rousseau points out, 'there could be no preference if there were not many that fail to find satisfaction'. To be above average is praiseworthy and satisfying; but we can attain this satisfaction only on condition that others are, or are deemed, below average.

The concern about where we stand in relation to others is an important feature of life at school. It is probably here that we are first confronted with the difference between the two kinds of 'preference'. The love of parents for their children is to a large extent unconditional, in the way described by Montaigne. We love our children because they are our children; this love is not contingent on how well they compare with others. But at school things are different. Here we have a 'competitive environment': to do well is to do better than others, and to be 'below average' is a deficiency.[16] Now it is true that enlightened teachers can do much to combat the ill effects of this. They will try to bring out the best in each child, making them all feel that they have something to contribute, are not a failure, and so on. But the problem cannot be eliminated altogether. For if we are to give praise to those who do well (if we describe their performance as 'doing well'), then there must be others who do not receive this praise. To some extent the problem can be overcome by giving good marks 'for effort', as indeed is done in many schools. However, there will be some who are below average in this respect too; while others will excel both in effort and in result. And so 'we begin to look round among our fellows; we begin to compare ourselves with them; there is emulation, rivalry and jealousy . . .'.

These attitudes and tensions are widespread in human life today and play an important role in the economic life of a nation. In his *Social Limits to Growth*, the economist Fred Hirsch has shown that among the most desired objectives of people today are 'positional goods', which yield their satisfaction only on condition that others go without. 'Offered to the majority, they are available only to a minority. Tensions and frustrations have inevitably resulted . . . What each of us can achieve, all cannot.'[17] In some cases (for example, top jobs) the advancement of the few entails that others are left behind. In other cases (suburban housing, holidays in unspoilt places, and the like), the goods are what they are only on condition of being confined to a minority. The economy of demand and satisfaction thus proceeds at two levels. At the level of basic needs, such as food and shelter, demands can be satisfied more and more with advances in technology and better social arrangements. Here there have been dramatic improvements in the satisfaction of needs, to a point at which, for many of us today, further advance is impossible because we have all we need, and, indeed, more than we need. But the economy of positional goods (which now becomes much more important) can never grow in this way; its tensions and frustrations cannot be overcome by an increase of production. And this economy has its roots in the economy of the emotions to which Rousseau draws attention.

3 BEFORE AND AFTER LANGUAGE

A more general criticism that may be levelled at Rousseau is that of practising armchair anthropology, which leads to a false account of empirical facts. He sometimes writes of 'Caribbeans' and other 'savages' as examples of original man.

But it is, nowadays, a familiar fact that so-called primitive people actually existing in the world have all kinds of elaborate beliefs and relationships, including a fair share of the emotions and attitudes comprised under *amour-propre*. As Rousseau himself points out, the possession of human language is a crucial factor in this; and the people in question have language. It also seems likely that Rousseau is wrong in his description of original man as a solitary creature 'roving the woods', and having no emotional capacities other than self-love and compassion. It is nowadays held that man and the chimpanzee descended from a common ancestor, who, like most primates today, lived in social groups. And studies of modern primates (and other animals) have revealed some quite complicated networks of emotional relations, including domination and servility and the marking of a certain territory as 'mine'.

However, such objections to Rousseau's position are largely beside the point. Rousseau should not be understood as offering a factual history of the development of man, even if he sometimes writes as if he were.[18] The story that he tells is essentially a story of how things *might* have happened. This enables him to present in a vivid historical narrative what are really differences of a logical nature between the condition of modern man and that of his forebears.

What Rousseau does not sufficiently bring out is the fundamental importance of language to the changes that he describes. The essential difference is that between linguistic and pre-linguistic man. The emotions that Rousseau subsumes under *amour-propre*, and to which he rightly attaches so much importance, become possible only for beings with a human language. We cannot, for example, 'live in the opinion of others' unless we have the concept of an opinion, and are competent in a language in which opinions are expressed and exchanged, with all that this implies.

From this point of view pre-linguistic man differs from ourselves in the same way as other species of animals. Why, asks Wittgenstein, 'can't a dog pretend to be in pain? Is he too honest?'[19] The difficulty about describing a dog as deceitful is not that dogs (or a particular dog) are generally very honest; it is that the appropriate 'logical surroundings' are lacking. It may be possible (as Wittgenstein goes on to point out) to train the dog 'to howl on particular occasions as if he were in pain, even when he is not'; but this would still not amount to *pretence*. The point about logical surroundings also applies to backward-looking emotions and attitudes, such as remorse and revenge. 'Why', to quote Wittgenstein again, 'can a dog feel fear but not remorse? . . . Only someone who can reflect on the past can repent.'[20] A motive mentioned by Rousseau, and the source of many atrocities, is that of revenge. Why is revenge found among human beings but not animals? It makes no sense to ascribe it to creatures that do not belong to a language-speaking community in which reference is made to past offences, and in which actions are *justified* (by reference to past events and also in other ways).

Now it may seem incredible that the existence of a feeling should depend on the possession of a suitable language. Of course an animal that does not have the relevant vocabulary would not be able to *say* that it has such and such a feeling; but may it not have that feeling all the same? An animal cannot say, 'I have a pain in my leg', but that is no reason for denying that it may have a pain in its leg. Why then should we not be able to ascribe remorse, for example, to a dog? Is it not conceivable, at least, that a dog may experience this feeling? (And if so, is it not likewise conceivable that a sponge or an oyster may experience it?)[21]

Let us consider what is involved in using such words as 'remorse', 'pride', etc. It may be thought that they are names of feelings in the same way in which 'bile' is the name of a fluid and 'dandelion' the name of a plant. On this view the feeling is a kind of 'inner object' which corresponds to the word (e.g. 'remorse') as bile corresponds to the word 'bile' and dandelions to the word 'dandelion'. Now the presence of dandelions in my lawn is a contingent matter; even if none is there, some might have been. Similarly, if there is no bile in my blood, one may still suppose that there might have been. And perhaps, if one wanted to make really sure, one would carry out observations. Is not the presence of feelings, in human beings or animals, contingent in the same way?

Given suitable circumstances, a person may or may not feel remorse; this is a contingent matter. What is not contingent is that he cannot have this feeling without the belief that there *are* such circumstances, or without being able to 'reflect on the past'. There is also a connection with behaviour. Someone who feels remorse would be expected to behave and express himself in suitable ways – including the ways provided by human language. 'Remorse' is the name of a feeling, but it is also more than that; and the same is true, in various ways, of other feelings.

We learn the names of feelings by being spoken to in certain ways. The child has done something wrong and the mother says: 'Aren't you ashamed of yourself?' (She speaks in a particular tone of voice and with signs of displeasure.) It is in such ways that we acquire the concept of shame and the capacity to feel ashamed – a feeling that is of central importance in our moral lives and evaluation of ourselves. But how, it may be asked, does the child know what shame *is*? Must he not be able to identify the feeling, before we can speak to him in this way? But shame is not some kind of inner object awaiting identification. We learn what shame is, not by identifying such an object, but by participating in what Wittgenstein called a 'language-game' – one that includes feelings, but also appropriate verbal exchanges, made in suitable circumstances.

We ascribe shame, remorse, fear and other emotions and attitudes in the first place to human beings; that is where our need for these concepts arises. Then we find it natural to extend some of these ascriptions to dogs and other creatures, because in some cases their behaviour resembles ours, and does so in suitable circumstances. It is also important that dogs and certain other animals have something like a human face; they look into our eyes and engage our emotions in a way that faceless beings could not. But in other respects dogs are not like ourselves. The possession of a human language, the ability to talk about the past and the future, to answer the question 'Why?', and so on – these are essential to certain feelings and motives, including those to which Rousseau drew attention as being the cause of so much disharmony and suffering. In acquiring the gift of language, man acquired the capacity to be proud, vain, vindictive and vengeful, thus losing the innocence of his pre-linguistic forebears.

The difference between the two kinds of feelings and motives – those that require language and those that do not – is important when comparing Rousseau with another investigator of early man, Thomas Hobbes. Rousseau, as we have seen, deplored the change of man from the natural to the social state. For Hobbes, by contrast, society is the great redeemer, rescuing man from a condition in which life would be hardly worth living. But the contrast is misleading, for Hobbes ascribes to 'the natural condition of mankind' motives which Rousseau would have regarded as factitious and unnatural. One of these is 'glory' – 'contemplating their own power in the act of conquest, which they pursue farther than their security requires'.[22] But glory, in this sense, is typical of the motives described by Rousseau under *amour-propre*. It is something that becomes possible, and perhaps inevitable, with the acquisition of language, but not before that. According to Hobbes, pre-social man, motivated by 'glory' and other feelings, but not yet restrained by the controls that society would provide, would be in a condition of 'war, where every man is enemy to every man'. 'The life of man', he concludes, would have been 'solitary, poor, nasty, brutish and short'.[23] But if we consider man in the original, animal state, as Rousseau does, then this description is not applicable. To see that this is so, we need only consider whether it could be applied to ordinary animals. To describe an animal as 'brutish' would be no more than to say that it is an animal. And what could it mean to describe the life of an animal species, such as the zebra, blackbird or chimpanzee, as 'poor' or 'nasty'? Perhaps these words would make sense if we tried to imagine *ourselves* taking up such a life, as far as this were possible or conceivable. But this is not an appropriate comparison, since we are creatures of a different kind, made in a different way. Again, it may make sense to describe the life of an individual animal as poor or nasty (or unduly short), using the normal life of the species as a standard. But there is no such standard by which to evaluate the life of a species as a whole; and the same is true of the original human species.

4 'MUST SOCIETIES BE ABOLISHED?'

In taking the fatal step into society (and into language) man became an artificial creature, no longer true to his nature, and at odds with himself. Such is Rousseau's diagnosis of what is wrong with the human condition today. But what is the cure?

> What, then, is to be done? Must societies be totally abolished? Must *meum* and *tuum* be annihilated, and must we return again to the forests to live among bears?[24]

The reader may think that the answer to all three questions must be 'yes'. But Rousseau's answer is more complicated. Let those who are able to give up their acquisitions, their 'restless spirits', 'corrupt hearts and endless desires' – let them 'retire to the woods', there to resume their 'ancient and primitive innocence'. As for himself, he will not follow this course. His 'passions have destroyed [his] original simplicity', he can 'no longer subsist on plants or acorns, or live without the laws and magistrates'.[25]

This is understandable enough. We cannot expect everyone to be equipped to follow the path of Rousseau's ideal, especially if one is as complicated and sophisticated as he himself was. There is, however, more to Rousseau's refusal to take to the woods than an inability to live on plants and acorns. The truth is that, having become the sort of being he is, having eaten of the tree of knowledge, he cannot really *wish* to go back to the state of happy innocence.[26] And the same will be true of those others, supposedly better equipped than himself, whom he admonishes to return to the life of nature. The difficulty is that to make the change, one would need to change inwardly, to become again the original man, without those complicated emotions which arise with the introduction of human language and human morality. Without this inward change, return to the life of nature would be an anomaly, combining the physical life of original man with the mentality of social man. About the former one has a choice – anyone can go to live in the woods if he or she wishes; and indeed, many people have, especially in recent years, chosen to live, in one way or another, in ways that are 'closer to nature'. But we have no such choice when it comes to our inward condition. Human beings cannot shake off the ability to compare themselves with others, nor can they choose not to experience certain emotions. (The point is similar to that made in discussions about disarmament, that even if all nuclear weapons were destroyed, the knowledge of making them could not be destroyed; they cannot be 'uninvented'. We cannot, therefore, go back to the position that existed before.)

5   THE VALUE OF NATURE

As we have seen, Rousseau attributes the preponderant unhappiness that he sees in modern life to man's departure from his original state. It is because we no longer live in the natural way that our lives are flawed. But behind this causal diagnosis is another, simpler idea. It is that the natural way is better in itself, and apart from any consequences. When he writes that 'society offers to us only an assembly of artificial men and factitious passions ..., without any real foundation in nature', he evidently thinks that these men and these passions are inferior merely by being artificial and contrary to nature, and not because of what follows from this. In making this assumption Rousseau could count on the understanding of his reader. Then, as now, the word 'natural' had a favourable connotation; to live one's life in a natural way was and is thought to be a worthy ideal. The appeal to nature is an important ingredient of Rousseau's argument. If he had claimed that we could lead happier lives by resorting to some yet more artificial mode of living, then his argument would have lost some of its appeal. A happiness that is obtained, say, by taking drugs, would not be esteemed as highly as one that comes naturally – even if there are no ill effects.

The preference for nature and the ways of nature, though variable to some extent, seems to be a perennial feature of human life. 'True wisdom', wrote Seneca in the first century, 'consists of not departing from nature and in moulding our conduct according to her laws and model'.[27] And similar sentiments have been expressed through the ages. Rousseau was neither the first nor the last to look to nature for his model. Yet the view that what is natural is good has not gone unchallenged. Mill, in particular, described it as 'one of the most copious sources of false taste, false philosophy, false morality, and even bad law'.[28] Like Rousseau, Mill is able to appeal to judgements that his readers are likely to share. 'Everybody professes to approve and admire many great triumphs of Art over Nature.' He lists such things as the building of bridges, the draining of marshes, and the invention of lightning conductors which will turn away Nature's thunderbolts.[29] 'The ways of Nature', he says, 'are to be conquered, not obeyed'; 'her powers are often towards man in the position of enemies, from whom he must wrest, by force and ingenuity, what little he can for his own use'.[30]

It is true that nowadays we are rather less confident than Mill could be about the benefits of draining marshes and other examples of the conquest of nature. Only too often the benefits are outweighed by long-term disadvantages and dangers. Or it turns out that the benefit of some people is bought at the cost of others. Even so, it remains true that we commonly admire achievements which are triumphs of art over nature. This description, after all, applies to the production of all sorts of beautiful things, useful inventions, and the alleviation of human suffering through medical science and technology. Again, if we would no longer speak of 'wresting what little we can' from a hostile nature, this is largely because we have learned (at least in the developed world) how to conquer nature more easily and effectively. But it remains true that without the wonderful skills of engineers, chemists and agricultural experts we would soon be in such difficulties that it would be idle and frivolous to talk about the admirable side of nature.

Turning to human nature, Mill admits that most of our natural instincts 'must exist for good ends', since otherwise 'the species could not have continued to exist';[31] but this, he says, is not enough to show that human nature is necessarily good, since some people have it in their nature to take pleasure in cruelty and other evils. Again,

> criminal actions are, to a being like man, not more unnatural than most of the virtues. The acquisition of virtue has in all ages been accounted a work of labour and difficulty, while the *descensus averni* on the contrary is of proverbial facility.[32]

Mill's claims are a good corrective to facile views about the goodness of nature. But would they affect Rousseau's position? Rousseau might reply that Mill addresses himself to the condition of man as he is and not in his original state. For in the case of original man there would be no such thing as crime (or virtue). He might, in a case of need, take something away from another being, as we saw, but this would not be a crime, any more than is the behaviour of animals towards one another. Again, in the state of nature there would be no place for the admirable triumphs of art over nature. Natural man would need neither the marvels of technology nor the creation of great works of art. It is true that he would be more prone to certain ailments and diseases (but less prone to others), and that his life would be shorter than that of civilized man (though this may not have been so until very recently). But, as Rousseau can easily show, he would be better off in various other respects.

Now as we saw in the last section, the 'return to nature', the abolition of society and the 'disinvention' of language – these are not really options for us, once we have eaten from the tree of knowledge. But what should be our attitude to nature and natural living in so far as we have a choice? Nowadays there is money in nature. An orange drink proclaims the following 'list of ingredients': no colouring, no flavouring, no preservatives, no sugar. Political parties gain popularity by campaigning about nature. Gardeners use natural compost rather than artificial chemicals and pest-killers. There is a desire to eat foods that have been produced in natural conditions as opposed to factory farms. To some extent these preferences are grounded on beliefs about superior quality or avoidance of dangerous side-effects. But these beliefs do not fully account for the preference. It is in any case easy to give examples of additives and other 'unnatural interference' which are beneficial according to the best evidence. Yet, when these factors have been taken into account, there remains a preference for what is natural, just because it is natural.

But is there a genuine distinction between natural and unnatural? According to Mill, there are 'two principal senses of the word Nature'.[33] According to the first, the word is all-inclusive – it means 'the powers and properties of all things'.[34] In this sense, he points out, acting 'according to nature' is not an alternative: it is 'what nobody can possibly help doing'. But according to the other, to us more familiar, sense, nature is contrasted with human action; it is 'only what takes place without the agency . . . of man'.[35] But, says Mill, this sense of the word still does not yield a suitable distinction. For in this sense, do we not interfere with nature whatever we do? 'The very aim and object of action is to alter and improve Nature . . . If the natural course of things were perfectly right and satisfactory, to act at all would be a gratuitous meddling, which as it could not make things better, must make them worse.'[36] In this way he disposes of 'the supposed practical maxim of following Nature'.[37]

But is it true that every human action is an alteration of nature? If a person picks blackberries and eats them, is that an alteration of nature? In one sense it is: the course of that part of nature, the blackberry bush, is thereby altered. But in another sense it is not. Such an action may be compared to that of a browsing animal (or of a person in the natural state); it is the action of one part of nature on another, rather than an alteration of nature. Someone who builds bridges or drains marshes, on the other hand, may be said to 'alter and improve nature'. Here we have a large-scale, permanent change in the natural world, brought about with a conscious purpose and differing in character from the actions of animals. It is by such criteria that we distinguish between natural and unnatural actions.

This is not to say that the criteria or the distinction can be sharply defined. We interact with nature in many different ways, and whether, or to what extent, a given action is unnatural, will often be a matter of judgement, and depend on the context in which the question arises. But a distinction that is not always easy to draw may be a valid distinction nonetheless. Hedges were introduced by man, for typically human reasons; but it makes sense to say that hedges are more natural than barbed wire. Gardening with organic compost is more natural than gardening with manufactured fertilizers, in spite of the fact that, from another point of view, gardening is altogether unnatural.

The distinction between natural and unnatural is not, as Mill maintained, inapplicable to human actions. But what is its moral significance? To prefer what is natural is not a moral obligation. If someone tells us that he does not care about nature, and that, other things being equal, he would just as soon use artificial products and follow unnatural methods, we cannot say that he must be morally depraved. Nor do those who prefer the natural alternative necessarily regard this as a moral matter. Nevertheless, there is more to this preference than mere individual taste. 'Because it is natural' is a reason, and one with which most people can sympathize to a greater or lesser extent; 'because it is unnatural' is not a reason at all, in this sense. We may choose what is unnatural because of the advantages it brings – but not 'for its own sake'.

NOTES

1 Rousseau, J.-J. (1973 edn) *Discourse on Inequality* in *The Social Contract and Discourses*, Dent, p. 106.
2 *Ibid.*
3 *Ibid.*, p. 104.
4 *Ibid.*, p. 66.
5 *Ibid.*, p. 66 note.
6 *Ibid.*
7 *Ibid.*, p. 68.
8 *Ibid.*
9 *Ibid.*, p. 73.
10 *Ibid.*, p. 81.
11 *Ibid.*, p. 87.
12 *Ibid.*, p. 12.

13 Rousseau, J.-J. (1964, French edn) *Émile*, Paris, p. 250 (my translation).

14 *Discourse on Inequality*, p. 89.

15 Montaigne, *op. cit.*, '*parce que c'est lui, parce que c'est moi*', p.97.

16 This point was previously made in connection with Schlick's remarks about the life of purpose.

17 Hirsch, F. (1977) *Social Limits to Growth*, Routledge & Kegan Paul, pp. 11 and 5.

18 In Rousseau's Préface he makes clear the difficulty of his undertaking, describing the natural state of man as one 'which no longer exists [and] perhaps never did exist' (*Discourse on Inequality*, p. 39).

19 Wittgenstein, *Philosophical Investigations*, section 250, p. 90 (my translation).

20 Wittgenstein, L. (1967) *Zettel*, Blackwell, sections 518–19, p. 91.

21 *Cf.* Chapter Four, Section 1.

22 Hobbes, Thomas (1651) *Leviathan*, Fontana, 1962 edn, p. 142.

23 *Ibid.*, p. 143.

24 *Discourse on Inequality*, p. 112.

25 *Ibid.*

26 In a sudden excursion into theology, he speaks of a 'voice from heaven' and a 'Divine Being' who has called mankind to partake in 'the happiness and perfection of celestial intelligences'. Those who have heard this voice will, apparently, not wish to return to the state of innocence, but will endeavour to become model citizens, obeying laws, honouring princes, and so on (*Discourse on Inequality*, p. 113). This is a confusing passage, but important in assessing Rousseau's position.

27 Seneca, 'On a Happy Life', *Moral Essays*.

28 Mill, J. S. (1875) *Three Essays on Religion*, London, p. 3.

29 *Ibid.*, p. 20.

30 *Ibid.*

31 *Ibid.*, p. 56.

32 *Ibid.*, p. 62.

33 *Ibid.*, p. 9.

34 *Ibid.*, p. 15.

35 *Ibid.*, p. 8.

36 *Ibid.*, p. 19.

37 *Ibid.*

CHAPTER EIGHT

Homo sapiens

1 THE 'POLITICAL ANIMAL'

On the title page of Rousseau's investigation of the nature
of man, a quotation from Aristotle appears as a motto: 'We
should consider what is natural not in things which are
depraved but in those which are rightly ordered according
to nature.' As we have seen, the depraved state of man,
according to Rousseau, is that in which we find him today,
having left his natural condition and come to live in societies.
However, Aristotle's opinion was exactly the opposite. He
believed that the depraved state of man is the pre-social one,
and that man is 'rightly ordered according to nature'
when he lives in society or, more precisely, in a political
organization such as the Athenian city-state or *polis*. Man,
he wrote, 'is by nature a political animal', one whose nature
is to live in a state.[1]

Whereas Rousseau regarded as natural the original state
of a thing, Aristotle took it to be what a thing is capable of
becoming. Thus if man in the pre-social state has it in him
to become a political animal, then he has not achieved his
true nature until he has become a political animal. As we
shall see, Aristotle's account is open to various objections.
But his overall conception of 'natural' must be taken into
account in any discussion of human nature and the good
life. To treat this word as if it meant no more than the
original or existing condition of man (or particular men)
would be inadequate. And when we speak of human nature

and 'self-realization', in educational contexts for example, we do mean what people are capable of becoming and not, or not merely, what they actually are.

However, when we widen the idea of nature in this way, we make the question of human nature, and its implications for the good life, much more complicated than it was before. The philosopher who looks to man's original nature for his ideal must try, like Rousseau, to give an account of this nature, which may be difficult enough. But the question of what human beings may become is far more wide-ranging and complicated. Which, among an infinite variety of possibilities, are relevant? Which represent the true nature of man? Which are most conducive to happiness and personal fulfilment? And which are commendable or objectionable from a moral point of view? Finally, is the question about the nature of man in general, or about the natures of particular men and women?

Aristotle, as we shall see, answered the question about human nature in a number of ways, one of them being in terms of membership of a political entity. The state, he wrote,

> exists by nature, as the earlier associations too were natural. This association is the end of those others and its nature is itself an end; for whatever is the end-product of the coming into existence of any object, that is what we call its nature – of a man, for instance, or a horse, or a household. Moreover, the aim and the end is perfection ... It follows that the state belongs to a class of objects which exist in nature, and that man is by nature a political animal.[2]

In reading this and other passages from Aristotle it is important to distinguish two different senses of 'end' and 'end-product'. Aristotle does not mean merely whatever happens to come in the end. Such an idea of 'end' would not imply that which is best, 'perfection'. What Aristotle means by an end is what a thing 'aims at being' and not merely the way it happens to turn out. A paradigm for this sense of 'end' (aim, purpose) is that which we find in human activities. A person has a certain end or aim in view, he does what is necessary to achieve it, and the activity is 'perfected' by the achievement of this end.

However, in this example the activity and achievement are conscious, in a way in which the development of political society is not. The person in the example knows what he wants and is conscious of working for that end. But man in the pre-political phase is not in this condition with regard to the state. He does not, he cannot, at that time conceive the creation of a state as his end, for he has no conception of a state.

We can, however, speak of the purpose of something even when that purpose is not attributable to any conscious or intelligent being. The purpose of an acorn is to develop into a tree; and this is not because that is what happens to the majority of acorns (the end-product, in that sense), but because the development into a tree is the natural one for acorns, in the sense that this is what they are designed for – even though we may not believe in the existence of a designer of any kind. It is, we might say, *as if* someone had designed it for that purpose.

Many animals and plants have conspicuous features which invite the question 'What is it for?' In some cases the purpose is obvious. It is obvious why birds have wings and why predators have fangs or poisons. What is the purpose of the jelly with which frogs surround their spawn? Or the huge claws of certain lobsters? The answer may or may not be known. What then is the purpose of the features that human beings have? And which are the features that matter? 'Nature', says Aristotle, 'does nothing without some purpose';

> and for the purpose of making man a political animal she has endowed him alone among the animals with the power of reasoned speech ... Speech ... serves to indicate what is useful and what is harmful, and so also what is right and what is wrong ... Humans alone have perception of good and evil, right and wrong, just and unjust, etc. It is the sharing of a common view in these matters that makes a household and a state.[3]

Now it may be accepted that if nature wanted man to be a political animal, she must endow him with reasoned speech, etc.; but from the fact that he has this endowment we cannot infer that this is nature's intention, or that this is where human beings find fulfilment according to their essential nature. For the city-state (the *polis*, as Aristotle knew it) is only one possible development. Not only are there many different kinds of state, but some people do not live in a state at all, or only in so far as it has been imposed on them from the outside. Must we say that the life of a nomad or jungle tribesman is not true to human nature? The fact that he could be converted into a member of a city-state, or something similar, does not prove that this is his true nature. Some species of birds have become adapted to life in cities; and perhaps others will do the same. They are endowed by nature with the means of leading such a life. But it does not follow that this kind of life is more natural for them than that which they led before.

2   THE RATIONAL LIFE

Among the order of mammals, certain species, including human beings, monkeys and lemurs, are classified as 'primates'. Among the higher primates, we find *Homo habilis*, *Homo erectus* and a number of others. The species, finally, to which we belong, is distinguished by the name '*Homo sapiens*'. In this matter the zoologists are in agreement with a long tradition, going back to Aristotle and beyond, whereby the most distinctive feature of man is his rational faculty.

According to Aristotle, a recipe for living can be deduced from this special feature of man; namely that we should develop it, or live in accordance with it, as much as possible. One version of this, as we saw in the last section, was that we ought to live in political societies, rather than in the original condition admired by Rousseau. But the rational life was and is recommended in a more general way, as representing the best fulfilment of human nature.

Is rationality the most distinctive feature of man, and if so, does this provide a recipe for living? Let us consider the first question. What is distinctive of a species may be a matter of judgement and will depend on the context of the question. What seems most distinctive to the layman may not be regarded so by the specialist in taxonomy. And the specialists may themselves be unable to reach agreement about the right classifications or principles of classification.[4] *Homo sapiens* is distinguished from other primates, not only by his cranial capacity (accommodating a larger brain), but also by, among other things, 'small canine teeth of spatulate form, the presence of a chin eminence', and 'limb bones adapted to a fully erect posture and gait'. Any one of these features might have served to provide a distinctive name for our species. We could also imagine man endowed with some more striking feature such as a single horn growing from the head. In that case, would he be classified by that feature rather than by his intellect?

The truth is that our classification of *Homo sapiens* by his intellect is due to our esteem for the intellect, rather than the other way round. It is not that we deduce the latter, and the implied recipe for living, from the fact that intellect is distinctive of man; but *because* of our esteem for the intellect, we select it as the most important feature. Our esteem for this feature would remain even if it were not distinctive of man. If it were discovered that other creatures (terrestrial or otherwise) can reason, talk, etc., it would make no difference to our esteem for these qualities. This shows that it is not their distinctiveness to man that gives them their special importance.

However, according to Aristotle, human happiness lies in the practice of man's special function or activity. He compared it to the fulfilment of an artist or craftsman in performing his special activity.

> If we take a flautist or a sculptor or any artist – or in general any class of men who have a specific function or activity – his goodness and proficiency is considered to lie in the performance of that function; and the same will be true of man, assuming that man has a function.[5]

He goes on to seek the peculiar function of man. It cannot be nutrition and growth, nor even sentience, since these are shared by 'horses and cattle and animals of all kinds'. The peculiar function of man, he concludes, is 'an activity of the soul in accordance with, or implying, a rational principle'.[6]

But what is wrong with nutrition, growth and perception is not that they are not distinctive of man; it is that they are not of the right type to provide a recipe for the good life. It would have made no sense to Aristotle to advise his students to follow a life of nutrition, growth or perception. Similarly, the fact that man is hairless, or has such and such an array of teeth, cannot yield a recipe for living. Such features may be very important to our survival, but no recipe for the good life can be deduced from them. The need to eat in a way suitable to our teeth, or to wear clothes if we live in a cold climate – these are prescriptions for survival, but not for a way of life that we can choose to take up and in which we can hope to find fulfilment and meaning.

Now the intellectual feature differs from the others in being essentially a *function* or *ability*. To say that human beings have reason is to say that they are able (or inclined) to do certain things, or do things in a certain way, and not that they have or lack certain physical properties. Thus a way of life is already implied by this feature. There is more to it than that, however. The way of life in question is one of progression and development; it conforms to the idea of 'self-realization', and to Aristotle's notion of a 'perfecting process', whereby a thing develops into that which it 'aims at being'. A human being, by nature, may find intellectual pursuits satisfying; but in engaging in them he can also change his nature – or, as Aristotle would hold, attain his true nature. He can acquire interests and ways of thinking that were previously outside his comprehension, and perform and enjoy activities that were beyond his reach when he began. He becomes a different person (or, as Aristotle would hold, the person he was really intended to be). In this way the intellectual life promises a kind of fulfilment that does not belong to other activities.

Another aspect of the 'intellectual' function is that there is a way of doing it well; and this was part of Aristotle's prescriptions for the good life and his argument for it. He compared the case of living well with doing well in other cases. The function of a harpist, he pointed out, is correlative with that of a good harpist; there is a 'distinctive excellence ... attached to the name of the function'.[7] Similarly, with the human function, that of the intellect; this too will be 'performed well when performed in accordance with its proper excellence'.[8] Hence, 'the good for man' turns out to be the life of reason, lived in accordance with the highest standards of reason.

As we have seen, Aristotle's derivation of this result from the distinctiveness of rationality to man is open to question. But let us consider the recipe in its own right. Is it a good recipe? Good in what sense? When Aristotle speaks of 'the good for man' ('the human good', etc.), this might be taken to mean what is good for us, in the sense of making us happy. But the goodness of a harpist (or a tanner or carpenter, to take Aristotle's other examples) is a matter of being good *at* something. In this case the goodness is relative to the demands and desires of others; a good harpist or carpenter will be one who is capable of satisfying these, and satisfying them well. But man in general cannot be cast in this role. Being human is not a profession or special activity, designed to satisfy the demands and desires of others. Hence 'the good for man' cannot be modelled on the goodness of a harpist or carpenter.

What is the connection between being good *at* an activity, and this activity being good for us? To describe a harpist as good is not to say that he or she is happy. Perhaps he would be happier doing something else. And the same is true of the rational activity. If someone is good at this, it does not follow that he or she will be happy in doing it. However, it seems to be true, on the whole, that someone who is good at a given activity, such as carpentry or playing the harp, will get pleasure from doing it well. Here we have an important ingredient of human fulfilment – 'doing one's own thing'. Many people today, who may not get enough of this fulfilment in their working lives, go in for activities such as sport, gardening or 'do-it-yourself', for which they have a special ability; and they find happiness in doing them well.

Similarly, someone who is good at the rational activity,

say in doing philosophy, may hope to get this kind of fulfilment by doing it well. But what of people who are not good at it? It is no use saying that they are good at it simply by being members of the species *Homo sapiens*. The fact that they are better at it than a horse or a caterpillar does not entail that they are *good* at it, or that they can obtain the satisfactions appropriate to excellence in this activity. Nor does it mean that it would come naturally to them to develop such excellence, or that they would be happier by doing so. The truth is that some people are not good at such activities, and they would be better advised to seek fulfilment in others for which they have an aptitude. Nor would it matter if the latter are not activities which human beings perform better than animals. A kangaroo can outclass a human being when it comes to long-jump; but this does not affect the human athlete's sense of fulfilment in doing well (by human standards) in this activity.

An important feature of Aristotle's account of the good life is its generality. He seeks a recipe for man as such – 'the good for man' – and neglects the variety of abilities of individual people. What, for example, should we conclude about those with a special talent for playing the harp? Does their happiness lie in their function as harpists or as human beings? If the function of man as such is the rational one, then it will not coincide with the function of the harpist as such. Hence, in this case, the functional approach to happiness will lead to two different answers. Should he devote himself to achieving excellence in harp-playing? Aristotle would have him give priority to the function of man as such. But it is not clear why this advice should be followed.

It might be said that the harpist, the carpenter, and other skilled workers are also engaged in the rational function, since these activities all require reason and intellect to some extent. But if Aristotle's prescription were taken in this way, then it would cover almost the whole of human activity, which would make it vacuous. He must have meant (and indeed did mean) certain activities that we would normally describe as intellectual, in contrast to others.

There is also another side to Aristotle's argument, apart from the point about intellect being distinctive of man. The 'rational principle' is to be followed also because it is 'the authoritative and better part' of man;[9] and we must 'do all we can to live in conformity with the highest that is in us'. The way in which reason is 'authoritative' was illustrated by Plato, who pointed out that a person may be 'thirsty and yet unwilling to drink'.[10] His 'irrational appetite' tells him to drink, but reason tells him to refrain. But we ought to obey the injunctions of reason, since this is the part that 'possesses knowledge of what is good' for us.[11]

Here we have a sense in which, as Aristotle claims, the life of reason is best. Obviously those who are tempted to drink when this would be bad for them would be well advised to 'listen to reason' and let their appetites be overruled. And in general such people are more likely to lead a happy life than those who give way to their appetites without reflection. However, this 'life according to reason' is not a matter of performing a certain kind of activity particularly well, as in the case of the harpist or carpenter. People do not need to be particularly good at reasoning in order to know when drinking is bad for them. The more important quality is strength of will to act on this knowledge. And those who are good at reasoning, or devote themselves to intellectual pursuits, will not necessarily be better at this than those who are not and do not. However, this quality, though certainly important for the conduct of life, is not such as to provide a recipe for living. That we should not give way to our appetites without reflection is good advice (though not without qualification); but it does not tell us what to do with our lives, or where to find meaning and fulfilment.

3   THE LIFE OF ENQUIRY

If we do opt for a 'rational' life, what exactly does this mean? A number of different qualities and activities were mentioned by Aristotle, or suggested by his remarks, as being important for *Homo sapiens*. One is curiosity – the desire to ask questions and acquire knowledge for its own sake. This quality was introduced in the opening sentence of the *Metaphysics*. 'All men', writes Aristotle,

> by their nature feel the urge to know. That is clear from the pleasure we take in our senses, for their own sake, irrespective of their utility . . .
>
> Philosophy (the love of wisdom) arose . . . as it arises still, from wonder . . . [Men] were evidently in search of knowledge for its own sake and not for any practical results they might derive from it. This is shown by the actual course of events; for philosophy arose only when the necessities and the physical and mental comforts of life had been provided for. Clearly, therefore, Wisdom is desired for no advantage extrinsic to itself.[12]

These observations contradict the view, often voiced or implied nowadays, that pure enquiry, whether in science, history or philosophy, is not a sufficient motive for these and other activities. In defence of scientific research having no obvious practical application, it is pointed out that such research has often led to material benefits which could not be foreseen at the time.[13] Historians try to defend their activity by claiming, for example, that it enables people to learn from past mistakes. And the study of philosophy is sometimes justified by the claim that it helps people to think more logically. However, the quest for such justifications is misconceived; for, as Aristotle pointed out, 'the urge to know' is a fundamental part of human nature; it is no more in need of defence or justification than is the urge to eat and drink. It is true that the satisfaction of this urge is not one of the 'necessities of life', in the sense that someone deprived of it would not cease to live as would someone deprived of food; nevertheless it is necessary to a full and happy life.

When Aristotle made his remarks, he was thinking of enquiries in the areas of philosophy and science. However, the urge to know is far more general than that. The asking of questions is a prominent (and sometimes irritating) characteristic of human children; a child that was not 'full of questions' would hardly be regarded as normal. And throughout our lives we want to find out what happened, why things are as they are, and so on. Of the many questions we ask every day, only some are for practical purposes; the rest are 'just for the sake of knowing'. One of the great satisfactions of life is that of having something explained to us; while a lack of explanation may make us feel frustrated. The urge to know is not confined to those who are engaged in research, or those who read books. It shows itself even at the level of the newspaper or conversation with a neighbour. Someone deprived of the means of satisfying this urge is deprived of the means of leading a normal life. This is one of the mental tortures to which prisoners in certain countries are subjected, when they are deprived of all newspapers, books and conversation.

The acquisition of knowledge can be said to invest our lives with meaning. This is so when the knowledge is systematic, either in the way of a narrative (as in history) or in the way of a scientific or causal or logical system. Such knowledge enables us to 'make sense' of our world, or part of it. We see that things can be fitted together in an orderly way, and as we follow the course of the explanation or narrative, we have the sense of being engaged in a meaningful progression. There is meaning in what we are doing and, to that extent, in our lives.

In another sense, the pursuit of knowledge gives meaning to human life as a whole. Human life, in contrast to that of the animal world, is characterized by a special kind of progress. In the evolution of other species there is progression and change; one species becomes extinct and another comes into being; a given species becomes better adapted to its environment, and so on. But this is not progress in the human sense. For all these changes are part of a fixed and permanent principle – that of ecological equilibrium. Adaptive change in the natural world is a case of running in order to stay in the same place. But with the arrival of man – especially literate man – a new kind of development becomes possible. The history of ideas is not merely a history of some ideas being replaced by others; there is an *accumulation* of knowledge and ideas, and a progress towards an ever greater understanding and richness. The works of past thinkers are available to us and future generations.

Scientists build on the work of their predecessors. New ways of thinking are devised, for example in mathematics, and are then available to future generations. In philosophy we return again and again to great works of the past and find fresh insights. *Homo sapiens* is richer, more developed in his special function, after these contributions, than he was before.

Someone who participates in activities of this kind leads a life whose meaning is not confined to his own lifetime. Such a life

> is not seriously disturbed by the thought that I myself shall never know how long my work has stood: or what superseded it. Just as I have inherited the work of others, so I let others inherit mine. The theoretic life is a conversation of fellow-workers who may belong to the same or to different ages. Knowledge (mathematical, scientific, historical) is both cumulative and impersonal.[14]

Man is by nature an inquisitive animal. A person who is not curious about anything would be regarded as deficient. Old people sometimes suffer a loss of curiosity, a lack of interest in the world, and we regard this as a decline. By contrast, a life of enquiry – such as that practised and recommended by Aristotle – is satisfying and meaningful in the ways I have described. However, these are extreme cases. It does not follow that a life devoted to systematic enquiry is the fullest kind of life, or that a person's happiness is proportional to how much of this there is in his or her life. In this matter, as in others, we must be careful not to lose sight of the many people who are *not* likely to read books by Aristotle, J. S. Mill or present-day thinkers – including the present book. Those who read such works will be people with certain mental traits, and they may be predisposed towards certain ways of living – such as those recommended by Aristotle. But they are not the whole of humanity; and we must remember those who are not listening as well as those who are. The life of systematic enquiry is one kind of meaningful life, but it is not the only one.

4   THE AESTHETIC LIFE

There is a passage in which Aristotle raises the question of the good life from the point of view of someone about to be born. Should he choose to be born a man or a beast? If the good life consisted of eating and sexual activity, then he might as well choose to be born a beast.[15] Why should he choose to be born at all? Aristotle quotes the reply of a respected predecessor.

> They say that Anaxagoras, when someone raised just these puzzles and asked him what it was for which a person would choose to be born rather than not, answered that it would be 'in order to apprehend the heavens and the order of the whole universe'. So *he* thought that it was knowledge that made the choice of life worth making.[16]

Aristotle spoke with approval of a life of 'contemplation', regarding it (as well as 'perception') as an 'activity';[17] and in general he recommended a life of activity. However, those who find meaning in contemplating the heavens and the order of the universe may not be engaged in any active enquiry or research. They may be contemplating what is there, as opposed to seeking knowledge about it. The contemplation may be done in a spirit of wonder and admiration, rather than one of enquiry.

The pursuit of knowledge itself has a passive as well as an active aspect. The pursuit, which may be more or less strenuous, may be crowned by the discovery and contemplation of some sort of order or regularity, as when we contemplate, with aesthetic satisfaction, some overall theory or explanation, or pattern in the world, as revealed by the enquiry. As we have seen, there is a human 'urge to know' – a fundamental urge to ask questions, regardless of practical utility. But there is also a human need for order – a craving for such qualities as order, system, regularity and harmony. (Thus it is the *order* of the whole universe' that we wish to contemplate.) There is also a remarkable readiness, on the part of most people, to accept the 'principle of causality' – that nothing exists or happens without a cause. We like to believe that everything has an explanation, some way of fitting into an order or schema; and one of the basic satisfactions of life is to have something explained, to learn that it 'makes sense' in a suitable context.

We also find order and aesthetic fulfilment, in that sense, in the non-scientific contemplation of nature. There is the pattern of colours in a flower, the beauty of a well-proportioned tree, the tiger's 'fearful symmetry'. And finally, there are works of art, created by man, in which there is what Clive Bell called 'significant form'.[18] The scientist enables us to make sense of the world, showing that there is order and logic behind the appearance, frequently, of hazard and amorphousness. (And the same is true, in a different way, of the historian.) But in works of art we find an order that has been created and not discovered. Listening to a piece of music by Mozart, the listener may feel that every note is 'just right': *this* was the way it had to go, no other would have been equally fitting. The same perfection can be found in the 'representative' arts, for example literature. This is why 'realism' can be a misleading term. A play or novel that is really like real life would have the same lack of form, the same random and 'meaningless' character as many of the events and sequences of real life. The work of art, by contrast, has an intrinsic order and is meaningful in that sense. And in giving ourselves up to contemplation of it, we participate in that meaning.

The creation of works of art is obviously an activity; but here again we find an interplay of active and passive. The artist, we may say, is a creator and not a discoverer. He brings into the world what was not there before, rather than contemplating what is already there. Yet in another sense he is also a discoverer. The point is that in composing his work of art the artist seeks to find out what is 'right', what exactly it is that would really satisfy him. This aspect was well described by R. G. Collingwood. The artist, he said, finds himself in a state in which 'all he can say about his emotion is: "I feel ... I don't know what I feel"'.[19] He sets about trying to find exactly the right expression, for which the ordinary names of emotions are usually inadequate; hence he 'gets as far away as possible from merely labelling his emotions as instances of this or that general kind, and takes enormous pains to individualize them'.[20] The activity of creation is at the same time a voyage of discovery.

Collingwood, an advocate of the 'expression theory' of art, made the point in terms of the expression of emotions. But the point is not tied to that theory. Consider the composer at the piano or the painter at the easel, trying out a note or chord here, a stroke of the brush there. They are discovering rather than inventing; trying to find out what is *right* in the context of the work, what exactly will satisfy them.

The passive aspect of artistic creation was described in another way by Shelley. 'A great statue or picture', he wrote,

> grows under the power of the artist as a child in the mother's womb; and the very mind which directs the hands in formation is incapable of accounting to itself for the origin, the gradations, or the media of the process.[21]

Some artists have thought of their works as being dictated to them by an outside power – 'the Muse'. Milton, according to Shelley, 'conceived the "Paradise Lost" as a whole before he executed it in portions. We have his own authority also for the muse having "dictated" to him the "unpremeditated song".'[22]

Shelley was talking about the higher flights of artistic creation, and of the experience of great artists such as himself. But it would be a mistake to think that artistic creation and contemplation are confined to a minority of professionals or people with a special taste. In almost every traditional society, there is widespread participation in music and dancing, the telling of stories, and various other kinds of 'folk art'. Artefacts made for a practical purpose are at the same time works of art. In our culture, the widespread need for artistic creation shows itself at the level of gardening, decorating and even cookery. The utilitarian idea that such things are done and made purely to serve an ulterior purpose is a myth.

The truth is that man is a compulsive artist, no less than a compulsive seeker after knowledge, as described by

Aristotle; an 'aesthetic animal' no less than an intellectual or political one. However, aesthetic contemplation and the pursuit of knowledge are not as distinct as may be thought; in both there is passivity as well as activity; and in both we can find meaning and fulfilment.

5   THE 'HIGHER' PLEASURES

Aristotle's account, as we have seen, is based on the superiority of the intellectual part of man, 'the highest that is in us', this being also the part that distinguishes man from other creatures. A similar view of the intellect was expressed by J. S. Mill. 'It is better', he wrote,

> to be a human being dissatisfied than a pig satisfied; better to be Socrates dissatisfied than a fool satisfied. And if the fool, or the pig, are of a different opinion, it is because they only know their own side of the question.[23]

Although Mill does not use Aristotle's 'functional' argument, he is thinking on similar lines, as can be seen from the way he juxtaposes his two comparisons. He thinks that the function in which we are superior to the animals is also that which we must do well, if we are to live the best possible life. And the function in question is that in which Socrates excelled – the intellect.

But was Mill right in his claims about the 'better' life? He was probably right in thinking that most of his readers would agree without further ado. But what reason can be given for regarding the human life as better than that of an animal, and the Socratic life as better than that of a fool? We must not be misled by Mill's examples and terminology. The words 'fool' and 'pig' have derogatory connotations. But what if we picked some other animal? Is it better to be a human being dissatisfied than a chimpanzee or a zebra satisfied? (Is it better to be a linguistic man than an original, 'animal' man?) It is not obvious that the answer must be 'yes'.

The difficulty with this question, as with others encountered in this book, is that its meaning is not clear. One way of understanding 'better' is with respect to some person or animal *for whom* the thing in question would be better. Thus to describe one wine as better than another is to say that it would be better for those who enjoy wine; and if I say that my holiday in Devon was better than my holiday in Wales, I refer to one person (myself) *for whom* it was better. But 'better' cannot be meant in this way when comparing the life of a human being with that of an animal. For in this case there would be no subsisting person for whom the one would be better than the other.

Again, when we describe one thing as better than another, we usually have in mind some quality or qualities with respect to which the comparison is being made. (A similar point was made about the word 'good', in discussing the question whether life is good – see p. 74.) These qualities may be obvious from the context, or they may need to be made explicit. 'Better in what way?', we ask in such cases. Thus, if a type of car is described as being better than another, we shall not understand what is meant unless we know the answer to this question. The same is true when we describe one sort of life as better than another. Is the life of a police officer better than that of a university lecturer? We need to know in what respects they are being compared, before we can make sense of the question.

In what respects, then, is a human life supposed to be better than that of an animal? Human beings can do certain things that animals cannot. For example, a human being can have an opinion about one kind of life being better than another, but a pig (contrary to Mill's rhetoric) cannot have such opinions. And in all sorts of other ways human beings have unique abilities and characteristics. However, this may be said of other species as well. A salmon, or a termite, can do things that other species cannot. It might be claimed that the characteristics of man are somehow more special, more unique, than those of other species. But how is this to be proved? There is no scale or standard of specialness to which we can appeal. But even if it were established that man is more special, this would still not mean that his life is *better* than that of another animal.

Is it better to be an intellectual person than a fool? 'Where ignorance is bliss, 'tis folly to be wise.' This statement is no less (and no more) self-evident than the claim made by Mill. The intellectual person may 'know both sides of the question', but does it follow that he will prefer his condition to that of the satisfied fool? Perhaps he will yearn for the steady satisfaction, the facile equilibrium in the seas of life, that many fools enjoy and many intellectuals are incapable of. Again, it is not right to say that the fool, like the pig, can 'only know his own side of the question'. For any normal person, however limited in intellect, must be able to make such comparisons, at least to some extent. (Here is an essential difference between human beings and animals, which Mill overlooks. A pig cannot make the comparison; a fool can, to some extent.) And if the fool – or let us say, the person not cut out for intellectual pursuits – makes the comparison, he may judge that his life is happier than the other.

One may also, like Rilke, reflect with envy on the oneness of animals with nature and with themselves, and on the 'instinctive knowledge' that guides their lives in accordance with nature's plan (*cf.* Chapter Two, p. 22). Animals have no need of religion. They are not troubled about the problem of evil, nor do they ask themselves what life is all about. The 'absurdity' of the cycle of generation, the insignificance of their lives and efforts in the whole scheme of things, the question of a life hereafter – these things do not trouble them. Nor are they conscious of a prospect of old age or of death. In these and similar ways their lives are more satisfactory than ours.

Yet is is likely that most people, most of the time, would agree with Mill in preferring the 'dissatisfied' alternatives. This judgement is also at work in our attitudes to education. To educate our children so that their minds are developed to their 'full potential' is regarded as a moral duty. To some extent, no doubt, this is justified by instrumental reasons – enabling them to make a living and so on. But it is also regarded as a good thing in itself, quite apart from any practical advantages. Yet it seems impossible to produce reasons to justify this preference or to prove that the human and Socratic lives really are superior to their alternatives.

Our preference for the life of reason cannot itself be supported by reason.

The question of higher and lower forms of life arose for Mill in the context of the 'Greatest Happiness Principle', according to which 'actions are right in proportion as they tend to promote happiness, wrong as they tend to produce the reverse of happiness'.[24] Having declared his adherence to the principle, Mill immediately turned to the objection that, according to it, it would be right to emulate the life of a happy pig, rather than live as 'a human being dissatisfied' – a consequence that he strenuously denied. Mill also had in mind the dictum of a previous advocate of the happiness principle, Jeremy Bentham, who insisted on 'quantity of pleasure' as the sole criterion of good. 'Quantity of pleasure being equal', he held, 'push-pin is as good as poetry'.[25]

This view of the principle was not acceptable to Mill. He believed that certain pleasures are superior to others in quality as opposed to quantity, and that this must be taken into account in applying the principle. It was, he claimed, 'quite compatible with the principle of utility to recognise the fact, that some *kinds* of pleasure are more desirable and more valuable than others'.[26] He went on to propose a criterion of value, which begins as follows:

> Of two pleasures, if there be one to which all or almost all who have experience of both give a decided preference, irrespective of any feeling of moral obligation to prefer it, that is the more desirable pleasure.[27]

Now this may seem a reasonable application of the utilitarian principle. If we are to decide (perhaps with the use of public money) between push-pin and poetry, then obviously those who have experience of both will be better qualified to tell us which is the greater pleasure. But this does not yet give us a distinction between quantity and quality; for those consulted may say that they get *more* pleasure from the preferred alternative. However, Mill goes on to make the distinction of quality as follows:

> If one of the two is, by those who are competently acquainted with both, placed so far above the other that they prefer it, even though knowing it to be attended with a greater amount

of discontent, and would not resign it for any quantity of the other pleasure which their nature is capable of, we are justified in ascribing to the preferred enjoyment a superiority in quality, so far out-weighing quantity as to render it, in comparison, of small account.[28]

This criterion is not, however, as neat as it may appear. Mill speaks of 'two pleasures', as one might speak of two poems or two apples. But how are pleasures to be individuated? Is poetry one pleasure, or a collection of pleasures? (One per poet, perhaps?) Is push-pin one pleasure, or are games (or games of that type?) one pleasure? Or are pleasures to be counted by *occasions* (of reading, playing, etc.)? If the pleasure on one side is defined in more general terms than that on the other, then its loss would be that much greater; but this is merely a matter of arbitrary definition.

However, when we look more closely at Mill's criterion, we find that this difficulty is swallowed up by a more fundamental one. For what Mill says, and needs to say, is that the superior pleasure would be preferred to *any* quantity of the other (and even though it were 'attended with a greater amount of discontent'). It is just by this dismissal of quantity that the breakthrough from quantity to quality is to be achieved. On this view, if poetry is a superior pleasure, and one with which I am 'competently acquainted', then I would rather give up a lifetime of push-pin than a single reading of poetry. Mill's criterion is more suggestive of an irrational addiction than a considered choice. An addiction to heroin would be more likely to pass the test than a love of poetry. Here we would have the required disregard of a greater amount of discontent, and the readiness to give up any quantity of other pleasures.

But let us suppose that the comparison is made, more plausibly, with a lifetime of poetry. Which would I choose in that case? Suppose I am really quite fond of poetry, and have a good understanding of it, but am not a frequent reader. Poetry is not a big thing in my life. Push-pin, on the other hand, is: I practise hard every day, take part in competitions, enjoy watching others, and so on. In short, I get a far greater *quantity* of pleasure from push-pin than from poetry. In that case, would it not be unreasonable for me to renounce push-pin?

There is a logical link between pleasure and desire: to say that X gives me pleasure is to say that, unless there are reasons to the contrary, X is what I desire. Similarly, if I say that X gives me more pleasure than Y, then I cannot go on to choose Y, unless there are special reasons (e.g. moral) for doing so. Now it may be thought that the special reason in the present context would be that Y is a 'superior' pleasure – superior in quality as opposed to quantity. But then the judgement that Y is superior must stand on its own feet: it must support the choice of Y, and not (as Mill's criterion would indicate) the other way round. Without some independent criterion of superiority (or some other reason for preferring Y) the person who chooses in accordance with Mill's formula would be acting unintelligibly. Now Mill proposed his criterion in answer to the question 'what I mean by difference of quality in pleasures'.[29] But in fact he had already answered this question, by implication, in the previous paragraph, where he spoke of 'the superiority of mental over bodily pleasures'.[30] (Although the discussion culminates in the claims about the human being *versus* the pig, etc., Mill's criterion was not designed to *establish* which are the superior pleasures, but to explain in what sense the mental ones are superior.)

But is it true that mental pleasures are superior to bodily ones? And which are the relevant pleasures? The mental/bodily division is not satisfactory. It is true that some human activities, for example digestion are clearly bodily, while others, such as mental arithmetic, are clearly mental. But most activities do not fit into the dichotomy. Consider push-pin, supposedly one of the inferior pleasures. It involves some bodily activity, but does that make it a bodily pleasure? Or take tennis, where the bodily work is more strenuous. Is tennis a bodily pleasure? It is essential to these and other games that the players be conscious of non-bodily aspects – the rules, the desire to win, etc. Does that mean that they are mental activities after all? Again, consider going for a walk. This is obviously a bodily activity; but one is also conscious of the scenery, observing the birds and so on. Is the pleasure of going for a walk mental or bodily? When people speak of bodily pleasures, they sometimes have in mind eating and drinking and sex. But these examples too are far from straightforward. In love between the sexes, mental and bodily elements are inextricably connected. And in eating and drinking there is the perception of different flavours and textures, the appearance of the food prior to eating and, perhaps, the convivial atmosphere of a meal eaten in company.

Where the mental/bodily division can be applied, it often does not coincide with our actual evaluation of pleasures. Consider such activities as reading and watching television, which might reasonably be regarded as mental pleasures. Does that make them superior to pleasures involving bodily exercise? Someone who watches soap-operas or reads trashy novels would not be regarded as spending his time in a particularly worthy way. To the child addicted to television we might say: 'Don't waste your time watching that rubbish; go out and get some exercise'. It is sometimes thought that what is special about the superior pleasures is that they are peculiar to human beings, since only they have a suitable mental equipment. But this point also applies to the pleasures just mentioned, and to other pleasures, such as gambling, which would not normally be regarded as particularly valuable. The fact that an activity or pleasure is peculiar to man does not entail that it has a superior value.

A feature that seems to belong to many of the favoured pleasures is that they do not come easily. This is especially true of the intellectual pleasures in which Socrates excelled. Discussion, thinking, mastering new ideas – these require exertion, which may be very strenuous. (Hence Socrates was more likely to be dissatisfied than the fool.) What about poetry? Some poems are very demanding, and we have to make an effort if we are to get pleasure from them. But not all enjoyment of poetry is like this; and the same is true of music, ballet and other arts (regarded as superior pleasures). However, it is often necessary to put in a considerable effort initially. One may need to learn a poet's language, or to concentrate hard on a piece of music, in order to get pleasure from them, without much effort, later. Physical activities too are often valued more highly if they require the mastering of a skill. On the other hand, we would not include a drug-induced pleasure among the superior ones, even if a considerable effort of perseverance and self-discipline were needed to get this pleasure.

Perhaps we are inclined to associate valuable pleasures with exertion because of the widely held conviction that the value of a thing is according to its price. (The false but popular maxim 'You get what you pay for' is fundamental to much of our commercial life.) But however this may be, it is hardly to be expected that our description of certain pleasures as superior can be explained by a set of conditions that they, and only they, have in common.[31]

There is, in any case, more to the evaluation of pleasures than the simple contrast between superior and inferior. Some pleasures are approved as being 'wholesome' or 'natural', with corresponding judgements on the negative side. Words like 'innocent' and 'spontaneous' may be used in approving of the pleasure of children or, again, of the pleasure that adults take in children. On the other hand, to describe a pleasure as 'childish' is not to approve of it.

Now one thing that is meant in describing a pleasure as superior is that we approve of it. In describing pleasure X as superior to pleasure Y, I am not (*pace* Mill) hazarding the prediction that anyone competently acquainted with both will prefer X. The point is, rather, that I would *wish* people to do so. I wish them to get *more* pleasure from X, and choose accordingly. I am also glad that I am myself able to appreciate these things, and get pleasure from them. Are these desires reasonable? The question is of political importance, because it may involve public expenditure. Is it right to subsidize 'good' music and drama with public money, or to provide evening classes in philosophy? What if these things are desired only by a minority? Should they not bear the cost, or if that is impossible, go without?

The description of certain pleasures as superior (higher, etc.) is not just a matter of personal taste. Even those who have no great interest in fine arts or intellectual pursuits generally agree about the higher value of these pleasures, perhaps regretting that they do not or cannot participate in

them. Someone who takes pleasure in soap-operas may
readily agree that this is a waste of time, and people who
play bingo would probably admit that it is no more than an
idle amusement. But these remarks would not be made by
those who take pleasure in the arts or intellectual pursuits,
about these activities.

The superior pleasures make our lives richer. People whose
intellectual and aesthetic capacities are well developed may
find it harder to take pleasure in activities which had
previously amused them, and in this way they have become
poorer as well as richer. But the balance will be on the
positive side, because the superior pleasures are generally
capable of more variation and more development in new
directions. These activities also make our lives richer by
enhancing those experiences which we would have anyway.
Art and literature teach us to perceive things in new ways,
making the world a more interesting place than it would be
without them. Our understanding of human beings is
deepened by psychological insights that we gain from works
of fiction and history. And in philosophy we are introduced
to questions that may not have occurred to us, and to new
ways of thinking about familiar facts and questions.

Does richer mean better? The pursuit and enjoyment of
new experiences are part of human nature, of the same kind
as the curiosity, 'the urge to know', to which Aristotle drew
attention (p. 136 above). 'I cannot rest from travel: I will
drink/Life to the lees.' Tennyson's Ulysses, even at the end
of his days, cannot bear to rest at home. For him every hour
that remains will be 'a bringer of new things'; he will 'follow
knowledge, like a sinking star,/Beyond the utmost bound
of human thought'. Not everyone is as restless as Ulysses,
and not everyone is interested to the same extent in enlarging
his life through new experiences or new knowledge. But
most people have such desires from time to time. The
widespread desire to travel, to 'see the world', is an example
of this. Again, many people are not particularly attracted by
the kind of enrichment that comes from the superior pleasures
or intellectual pursuits; or they may not be prepared to put
in the effort that is required. But those who are, and who
do put in the effort, have often experienced an enrichment

of life that goes further than that of other pursuits. But these activities, just because they do not yield up their benefits easily, may need special protection and encouragement. Without these they are liable to wither away, to the impoverishment of the whole culture.

6   THE MORAL LIFE

Most people would expect 'the good life' to have some connection with moral virtues directed towards other persons. For Aristotle, as we have seen, the best life is that of enquiry or contemplation. And in our society, intellectual pursuits and abilities are highly valued, and valued for their own sake as distinct from any advantages they may bring. It is sometimes thought that people with these abilities are more valuable, more worthy of respect, than others. But are intellectual virtues more important than moral ones? The issue was presented in a striking way in Schopenhauer's essay 'On Women', which is notorious for its disparaging remarks about them. Women, he said, are suited to looking after children because 'they themselves are childish, silly and short-sighted, in a word big children'.[32] (Perhaps he thought these qualities would exclude them from reading his essay!) However, Schopenhauer does not conclude that women are inferior. Women, he says, 'display more pity, and consequently more philanthropy and sympathy with the unfortunate, than men do'. 'Thus,' he concludes, 'while they possess the first and chief virtue, they are deficient in the secondary one'.[33] This ranking of virtues is the opposite of Aristotle's.

Notwithstanding its sweeping claims and crude stereotypes, Schopenhauer's essay brings out an important tension in the advocacy of feminism. There are those who claim that women should have the same treatment as men because their intellectual and emotional qualities are the same, or virtually the same. Others, however, draw attention to the positive qualities associated with women (like those mentioned by Schopenhauer); they point out what a mess men, with their characteristic qualities, have made of the world, and conclude that women are *more* deserving of respect, and of positions of leadership, than men. The first argument requires the premise that the difference between women and men is unimportant; the second, that it is highly important.

Aristotle also gave an important place to the moral virtues, as when 'we act justly and bravely and display the other virtues, observing what is due to each person in all contracts and mutual services and actions of every kind and in our feelings too'.[34] A life in accordance with these virtues would, he said, be 'happy in a secondary degree'. Why only in a secondary degree? One reason was that the life of contemplation, unlike that of moral virtue, was godlike. We may assume, argued Aristotle, that the gods are 'supremely happy and blessed';[35] hence they may serve as our model of the good life. But how do the gods spend their time? Surely not, he argued, in 'making contracts and returning deposits and all that sort of thing'.[36] Nor would it make sense to ascribe to them virtues such as bravery, generosity and temperance, since they would have no bad appetites, no need for money, etc. The life of contemplation, by contrast, could be ascribed to the gods.

These speculations about the gods may strike the modern reader as quaint; but Aristotle's point can be put in another way. In a 'perfect world', we may say, there would be no bad appetites, and no place for money or for virtues like generosity, since no one would be in *need* of anything; there would be no needy people who could be the object of such virtues. (The original ideal of communism was rather like this.) Again, there would be no need for such safeguards as contracts or deposits, since no one would be disposed to dishonesty. Nor would there be a need for those admirable people who devote their lives to a great moral cause, such as the Swede Raoul Wallenberg, who worked for the rescue of hundreds of thousands of Jews in Hungary during the Second World War.[37] Such a life is correlated with the pain and suffering of those who need help.

However, the fact that help implies need, and that virtues imply corresponding vices or evils, does not entail that a life devoted to the relief of others is less good or meaningful than the intellectual life. It is true that such a person cannot enjoy the 'perfect happiness' that Aristotle ascribes to the gods. But this is not an option for human beings anyway. We are not able, like Tennyson's 'Lotos Eaters', to 'lie reclined/On the hills like Gods together, careless of mankind/ . . . Where they smile in secret, looking over wasted lands'. Admittedly, we may not, and should not, be thinking all the time about the suffering of others; and we may devote ourselves to a large extent to a life of contemplation or enquiry, in one sense or another. But no normal human being can be unaware or completely insensitive to the needs and sufferings of others. Nor can he be unaware that in the eyes of others he will be valued, at least to some extent, by his response to such needs.

In any case, a life of virtue and devotion to others does not always imply the existence of evil or suffering. One of the great sources of fulfilment in life is the knowledge that one is needed. But this need arises in ordinary contact with members of one's family, people at work, and so on. The knowledge that another person is counting on me is one of the most satisfying reasons I can have for action. But this kind of need does not mean that there is evil or suffering from which someone needs to be rescued. The relationship existing, for example, between parents and children, calls for moral qualities that are not, or not necessarily, correlated with such evils. Yet these relationships, and the virtues and duties that go with them, are part of what we mean by a meaningful life.

It would be misleading, however, to regard 'the life of moral virtue' as an alternative to the enquiring or contemplative life. The moral virtues cannot yield a recipe for living in the sense that enquiry and contemplation can. The latter are activities, occupations; one can be advised to take them up (or take them up to a larger extent), as one might be advised to take up music or physical exercise. But one cannot be advised to take up moral virtues in this sense. Morality is not an activity, but something that qualifies our activities. When we say of someone that he behaves justly or bravely, we are not saying *what* he does, but that his actions, whatever they may be, have these qualities.

There is also an ambiguity in the expression 'the good life', which must be noted when trying to compare a moral life with a life of contemplation. The latter may be put forward as being good for the person concerned – a recipe for personal happiness, fulfilment and self-realization. But this is not what we have in mind when we speak of 'a good life' in the moral sense. In this case we are concerned (or largely concerned) with virtuous behaviour affecting others. Thus our reason for approving of such qualities as kindness and honesty is not that they bring about self-realizations for the agent, but that they are of importance in his dealings with others. This again makes morality unsuitable for the role of providing a recipe for the good life. When we admonish children to 'be good', this usually means that we want them to behave in some particular way, rather than giving them a recipe for personal happiness. It is true that virtue and happiness may coincide, but sometimes they do not. In any case, they are (as Kant insisted) different motives. (This is not to deny that a general disposition to virtue may be an essential ingredient of happiness, as will be seen in the next chapter (Section 5).)

7   MEN AND WOMEN

'Nature', wrote Aristotle, 'recognizes different functions . . . every instrument will be made best if it serves not many purposes but one'.[38] Aristotle was speaking, not of men and women, but of women *versus* slaves. Barbarian communities, he complained, treat women and slaves alike, but this was a mistake because their functions are different. But that women should be treated differently from *men* was a point that could be taken for granted. Nowadays, of course, the discussion is about women *versus* men and not slaves. But the terms of the discussion are still to a large extent those of Aristotle. What is at issue is whether women are fulfilling their true function or potential in the social roles that are generally assigned to them. The actual ill-treatment of women, where it occurs, is obviously a wrong that needs to be corrected, whether in the private or the public sphere.

But the more interesting questions are about what is potential rather than actual – whether, for example, women who are tolerably satisfied with their lives, ought to be so.

There is also a question about actual and potential uses of language. In the course of writing this book I have been under editorial pressure to conform to the new 'gender-neutral' usage, whereby traditional uses of words such as 'man' and 'he' are to be replaced by various non-masculine substitutes. To some extent I have tried to meet this demand, sometimes preferring 'person' to 'man', and writing 'he or she' rather than 'he', especially where this seemed natural or preferable for a particular context. But I realize that in general I am heavily on the masculine-gender side, and I hope this will not cause offence to too many readers.

This offence should, however, be balanced against other considerations. To many readers (including myself) the new usage often seems inelegant or intrusive, and sometimes positively repellent. It is also liable to prevent a writer (such as myself) from giving precise expression to his ideas – which may be difficult enough anyway. An example of the latter difficulty arises with the use of 'man' to denote the human species, as has been done in this book (in speaking of 'rational man', 'social man', etc.). A number of substitutes for this word (humans, people, humanity, humankind) are given in guides on gender-neutral usage; but, in many contexts at least, none of these hits off precisely what one wishes to convey. Sometimes, again, the results are clumsy or ungrammatical, or one may be forced to change terms ('humanity', 'people', etc.) in mid-sentence, thus spoiling the continuity. There is also a loss of resonance with past writers, such as those discussed and quoted in this book, who conduct their discussions of the human condition in terms of 'man' and other masculine words.

Now some of these comments apply only to the English language as it is today. It may be that, if the reformers have their way, and if the new usage is adopted sufficiently widely, and for a sufficiently long time, it really will supersede the old – not merely in the sense of being substituted for it, but in coming to be regarded by everyone as the more natural usage, and without any sense of the loss of style, clarity and continuity. In the meantime, however, there is such a sense – though this will obviously vary according to one's sensibilities and other factors.

One of these concerns the issue of feminism itself. The new usage is described as 'gender-neutral' because it refers in equal proportions to males and females. But in another sense it cannot be neutral. Consider, for example, the use of 'he or she' (or 'she or he') to replace the traditional 'he'. This replacement cannot – as the English language is today – be regarded simply as an alternative expression without any distortion of meaning. For what was meant in using 'he' was to refer to some hypothetical individual whose sex is irrelevant to the discussion, and far from the minds of the writer and reader. By contrast, in introducing the new terminology, the writer draws attention to gender, and indeed sounds a note in favour of feminism (or rather, a certain type of feminism). He will indicate, by choosing it, that the new usage is preferable; and since it is not preferable for reasons connected with the context (if it were, he would want to choose it anyway), it will be taken by readers to express sympathy with the feminist cause. In this sense, then, the usage is not neutral; and for the writer who is not in sympathy with feminism (or rather, that type of feminism) it will go against the grain of his beliefs on an important issue. And this will be especially so if his book happens to be about moral questions, and the question of self-realization in particular.

The issue of feminism is largely about self-realization, involving the distinction between actual and potential. Today many women feel resentful about the place of women in society. But these feelings are, to a large extent, of quite recent origin. Before the present wave of feminism it would not have occurred to most women to complain about their role in society, and they would have regarded as ridiculous the introduction of gender-neutral terminology. Were such women, and are such women today, lacking in self-realization? Was it better that they should be roused from their contentment with the existing arrangements? This is not a question about those who suffered gross cruelty at the hands of men, or those who were (or are) made destitute through the operation of bad laws; nor is it about particular women who show a clear desire and ability to perform and excel in occupations traditionally associated with men, and who are prevented from doing so by existing arrangements. The question is about whether, in general, women should be brought up to *have* the same desires and expectations as men (and *vice versa*). It is a question, not about the satisfaction of existing desires, but about what sort of desires should be instilled and encouraged.

It is sometimes claimed that the state of equality is the *natural* one, and the traditional state of affairs a perversion of nature, brought about by social pressures. On this view, women are (or have been up to now) satisfied with the traditional roles only because these have been instilled into them from an early age. Girls are given dolls to play with, encouraged to help mummy with household tasks, and so on. The contrary view would be that girls are given dolls, etc. because that is what they prefer. But if they have this preference, is this not already due to 'stereotyping' which took place at a very early age, perhaps in subtle and unconscious ways? When does stereotyping really begin? Are the different preferences of boys and girls, men and women, due to nature or nurture?

To a large extent we are, all of us, products of a particular social environment. Our desires and interests, and our very concepts, are shaped by the environment into which we are born; and this must also apply to our personalities as members of one sex or the other. The same child brought up in a different environment would become a different person, and this is also true of his or her gender-related attitudes. But what are we like originally? What are the 'real' preferences of boys and girls, as distinct from any social conditioning?

Could these questions be answered in a scientific way, by conducting experiments? Obviously we cannot experiment with human beings as we can, for example, with different strains of barley. Perhaps it will be said that the relevant experiment with human beings is the one that is actually taking place, i.e. the present movement towards equality between the sexes. But if equality were achieved, what

would this prove? If women came to be represented in the
relevant positions in the same numbers as men, and to be
performing equally well, would this show that this had been
their true nature all along? No; for we could then suppose that
this, the new state of affairs, was itself due to conditioning. 'If
we bring the daughters up . . . to think that there should be
no sex roles, that does not free them from conditioning: it
only brings them up with a different sort.'[39]

On the other hand, there are obviously differences between
men and women which are prior to any conditioning. Apart
from the sheer physical differences, there is a range of
emotions and experiences which are different as between the
sexes. (The experience of having a baby is an obvious
example.) Again, the sexual behaviour of the sexes is
different, and not merely in the physical sense. We may
assume that, as with other animal species, *Homo sapiens* (and
other hominids) evolved so that the male is stronger and
more aggressive, with competition for sexual advantage
taking place between males rather than between females,
and so on; and here again, different emotions are at work.

These differences are part of human nature if anything is.
But what are their implications regarding self-realization?
There is no syllogism which runs: women have such and
such physical and emotional lives, therefore they are not cut
out to be company directors. Nevertheless, the idea that
there are *no* relevant differences between men and women,
which might affect their suitability, in general, for a given
way of life, is not plausible. The differences to which I have
drawn attention are not superficial like 'the colour of one's
skin'. (Hence it may be wrong to assimilate 'sexism' to
racism.) They are deep differences, not brought about by
social conditioning; and they affect the attitudes of men and
women to the world and to other people.

But what if it could be proved that there are no such
differences, that the existing differences between men and
women are entirely due to conditioning, and not natural in
any sense? As we saw in the last chapter (p. 122), and as
Mill pointed out, the fact that a certain kind of behaviour
is natural does not entail that it is good. In devising
educational policies we must consider which kinds of

behaviour are desirable, and not merely which ones are
natural. Similarly, if men and women are different by nature,
it does not follow that this is the best way for them to be;
and conversely, if they are not, or not very, different by
nature, it might be thought desirable to make them *more*
different.

In favour of minimizing the difference is the fact that in
the history of human affairs the assignment of individuals
to different types or classes has often been accompanied by
oppression and deprivation; and it may be said that, on the
whole, women through the ages have had a bad deal.
However, this is more true of past centuries than of our
own, which has seen steady and substantial improvements
in the condition of women. Moreover, such improvements
can be achieved without the ideal of equality. A decent life
for all is not incompatible with large inequalities (say between
the very rich and those who have just enough). And a decent
life for women is not incompatible with a large measure of
stereotyping and the assumption of different roles for men
and women.

But is there anything to be said in favour of such
stereotyping? J. R. Lucas has argued that differentiation
between the sexes is important in cementing the marriage
relationship. 'A division of labour is not only often economi-
cally more efficient but emotionally more enjoyable: each is
doing something for the other, each is more needed by the
other.'[40] He describes how, in a typical marriage, the man
may *lose* his 'bachelor abilities to darn socks and boil eggs'
and the woman her 'facility at filling in forms or cleaning
sparking plugs'. Here is a process of differentiation that is
neither natural nor social in the usual sense. It is brought
about, or enhanced beyond its original degree, by the
emotional satisfactions of division of labour. The man is
needed, and perhaps admired, for doing things that the
woman could probably have done or learned to do, and
conversely. It does not matter very much to this differentiation whether the pre-marriage abilities were due to nature
or social stereotyping; its value lies in its role in the marriage
and is not dependent on its origin. Nor is it important or
inevitable that the accepted stereotypes be precisely those

existing in our society. (Lucas quotes an ancient Greek saying, 'Nobody ever saw a woman cook'.)[41] The point is that the existence of *some* assumptions about the respective roles of men and women in a given society is a good thing, because this promotes stable and satisfactory sexual relationships. With this assumption, the satisfactory division of labour comes about in a 'natural' way, by following the stereotype; without it, there may be uncertainty about what to expect from one another, and suspicions by one partner or the other about whether he or she is getting 'a fair deal'.

This argument presupposes, of course, that the marriage relationship (or a stable relationship of that kind) is itself desirable. Some people nowadays believe that it is, or might be, better for people to live in loose, impermanent relationships with the opposite sex, rather than being tied to one partner. This question again raises problems about nature *versus* convention, and about actual *versus* potential people and preferences. And here again it will be impossible to establish by empirical investigation whether people are, on average, happy or unhappy (and to what degree) in and out of marriage; whether those who are married *would* be happier out of it, and conversely; and so on. To a large extent marriage is obviously a conventional arrangement, not only with regard to the outer trappings, but also in the sense that in a society in which it is the standard practice, people will be brought up with appropriate expectations. On the other hand, it seems likely that marriage – or let us say, a long-term union between man and woman – is of advantage in natural selection. (The formal aspects of marriage could then be defended as helping to maintain such unions.) Human children need a long period of care and protection, and this is efficiently brought about if there is a suitable bond of affection between them and their parents – fathers as well as mothers. And if there is to be a long-term cohabitation of children with their parents, this will work best if there is also a long-term affection between the parents. It will not be surprising, then, if many men and women get satisfaction and fulfilment from a long-term relationship – even if no one can say just how many or how much.

As we saw in Chapter Six, there are various difficulties

about 'self-realization' as a prescription for the good life. Which is my true self? The one that would exist if I were not subject to any social conditioning? This is an idle abstraction, which no real person could conform to – 'unless we are to suggest that people should be sent to grow up among wolves (and anyway there are social pressures even among wolves)'.[42] Should I accept the way I am, and develop myself in accordance with this nature, or should I try to change myself, and encourage others to do likewise? If so, should the change consist, for example, in renouncing the sexual stereotype or, on the contrary, in confirming and strengthening it? To answer these questions, we need to go further than the mere principle of self-realization.

8   CONCLUSION

This chapter has been mainly about attempts to deduce a recipe for the conduct of life from particular features that distinguish *Homo sapiens* from other animals. I have argued that distinctiveness is not a sufficient reason for preference. While it is true that we value intellectual activities, we would not value them less if other beings were capable of them as well. I have also tried to show that other activities and aspects of life may be put forward as being 'good for man', besides that advocated by Aristotle (which itself is not as unitary as he seemed to think). There is indeed no need to assume that there must be some single activity (corresponding to 'the' distinctive feature of man) in which the good life is to be found (and that it is up to the philosopher to discover what this is). We may just as well assume that the good life will be a mixture of various activities, experiences and ways of behaving, disposed in various ways and proportions, and depending on the individual.

Again, the question of self-realization is not merely a question about so many separate individuals, but about individuals who are members of a society in which there are divisions of labour. This point arises, as we saw in the last section, in connection with sexual partnerships, where the best way to fulfilment and happiness may be by emphasizing the *different* roles of the partners. But the point can also be made about division of labour in general. A society in which some people specialize in playing the harp, others in being carpenters, and so on, is more likely to bring fulfilment and happiness to all of its members, than one in which everyone wants to be a philosopher or scientist, believing that this is *the* best life for human beings as such.

It is true that we place a high value on intellectual activities, but no proof has been given that we ought to value them more than others. Eating and sex, as Aristotle pointed out, are not suitable as reasons for wanting to be born a man rather than a beast, but it does not follow that they are unworthy or second-class activities for human beings to engage in. The intellectual activities would not be less valuable if we shared them with other beings; similarly, the fact that we share eating and sex with other beings does not diminish their value.

However, the treatment of these activities, and of those discussed in previous sections, as so many separate alternatives from which we might choose 'the good for man', is anyway misconceived. For the different activities and aspects of life interpenetrate one another. This is true of those discussed earlier – enquiry, contemplation, morality and aesthetic pursuits. They are connected with the intellect, and with one another, in various ways. But the same is also true of eating and sex. For although we share these activities with animals, we do them in a different way. The human attitude to sex, for example, is conditioned by our nature as *Homo sapiens*; it is a complicated mixture of animal instinct with thoughts, concepts and aesthetic experiences, such as cannot be ascribed to animals other than ourselves. This was perceived by Rousseau, who spoke of 'the moral part of love' as one of the 'factitious' feelings, 'being founded on certain ideas of beauty and merit' which could not be part of the endowment of original man.

There is one sense, however, in which the intellectual function of man (as he is now) is of peculiar importance in regard to the conduct of life. With this function there arose the possibility of a new kind of fulfilment. An acorn grows into a tree, a caterpillar changes into a butterfly. Each in its way achieves, as Aristotle put it, what it 'aims at being', an 'end-product or perfecting process'. But with human beings there is fulfilment – self-realization – in a different sense. In this case there is not merely self-realization *of* ourselves, but deliberate activity *by* ourselves, to bring this about; 'self' is both object and subject. Human beings can 'aim at being' something, not merely in the sense of blindly following a causal process over which they have no control, but by consciously working for an aim of self-realization that they judge to be good. That is why self-realization can be a *problem* for human beings, unlike acorns or butterflies. The intellectual function leads us to pose the question – but its existence does not, as Aristotle thought, provide the answer.

NOTES

1   Aristotle (1981 edn) *The Politics*, Bk I.2, Penguin, p. 59.
2   *Ibid.*
3   *Ibid.*, p. 60.
4   See Pratt, Vernon (1972) 'Numerical Taxonomy – a Critique', *Journal of Theoretical Biology*, 36, pp. 581–92.
5   Aristotle, *Nicomachean Ethics*, p. 75.
6   *Ibid.*, pp. 75–6.
7   *Ibid.*, p. 76.
8   *Ibid.*
9   *Ibid.*, p. 331.
10 Cornford, F. M. (trans.) (1941) *The Republic of Plato*, Oxford University Press, p. 136.
11 *Ibid.*, p. 140.
12 Aristotle (1961 edn) *Metaphysics*, Dent, Everyman edn, pp. 51 and 55.
13 A more ambiguous example is the splitting of the atom. When this was achieved in the 1930s by Rutherford, he declared that here was one piece of pure research which could never be put to any practical use!
14 Britton, Karl (1971) *Philosophy and the Meaning of Life*, Cambridge University Press, pp. 65–6.
15 Aristotle (1982 edn) *Eudemian Ethics*, 1215b, M. Woods (trans.), Oxford University Press, p. 5.
16 *Ibid.*, pp. 5–6.
17 *Nicomachean Ethics*, pp. 328–9.

18 Bell, Clive (1923) *Art*, Chatto.
19 Collingwood, R. G. (1963) *The Principles of Art*, Oxford University Press, p. 109.
20 *Ibid.*, p. 113.
21 Shelley, P. B. (1926) *In Defence of Poetry*, Macmillan, pp. 93–4.
22 *Ibid.*, p. 93.
23 Mill, *Utilitarianism*, p. 260.
24 *Ibid.*, p. 257.
25 *Ibid.*, p. 123. What Bentham actually said was:

> Prejudice apart, the game of push-pin is of equal value with the arts and sciences of music and poetry. If the game of push-pin furnish pleasure, it is more valuable than either. Everybody can play at push-pin: poetry and music are relished only by a few. (Bentham, J. (1843) *Works*, J. Bowring (ed.), vol. II, Tait, p. 253.)

See Gibbs, B. (1986) 'Higher and Lower Pleasures', *Philosophy*, 61, p. 43.
26 *Utilitarianism.*, p. 268.
27 *Ibid.*, p. 259.
28 *Ibid.*
29 *Ibid.*
30 *Ibid.*, p. 258.
31 Wittgenstein has shown that this kind of explanation is not available for ordinary words (such as 'chair' and 'game'), and that in general the use of language does not require the existence of such conditions or explanations. See *Philosophical Investigations*, section 66 ff.
32 Schopenhauer, *Essays and Aphorisms*, p. 81.
33 *Ibid.*, p. 83.
34 *Nicomachean Ethics*, p. 331.
35 *Ibid.*, p. 333.
36 *Ibid.*
37 His astonishing story is told in Bierman, John (1981) *Righteous Gentile*, New York.
38 *The Politics*, p. 57.
39 Richards, Janet Radcliffe (1982) *The Sceptical Feminist*, Penguin, p. 88.
40 Lucas, J. R. (1978) 'Vive la Différence', *Philosophy*, 53, p. 365.
41 *Ibid.*, p. 368.
42 Richards, *op. cit.*, p. 80.

CHAPTER NINE

Happiness and desire

1 DESIRE AND SATISFACTION

To a large extent, the question 'How ought I to live?' is settled for us from the moment we are born. Nature has endowed us with certain needs and desires, which prescribe appropriate courses of action to us. We come into the world needing food and shelter, desiring comfort and the absence of pain. From early infancy we give expression to these needs and desires in positive and negative ways. The vocabulary in which we speak and think about questions of conduct – words like 'happy' and 'unhappy', 'good' and 'bad' – are acquired largely in the context of such needs and desires. 'Whatsoever is the object of man's appetite or desire, that is it which he for his part calleth good.'[1]

As we grow older, our desires become more varied and more complicated. We learn to balance one satisfaction against another, the long term against the short term, the selfish against the altruistic. But we are still, by and large, happy when our desires are satisfied and unhappy when they are not.

We come into the world wound up, as it were, like a clock. Our desires are the springs of action, action leads to fulfilment, and thus the desires are 'wound down'. But the clock is self-winding. New desires appear; and so there is a cycle of desire, action, fulfilment and fresh desire. Here we have a simple schema with which to answer questions about the purpose of life and the way we ought to live – a schema that is laid down by our nature. The purpose of life, on this view, is to satisfy our desires; and to determine how we ought to live we need only to identify these. This is not to deny that the balancing of different desires, the prediction of consequences, etc., may be very complicated. (Clocks can also be very complicated). But these complications do not affect the simplicity of the underlying model.

But if I desire X, does it follow that X will be good for me? Will it make me happy? If X has bad consequences, then it may make me less happy in the long run. However, this can be accounted for in terms of other desires I have. Thus if Y and Z are the bad consequences, then they will be objects towards which I have a negative desire; and if they are very bad, then my desire against them will, if I act rightly, override the desire I have for X.

Now one problem that may arise, and is not reflected in the analogy of the clock, is that my desires pull in different directions with equal force. But let us consider the case in which my desire is for one thing only. If I desire X, and X has no bad consequences, does it follow that X will be good for me? Perhaps, when I get it, I shall find that it is not good, or not as good as I thought; I may conclude that I was wrong to desire X. Conversely, we sometimes find that something we did not desire (or even, desired *not* to have or do) turns out to be good and to make us happy. 'I never had a desire to do Z; one day I was persuaded to do it and found to my surprise, that I enjoyed it very much.'

It may be thought that these discrepancies are due to mistakes about the object. I may desire and obtain a particular bottle of wine, and then discover that it is too dry for me. But in this case, it may be said, I am not really getting what I desired; it was a case of desiring X and getting Y. I desired this bottle, assuming that the wine would not be unduly dry, and this was a mistake. However, not every disappointment is like this. It may happen that X is not different from what I took it to be, and yet I am not happy when I get it. The wine tasted as I thought it would, and yet I did not enjoy it, or not as much as I thought I would. I decide to listen to some music, and find that I do not enjoy it, or not as much as usual. Perhaps I am not in the right mood. Or

I may be in a state of mind in which nothing seems to give me satisfaction: 'With what I most enjoy, contented least'. The discrepancy is in myself, and not between the nature of the object and my belief about it. Satisfaction of my desire may not give satisfaction to *me*.

Indecisive people are sometimes admonished 'You must know what you want'. Here we have a truism about the word 'want'. It is part of the logic of this word that the individual has a special authority in saying what he wants. On the question whether Smith wants tea or coffee, we cannot do better than to ask Smith. But this is a misleading model. To choose what is best for me, I need to know what will give me satisfaction, and not merely to 'know what I want' in the sense of the truism. And in this matter it may be very difficult to form a judgement, especially in the case of more important questions. Suppose I have a desire to take up a certain career or course of study, and then find I am not satisfied (even though my desire is satisfied). The discrepancy may be in myself and not in my belief about the object. I discover, not that these activities are different from what I thought, but that I am not cut out for them. (In practice the two kinds of discrepancy may be hard to separate, but they are distinct nevertheless.) The English expression 'I would like . . .' ('what would you like?', etc.) reflects the ambiguity of the concept of desire. On the one hand, it is simply a way of expressing desire, an alternative to 'I desire' or 'I want' – a categorical statement about my present condition. But its hypothetical form reflects the *predictive* aspect of desire. Literally, 'I would like X' means that *if* I had X, I would be happy or satisfied; and this hypothesis may turn out to be false. Now in some cases we can learn from experience. Experience may teach me that when I desired X in the past (or desired it in certain circumstances), I did not get satisfaction from the satisfaction of this desire. But many of our decisions, especially the more important ones, are not repeatable and we cannot learn from experience in this way.

This difficulty also affects collective desires, as in the case of democratic institutions. It is essential to these that their members know, and are able to indicate, what they desire.

These desires are the fundamental data on which policies are to be based, and in which they find their justification. It is assumed that the best outcome is that in which most people get what they desire, most of the time. Yet this may not produce the greatest satisfaction. Some years ago the people of Britain were asked whether they would like British Summer Time to be maintained throughout the year. The majority said 'yes', and the change was made. But then it was found that most people were less happy with the new arrangement and desired a return to the old; and this was done. Were people less happy with the new arrangement because it was not what they had taken it to be? Perhaps some of them forgot that it meant losing an hour of daylight in the morning as well as gaining an hour in the evening. But most people knew this perfectly well. Their mistake was about themselves and not about the object of their desire. In this case rectification was easy enough. But in other cases, often of far greater importance, it may be difficult or impossible to revoke what has been done.

2   ACTUAL AND POTENTIAL DESIRES

The question 'What do I desire?' may also turn into a question about my identity. Suppose I have decided to take up a certain career, or to live in another country, etc., and find myself reasonably contented with the resulting position. Did I make the best decision? Perhaps I would have been happier living a different sort of life. In cases of this importance, the opportunity to try an alternative will probably never present itself again. But even if it did, would I still be the person I was? We are altered by what we do. With decisions of this importance, there is no returning to the original state of affairs. (This is similar to the difficulty about returning to the 'natural state' of man). It is true that happiness is connected with the satisfaction of desires. They do not always coincide, but in general and subject to certain qualifications, we shall do well to follow our desires if we want to be happy. But should I rely on the desires I actually have, being the person I am? Or should I also take into account those I might acquire after embarking on such and such a life, and becoming to some extent a different person? This question cannot itself be answered by consulting the desires I have.

What should be our attitude towards the desires of others? Should we help them to get what they desire (assuming there are no ill effects)? Perhaps they would be better off with different desires – which, perhaps, they cannot even conceive of. A good deal of school education consists in arousing such desires in the children – desires for 'higher' things, such as scientific knowledge and appreciation of the arts. These are desires that young children could not conceivably have, but we consider it good that they should acquire them. But will this make them happier? As Mill remarked, 'a being of higher faculties requires more to make him happy, [and] is capable probably of more acute suffering'.[2] (In spite of this he maintained, as we saw in the last chapter, that it is 'better to be Socrates dissatisfied'.)

A more controversial case is that of primitive societies. Having lived, as long as anyone can remember, with a more or less fixed perspective of desires, the members of such a society are introduced to Western ideas and goods. They acquire new desires, and new possibilities of satisfaction and dissatisfaction. Suppose they tell us that, on the whole, they are now more happy and would not return to the old life. Does it follow that the change was for the better? The difficulty is that after the change they are no longer the same people, and can no longer see things in the old way. They cannot divest themselves of their new personalities in order to make a true comparison.

This example raises problems of value as well as identity. A human being can reflect, not merely on the best means of getting what he desires, but also on the value of these desires. Desiring X, Y or Z, I may be expected to do what I can to get these objects. But is it good that I should have these desires? This takes us back to the difficulties encountered in the last chapter, about what kind of person, or being, it is 'better to be'. The problem is well illustrated in V. Sackville-West's novel *The Edwardians*, whose hero is a well-to-do young man, enjoying the typical life of an officer in one of the famous regiments. Is it good that he should do so? Is that what he really wants?

> Every time he met a detachment of his regiment, their red cloaks spread magnificently over the rumps of their horses, riding through the mist of London down St James's Street, he revolted against the connection which linked him with such picturesque foolery. He liked it, and he hated himself for liking it. He liked himself for hating it, and hated himself for submitting to it.[3]

What should this person do, to satisfy his desires? The desire for picturesque foolery ('He liked it') is being satisfied already. The desire not to have such desires ('He hated himself') would be satisfied if he could become a different kind of person. Finally, the desire to be the kind of person who 'likes himself for hating it' can only be satisfied by remaining as he is. But – what kind of person does he really want to be?

Another difficulty about the precept of following one's desires was brought out by Socrates in his argument with Callicles, who was advocating a life of strong appetites. 'The man who is going to live as a man ought should encourage his appetites to be as strong as possible', and use his abilities 'to satisfy them in all their intensity'.[4] In that case, asks Socrates, 'can a man who itches and wants to scratch and whose opportunities of scratching are unbounded be said to lead a happy life?'[5] This passage is obviously about the valuation of desires according to their objects; but it also raises questions of a quantitative kind. Which is better, to get what I want, or not to want what I cannot get? Is it better to have few desires or many, assuming an equal proportion are satisfied? Again, in the balance of satisfied *versus* non-satisfied desires, is it better to have large scores on both sides (say 100 to 50), or a small or zero score on the negative side, even if the positive balance is smaller (say 20 to 0)? In Plato's dialogue the argument seems to go against the maximization of desires, with Callicles being made to look ridiculous. But Callicles also makes a good point in the discussion. When Socrates puts to him the view that, contrary to the maximization view, 'those who have no wants are happy', Callicles is able to reply: 'at that rate stones and corpses would be supremely happy'.[6] This comparison is not as far-fetched as it may at first appear. It may be said that the having and satisfaction of desires is an essential part of a full life; that the minimization of desires (as practised by certain Eastern sects, for example) is a change in the direction of *less* life; and that a creature with literally *no* desires would hardly be living at all. (This would not, however, amount to an argument for the other extreme, as advocated by Callicles.)

These questions are relevant to the 'consumer society', in which there is an ever greater arousal and satisfaction of desires. Things that no one would have dreamt of desiring, or desiring in such quantities, a generation or two ago, are nowadays desired and taken for granted by a large part of the population; and the expansion continues. In this respect we are followers of Callicles rather Socrates. The greater part of a modern economy depends, not on the satisfaction of existing desires, but on the creation of new ones, largely through advertising. It is true that in some cases the new object is really a better way of satisfying existing desires; and the advertiser or salesman may perform a useful service in getting us to see this. But in other cases it is not so. We are persuaded, by one means or another, to want the new machine (for example, a word-processor); once we have it, we change our habits, and the organization of our activities, sometimes with considerable disruption and frustration of existing desires. New desires come into being, and old ones may have to be suppressed; and after a time we find ourselves neither willing nor able to do without the new machine. We are adapted to the machine rather than *vice versa*.[7] Are we now better off? How did people manage before? Were they less happy? Was the quality of their work, for example, inferior to ours? Did Plato and Aristotle need (and have) better memories than writers of today? If so, was that bad or good?

Such problems also arise when what is being 'sold' is not a product but an ideology. Marxism, for example, teaches people not merely to get what they desire, but to acquire new, class-conscious desires which otherwise would not have occurred to them. The same is true of such movements as nationalism and feminism, the very concepts of which did not exist until recent times. In many parts of the world, and for long periods of time, people have been content to live, for example, under an oligarchy of foreigners, and with no political rights of their own, regarding this as a normal and acceptable state of affairs. Then, by one means or another, ideas of nationalism and political rights are introduced, and new desires spring into being. The results may be clearly beneficial in terms, say, of an alleviation of suffering, but only too often this has not been so. Similarly, many women today ask themselves, for the first time, whether they resent such and such sexual arrangements, and perhaps come to feel that they do. New desires are created, with new possibilities of satisfaction and dissatisfaction; and whether the change is for the better or the worse, cannot be deduced from existing desires.

It is sometimes thought that democratic institutions are good because they lead to the greatest satisfaction of desires. Is this true? Consider a democratic meeting at which people have opposing views on a certain question. Perhaps, if the question had not been put to them, they would not have thought or cared about it very much, being content to leave it to others to make the decision. But as it is, they think about the matter and perhaps argue at length in favour of one alternative. Their emotions are engaged, and there will be satisfaction for some and frustration for others. Perhaps, if the choice is between two alternatives, there will be as much of one as of the other. But if there are three or more alternatives, each with one advocate, then more people will be frustrated than satisfied. (Of course, the degrees of frustration and satisfaction will vary from case to case.) This is not to deny that democracy may be the best arrangement – especially at the national level. (It has been well said that even if democracy is not a good form of government, every other is worse.) The point is, however, that its benefits cannot consist simply in the direct satisfaction of desires.

The enlargement of desires also leads to a greater variety of desires within the individual. Is this good? I find myself having to choose between A, B and C, all of which I desire.

Now if the way to happiness is to follow one's desires, then I must judge which I desire most (or, following the argument of the last section, which satisfaction of desire will satisfy me most). But if I choose A, then I must forgo B and C, which may be a matter of considerable regret. Thus my satisfaction in getting what I wanted will be tainted by regrets at not getting what I wanted. (In practice such regrets are often exacerbated by doubts about whether I really made the right choice.) For a person whose desires are less developed these difficulties are less likely to arise.

Aristotle describes a person whose desires are always in harmony. 'He is completely integrated and desires the same things with every part of his soul ... It is always the same things that vex or please him, and not different things at different times.'[8] Here is a twofold harmony: his desires are always unanimous, and there is a constant match between what he desires and what pleases him. This condition was contrasted by Aristotle with that of wicked people, whose 'soul is in a state of conflict'. But the difficulty is not confined to the wicked. The blessing of integration is given to different people, virtuous or wicked, in different measures. It is, however, *less* likely to exist among those affected by views of the kind advocated by Aristotle and Mill, in which the development of human potential is given great importance.

3   DESIRE AND THE 'GREATEST HAPPINESS PRINCIPLE'

In the preceding discussion the principle of following one's desires has been criticized partly by reference to results in terms of happiness. Will I be happy if I get what I desire? Not necessarily. Would I be happier if I had different desires? Would the members of a primitive society be happier if their desires were enlarged, or are they happier left alone? Such questions cannot be answered by reference to existing desires. But why should happiness be the criterion? Does the value of happiness not depend on the fact that it is itself desired? Thus it may be said, in the case of the examples discussed above, that the desire is really twofold: my desire for X entails or includes another – that I shall be happy when I get X. (I may indeed believe, on the basis of past experience, that fulfilment of the first desire may not bring fulfilment of the second.) Thus the problem can be seen as being about discrepancies between desires, rather than between desire on the one hand and happiness on the other.

Mill regarded happiness as 'the foundation of morals' – 'actions are right in proportion as they tend to promote happiness, wrong as they tend to produce the reverse of happiness'. But in support of this, the 'Greatest Happiness Principle', he appealed to a fact of human desire: 'No reason can be given why the general happiness is desirable, except that each person . . . desires his own happiness'.[9] So we are brought back to a fact of desire as the foundation of all value.

But which comes first, desire or value? According to Aristotle, 'we desire the object because it seems good to us, rather than the object's seeming good to us because we desire it'.[10] This ordering may seem more plausible than Mill's. Suppose my desire is to see a certain film. Asked why I desire this, I can reply that I believe the film to be good, perhaps on the testimony of others: I desire the object because 'it seems good'. But I cannot, conversely, reply to 'Why does it seem good?' by saying that I desire it. The 'because' works in one direction but not in the other. There is a reason why the direction should be as it is. The description of X as good (giving this as a reason for desiring it) opens the door to further, more interesting information; for we could go on to ask *why* X is regarded as good.

In this way, then, Aristotle's dictum is closer to the truth than Mill's. But in other ways Mill is right; there are contexts in which the reasoning is from desire to value. This is especially clear if the desire is not one's own but that of others. Thus if someone, or people in general, desire X – for example, the preservation of wild habitats, as discussed in Chapter Seven – then that may be a reason for regarding X as morally desirable; or if we are asked why it is *good* to provide X, the answer may be that X is what people desire. Respect for the desires of others is, indeed, one of those fundamental moral values that we should expect to find wherever human beings live in the company of others. This is not to say that there is a strict entailment from 'desired' to 'desirable'. Of course, one may hold that even if most people desire the institution of capital punishment, or prefer Bingo to Beethoven, these things are not desirable or right. Nevertheless, these desires must have *some* moral force, and reasons would have to be given for overriding this.

What is wrong with Mill's argument is not that he argues from 'desired' to 'desirable' (from fact to value, contrary to a widely accepted but false dichotomy), but that his statement of what *is* desired is obviously and outrageously false. For, having defined happiness as 'pleasure, and the absence of pain', he goes on to claim that 'mankind do desire nothing for itself but that which is a pleasure to them, or of which the absence is pain'.[11] But while it might be plausible to make such a claim about happiness, it is hardly so for the case of pleasure (and the absence of pain). Moreover, it is just in the case of pleasures that one would wish to apply the *distinction* between 'desired' and 'desirable', pointing out that, in this area especially, what is desired may not be what is good.[12] If Mill had said that *some* things desired for themselves are desired for the pleasure they give us, then he would have been obviously right. This would not, of course, have enabled him to regard the production of pleasure (and the absence of pain) as 'the foundation' of morals; but he could certainly have claimed, or reminded us, that it is morally desirable to give people pleasure (unless there are countervailing reasons).

But if this had been Mill's argument, then there would have been no need for it. It needs no great philosopher to prove that pleasure – or, *a fortiori*, happiness – are desirable and good. Now it may be doubted (on the basis of certain passages) whether Mill was really trying to *prove* his principle. According to one commentator, 'the question of proving what is an ultimate end cannot arise; but you can find out what people recognise as ultimate ends by finding out what they desire', and this is what Mill was attempting to do.[13] But such a procedure would make no sense in the case of happiness. There cannot be such a thing as *finding out* whether people desire happiness or regard it as good. Anyone who understands the meanings of these words must be aware that happiness is both desired and good.

Nevertheless the introduction of happiness as the *only* ultimate object of desire may seem (if accepted as true) to simplify our quest for the good life. On this view there would be a single and constant point of reference to which all our desires, however varied on the surface, would be accountable. It would be like regarding the making of money as the sole criterion in running a business. In a business firm we find many different desires and activities, interrelated in all sorts of complicated ways. But if the only ultimate desire is to make money, then they can all be evaluated as means to that end. This may be difficult in practice, but at least the overall objective would be clear.

But this is not a good analogy for the case of happiness and the good life. The difficulty here is not, or not merely, about the means of achieving a given end; it is also about *what* that end consists in. We ask about the constituents of happiness, and not merely about the means of attaining it. The proverbial 'What is happiness?' is an expression of this difficulty. There is no corresponding question 'What is money?'; and we do not ask ourselves what money consists in.[14]

In desiring happiness, we do not really know what we desire. 'It seems that to be happy is something that it is safe to want, but too safe: safe because it is sufficiently non-specific to be non-significant as an object of wanting.'[15] The problem about attaining happiness is not merely about conditions, favourable or otherwise, in the world outside ourselves; it is also a matter of self-examination, about what it is that we would regard as a happy life.

Mill's reduction of happiness to pleasure (and the absence of pain) is also likely to strike the reader as implausible; and one reason for this is that these questions do not arise about pleasure as they do about happiness. There is no adjective 'pleasant' which is descriptive of a person's condition as the word 'happy' is. And if we speak of 'a pleasant life', this will not mean quite the same as 'a happy life'; while 'a life of pleasure' is certainly something else. When people think about what would make them happy they may indeed reflect that there must be more to it than mere pleasure.

The discrepancies between desire and happiness constitute a difficulty for more recent versions of utilitarianism, which are based on desire or preference ('preference utilitarianism'). These versions have the advantage of avoiding difficult questions about the nature of happiness, its relation to pleasure, etc., by locating the good in the particular desires of human beings (or of sensitive beings, human and otherwise). But it may be argued, and argued by a utilitarian, that the maximization of happiness is more important than the satisfaction of desires; that the production of *good consequences* is the criterion of right action, rather than the satisfaction of an antecedent condition (an existing desire or preference). It may be thought that the two objectives coincide, since happiness is what we desire in all cases; but, as we have seen, the desire for happiness in the abstract cannot be identified with particular desires for X, Y or Z.

4 HAPPINESS AND TRUTH

But is it true, after all, that happiness is the only ultimate object of desire? It would be surprising if all the objects of human desire could be reduced to one – even one as non-specific as happiness. The desire for a cup of tea, for example, could hardly be regarded as a desire for happiness. Such desires accord better with Mill's wording after the switch from 'happiness' to 'pleasure', for it is true that I would expect the tea to be 'a pleasure to me'. But are there objects of desire which might be set *against* happiness? If someone chose to be a Socrates dissatisfied rather than a fool satisfied, then his choice would be contrary to happiness (and contrary to the Greatest Happiness Principle); for we would not describe a dissatisfied person as happy.[16] Another example is that of a person who has suffered brain damage and is reduced to a 'vegetable' condition. He feels no pain, has all his needs satisfied, and gives every sign of being happy. We may indeed say of such a person that he is happy. Yet we would probably not wish this condition for ourselves. It is true that in this case there has been damage, unlike (we may assume) the pig and fool in Mill's statement; and damage is not normally desired. However, we can consider the matter from the point of view of this person's present condition, without regard to its cause.

What is it we desire, apart from happiness? It might be said that the brain-damaged person would not be capable of as wide a range of experience as ourselves, and that this is what makes the difference. Suppose, however, that he could somehow be given the illusion of having a wide range of experience; then his happiness would be adequate in this sense as well. From his point of view it would be just like that of normal people with a normal range of experiences. But would we desire such a life? Would we want a kind of happiness that is based on an illusion?

The question is highlighted by Robert Nozick, who asks us to imagine an 'experience machine', which has the power to act on our brains so as to give us any desired sequence of experiences. 'You would think and feel you were writing a great novel, or making a friend, or reading an interesting book. All the time you would be floating in a tank, with electrodes attached to your brain.'[17] We are given the choice of plugging ourselves into this machine. Before doing so, we can programme it for any desired sequence of experiences. From time to time we get a chance to re-programme it, and so on. Supposing the details can all be worked out, 'would you plug in? What else can matter to us, other than how our lives feel from the inside?'[18] However, Nozick points out that this would not be enough. First, 'we want to *do* certain things, and not just have the experience of doing them'. Secondly, 'we want to *be* a certain way, to be a certain sort of person'. Can we say of the person in the tank that he is 'courageous, kind, intelligent, witty, loving? It's not merely that it's difficult to tell; there's no way he is. Plugging into the machine is a kind of suicide.'[19]

Various other machines, which might seem to overcome these difficulties, are introduced by Nozick. There is the 'transformation machine, which transforms us into whatever sort of person we'd like to be', and the 'result machine, which produces in the world any result you would produce'.[20] What is wrong with these and other machines? It is, says Nozick, 'their living our lives for us'. 'What we desire is to live . . . ourselves, in contact with reality. And this, machines cannot do *for* us.'[21] Here is a desire that is more fundamental than the desire for happiness. A happiness that is based on illusion is not what we desire.

The concern about truth is also retrospective. Someone who discovers that his happiness *has been* based on a falsehood (he has been 'living a lie') may feel that his happiness was unreal, even though it seemed real enough at the time. It might be thought that a person who makes this discovery near the end of his life will have had a good bargain. What is a short period of unhappiness, due to learning the truth, in comparison with an almost lifelong happiness? Yet we may feel we would rather have known the truth all along – that if we could have our life 'all over again', this is what we would choose, rather than the happy life of falsehood. In Tolstoy's story 'The Death of Ivan Ilyich', the hero has thoughts of this kind as he lies in the throes of his fatal illness. Ivan has been leading a respectable and satisfying life as a family man and distinguished lawyer in nineteenth-century Russia. All in all, he is not a bad man or a hypocrite, but someone who behaves well according to the standards of that society. But that society, as Tolstoy portrays it, is shallow and deficient in moral concerns. During his final agonies, Ivan feels that there is still something he needs to get right, to understand properly about his life, before he dies. But he is hindered from this 'by his conviction that his life had been a good one. That very justification of his life held him fast and prevented his moving forward.'[22] Suddenly he seems to experience a physical shock; and then

> he fell through the hole and there at the bottom was a light. What had happened to him was like the sensation one sometimes experiences in a railway carriage when one thinks one is going backwards while one is really going forwards and suddenly becomes aware of the real direction. 'Yes, it was all not the right thing', he said to himself.[23]

Again, we can sometimes make a person happy by means of falsehood or withholding the truth. Yet this may not be what he desires. He may want to know what we really think, rather than to be made happy by false flattery. Or to take another example, we may want the doctor to tell us the truth about ourselves or someone close to us, rather than to 'spare our feelings', even if this would leave us in a happier condition.

One may also derive happiness from adherence to a religious belief, and it is sometimes thought by advocates of religion that this is a point in favour of belief. Human beings, it is claimed, need religion; they cannot attain full happiness without some kind of religious belief. Now whether this is true is a difficult and complicated question. But if it is true, it cannot serve as a *reason* for belief. To have a reason for believing that *p*, is to have knowledge of something that proves, or makes it likely, that *p* is *true*. And the fact that a belief would make us happy has no bearing on its truth. Moreover, we may not want that happiness unless it is based on truth.

In recent years there has been a spate of quasi-religious and quasi-philosophical movements, which promise their adherents a sense of meaning and purpose in life, sometimes at a considerable sacrifice, financial and otherwise. Some of these 'philosophies of life' are couched in obscure and pretentious language, often employing words and ideas from physics or psychology. The candidate may feel that here at last he or she can find answers to the great questions of life, answers that may not be provided by a philosophy that is subject to the constraints of critical argument and plain language. What should be our reaction to those who get satisfaction in this way? One reaction would be to leave them alone. What does it matter, as long as they are happy? We may feel, however, that it does matter; and that a happiness obtained in this way is not worth having.

5   HAPPINESS AND DUTY

Another choice that may be contrary to the desire for happiness is that of moral duty. A person may choose to sacrifice his or her happiness in order, for example, to look after an elderly parent. It is sometimes thought that duty and happiness are not really distinct, because the moral choice will always be to one's advantage in the long run. 'Honesty is the best policy.' But this saying may be criticized both for being false and for being immoral. Honesty may be to one's advantage where dishonesty is liable to be discovered and punished; but this is not always the case. Similarly, if we fail to do unto others as we would have them do unto us, then the day may come when they will pay us back for our bad behaviour; but again, this day may not come, and sometimes it will be safe to assume that it will not. In short, it happens not infrequently that, as far as personal happiness is concerned, honesty is not the best policy, and immoral behaviour can be practised in one's own interest without fear of reprisal. On the other hand, the saying that honesty is the best policy may be described as immoral because it distorts the moral motive, implying that we are to be honest *because* this is the best policy. But what morality requires of us is that we should be honest whether it is to our advantage or not. That a particular action would be dishonest is a sufficient reason for not doing it; and the moral motive is distinct from any considerations of personal happiness.

Kant was emphatic about the distinctiveness of the moral motive, rejecting especially the idea that it could be reduced to the desire for happiness. 'The principle of *personal happiness*' was to be rejected

> not merely because it is false and because its pretence that well-being always adjusts itself to well-doing is contradicted by experience; nor merely because it contributes nothing whatever towards establishing morality, since making a man happy is quite different from making him good ... but because it bases morality on sensuous motives which rather undermine it and totally destroy its sublimity.[24]

However, the extent to which morality and happiness actually present themselves as rivals will depend on circumstances – and also on the character of the individual. There are those who take pleasure in virtuous behaviour of one kind or another, and for them the choice between duty and happiness may be hard to distinguish in practice. Others, of a different disposition, may encounter the conflict more frequently and sharply, and for them the path of duty is more likely to entail a renunciation of happiness. Which kind of person is it better to be? According to Kant, the second is more admirable. He asked the reader to consider two kinds of person. One is by nature sympathetic and finds pleasure in helping others; the second also helps others, but he does it, 'not from inclination, but from duty'.[25] According to Kant, the action of the first, 'however right and however amiable it may be, has still no genuine moral worth'; it is the second who shows a moral 'worth of character' – one that is 'beyond all comparison the highest'.[26]

This view may be illustrated by a real example. The philosopher G. E. Moore was admired for a certain childlike innocence, including a complete absence of vanity about his own achievements. Asked whether he could understand the resentment displayed by another philosopher about criticism of his work, he replied, after a little thought, that he could not. This conversation was reported in a letter to Wittgenstein by Norman Malcolm, who commented favourably on Moore's character. But Wittgenstein took a Kantian view.

> As to its being to his *credit* that he is childlike – I can't understand that; unless it's also to a *child's* credit. For you aren't talking of the innocence a man has fought for, but of an innocence which comes from a natural absence of temptation.[27]

Which is better, a natural goodness or one that has been fought for? Which kind of person is more to be admired? Many people today, perhaps influenced by Kant or Kantian ideas, would favour the second. This has the paradoxical consequence that the person who is good by nature could *never* achieve the same moral standing as is possible for the one who is bad by nature. Perhaps, if there are rewards in heaven, the former would be well advised to try to *become* mean by nature, so that he could attain the higher moral standing by acting well in spite of his nature! Conversely, those for whom duty and inclination are clearly opposed (like the person in Kant's example) had better take care to preserve this opposition. The difficulties of this view were illustrated in an episode in George Eliot's *Middlemarch*, in which the high-minded Dorothea announces that she will give up riding.

> 'No, that is too hard', said Sir James . . . 'Your sister is given to self-mortification, is she not?', he continued, turning to Celia . . .
>
> 'I think she is,' said Celia, feeling afraid lest she should say something that would not please her sister, and blushing as prettily as possible above her necklace. 'She likes giving up.'
>
> 'If that were true, Celia, my giving-up would be self-indulgence, not self-mortification. But there may be good reasons for choosing not to do what is very agreeable,' said Dorothea . . .
>
> 'Exactly,' said Sir James. 'You give up from some high, generous motive.'
>
> 'No, indeed, not exactly. I did not say that of myself,' answered Dorothea, reddening.[28]

The person who is good by nature and acts accordingly, leads a good life both in the self-regarding and in the moral sense. The other kind of life, regarded as superior by Kant, is more admirable in one way, but inferior in terms of internal harmony and happiness, as we have seen. A third kind of life remains to be considered: that of the person who is bad by nature and acts accordingly. His life will obviously be inferior in the moral sense, but will it be so in the self-regarding sense?

According to Aristotle, virtue is an essential condition of happiness in the sense of internal harmony. As we saw, he contrasted the 'integrated' man, whose desires are always in harmony, with the wicked, whose 'soul is in a state of conflict'.

> One part of it through depravity feels pain in abstaining from certain things, and another feels pleasure; one pulls this way and the other that, as if they would tear it apart . . . Such a person is very soon sorry that he was glad, and wishes that he had never taken pleasure in such things; for bad men are full of regrets.[29]

Such people, he said, 'feel no affection for themselves', for they have 'no lovable quality'.

Aristotle's point is not merely that the pain of regret may outweigh the previous pleasure. This may be so in some cases but not in others. (Similarly, honesty may be the best policy in some cases but not in others.) Repentance is a quality that may not be very much in evidence in the case of a thoroughly wicked person. If the latter is single-minded enough in his wickedness, may he not achieve the same degree of integration as the virtuous man? Aristotle's answer is that he cannot; for he cannot contemplate himself with the same satisfaction as the virtuous person. Having 'no lovable quality', he 'feels no affection for himself'.

In many cases the wicked person will be better off than the virtuous. As Kant observed, the idea that 'well-being always adjusts itself to well-doing is contradicted by experience'. Yet the wicked person may reflect on his life, on the kind of person he is and would wish to be, and this may make him pause. Such a person is described in a novel by L. P. Hartley, in which the hero, a car-hire driver with little sense of morality, would nevertheless not steal from his clients, 'because he didn't see himself as that sort of man'.

> It wasn't so much that he disapproved of stealing as that he despised the kind of man who stole. If he had stolen, he would have had to despise himself, and that he couldn't do.[30]

Rousseau, as we saw in Chapter Seven, complained that man in the social condition 'only knows how to live in the opinion of others', regarding this as the source of those harmful passions which he subsumed under 'amour-propre'. But this living in the opinion of others is also an important source of morality. A human being, good or bad, has the ability to survey and evaluate his own life as he may survey and evaluate the life of another; and he will be satisfied or dissatisfied by what he perceives. But what is to be his standard of evaluation? Admirable qualities are those that we admire in others; and these must be qualities like kindness and honesty, rather than their opposites. Hence, if I can find these qualities in my behaviour, I can be satisfied and at peace with myself. In this sense, as Aristotle puts it, 'it is right for the good man to be self-loving'.[31] But this satisfaction is not available to the wicked person.

The wicked person would not necessarily be unloved by others, for he might gain their love or esteem through dissimulation. But this, again, cannot give him the same satisfaction as love or esteem gained *without* dissimulation. The crooked politician may be heaped with honours and high offices; the cheating student warmly congratulated on his or her exam results; but they cannot avoid the knowledge that their achievements are a sham, and that these honours and congratulations are not the real thing. The point was well expressed in a recent *Punch* cartoon: 'Anyone who sends for a fake diploma deserves a fake diploma.' Such a person can 'feel no affection for himself' – or, at least, his affection for himself cannot be unqualified like that of the virtuous person. He also faces a difficulty about the affection of others. Rousseau, expatiating on the sweetness of love, drew attention to our desires to be 'worthy of love', seeing in this a route to jealousy and dissension. But again, there is also a positive side to this. For what I desire is to be loved for qualities I have and not qualities I merely seem to have; to be loved or admired for what I really am, by those who really know me. In this way the path of virtue and the path of happiness coincide.

It might be objected that the dishonest person may also be admired, or feel pleased himself, for his skills in cheating – assuming, perhaps, that the results are not unduly harmful. But in this case he would be admired because of his skill (perhaps in outwitting a clumsy, impersonal bureaucracy), and not because of the cheating as such. Someone who displayed equal skill, but in an honest cause, would still have the advantage over the cheat. It is also worth noting that those who are convicted of cheating and other crimes (gangsters, mafia bosses, etc.) often go to great lengths to justify themselves in their memoirs, trying to prove to the reader, and perhaps to themselves, that they really had nothing to be ashamed of. This is part of the tribute that vice pays to virtue.

However, the distinction made at the start of this section, between happiness and duty, remains in force. These motives are distinct in logic, and will *sometimes* be distinct in practice, given the nature of human beings and the world in which they live. If happiness is one of the main categories of desires, morality is another. We desire to be happy, but we also desire to live in a way that is morally satisfactory; and the two desires are distinct.

It may be said that in the case of morality desire itself is liable to be overridden. 'I don't want to do X, but I ought to' is an essential part of our moral life. We may also experience the moral requirement as a peculiar kind of 'imperative' (to use Kant's term), as when we say 'I *had* to do X – it was my duty', in spite of the fact that it was in one's power not to do X (and X was not what one desired to do). However, it is still correct to say, from a more general point of view, that to conduct our lives in a morally satisfactory way – whatever that may be – is one of our desires.

NOTES

1   Hobbes, *op. cit.*, p. 90.
2   Mill, *Utilitarianism*, p. 288.
3   Sackville-West, V. (1930) *The Edwardians*.
4   Plato (1971 edn) *Gorgias*, Penguin, p. 90.
5   *Ibid.*, 494, pp. 94–5.
6   *Ibid.*, 492, pp. 91.
7   Mr Katz fitted on the made-to-measure suit and cried in dismay:
     'Look at this sleeve! It's two inches too long!'
        'So stick out your elbow,' said the tailor, 'which bends your arm – and the sleeve is just right!'
        'The collar! It's half way up my head!'
        'So raise your head up and back – and the collar goes down.'
        'But the left shoulder is two inches wider than the right!'
        'So *bend*, this way, and it'll even out.'
     Mr Katz left the tailor in this fantastic posture: right elbow stuck out wide, head far up and back, left shoulder tilted. A stranger accosted him.
        'Excuse me, but would you mind giving me the name of your tailor?'
        '*My* tailor?' Katz cried. 'Are you mad? Why would anyone want my tailor?'
        'Because any man who can fit a *kalikeh* [cripple] like you is a genius!' (Rosten, L. (1971) *The Joys of Yiddish*, Penguin, pp. 167–8.)
8   *Nicomachean Ethics*, 1166a, pp. 293–4.

9   *Utilitarianism*, p. 288.
10 *Metaphysics*, 1072a.
11 *Utilitarianism*, p. 292.
12 Mill is also criticized for comparing the relation between desired and desirable to that between seen and visible, heard and audible, etc. It is pointed out that 'desirable' (unlike visible, etc.) means *worthy*, and not merely able, to be desired. But the inference from desired to desirable may be correct in spite of the weakness of this comparison.
13 Warnock, Mary, 'On Moore's Criticism of Mill's "proof"', in J. B. Schneewind (ed.) (1968) *Mill*, Macmillan. See also the introduction to Warnock's edition of *Utilitarianism* (cited above).
14 This is not to say that if we did ask ourselves this question, we would find it easy to answer. The question is raised, and an answer given, in Crowther, G. (1948 Rev. edn) *An Outline of Money*, Nelson, chapter 1.
15 Austin, Jean, 'Pleasure and Happiness', in Schneewind, *op. cit.*, p. 238.
16 Mill's terminology in this crucial passage is not as clear as might be wished. At one point he warns us not to confound 'the two very different ideas, of happiness, and content' (*ibid.*, p. 260); and here he seems to imply that the 'superior being', though less *contented*, would not thereby be less happy. Perhaps he intended a similar distinction with the word 'satisfied', which he introduces in the passage about Socrates. In any case, his argument in these pages may just as well be taken to point to a conclusion about more and less *happiness* – better to be an unhappy, or less happy, Socrates, etc. Mill's argument would work better with Aristotle's term '*eudaimonia*' – translated as 'happiness' but having the connotations of 'flourishing' (and also 'prosperity'). It is more natural for Aristotle to claim that only a fully-developed person can be happy, than it would be for us to do so, in the modern sense of the word.
17 Nozick, R. (1974) *Anarchy, State and Utopia*, Blackwell, p. 42.
18 *Ibid.*, p. 43.
19 *Ibid.*
20 *Ibid.*, p. 44.
21 *Ibid.*, p. 45.
22 Tolstoy, L. (1982 edn) *The Raid and Other Stories*, Oxford University Press, p. 278.
23 *Ibid.*
24 Kant, *op. cit.*, p. 103.

25 *Ibid.*, pp. 63–4.
26 *Ibid.*, p. 64.
27 Malcolm, N. (1966, 2nd edn) *Ludwig Wittgenstein*, Oxford University Press, pp. 115–16.
28 Eliot, George (1970) *Middlemarch*, Penguin, chapter 2.
29 *Nicomachean Ethics*, 1166b, p. 295.
30 Hartley, L. P. (1973) *The Hireling*, Penguin, p. 149.
31 *Nicomachean Ethics*, 1169a, p. 302.

CHAPTER TEN

Who am I?

1 THE INDIVIDUAL AND SOCIETY

According to Aristotle, as we saw at the start of Chapter Eight, man realizes his true nature by living in a political society, this being the 'aim and end' or 'perfection' of human nature. Having attained this condition, what is the relation between the individual and society? 'The state', wrote Aristotle, 'has priority over the . . . individual. For the whole must be prior to the part.'[1] His point was that the part is what it is in virtue of the whole to which it belongs. A draughts piece would not be what it is in isolation from the game of draughts.[2] Similarly, 'separate hand or foot from the whole body, and they will no longer be hand or foot except in name . . .'[3] A hand or foot is what it is in virtue of its 'capacity and function' relative to the whole organism, and when this is broken, 'we cannot say that they are, in that condition, the same things'.[4] And the same is true of the individual person and the organism – the city or state – of which he is a part, and in which he exercises power or function. Aristotle's analogy seems to be confirmed by our use of the word 'member' to mean both a part of the body (e.g. a hand or foot) and an individual belonging to some association, such as a club, a firm or a state.

F. H. Bradley, writing in the nineteenth century, held that a thing is what it is in virtue of its relations.

> The 'individual' man, the man into whose essence his community with others does not enter, who does not include relation to others in his very being, is, we say, a fiction.[5]

A child, he pointed out, 'is born not into a desert, but into a living world'.[6] 'He is what he is because he is a born and educated social being, and a member of an individual social organism.'[7] Man, he concluded, 'is a social being: he is real only because he is social, and can realize himself only because it is as social that he realizes himself'.[8] He cannot

> find the function, which makes him himself, apart from the whole to which he belongs; to be himself he must go beyond himself, to live his life he must live a life which is not *merely* his own ... I am myself by sharing with others, by including in my essence relations to them, the relations of the social state.[9]

Aristotle's remarks were about man as such; man is a 'political animal', and finds fulfilment by being a member of a city or state. But Bradley was concerned about the situation of individual men and women. Human fulfilment is to be found, he held, not merely by being a member of society, but by living in accordance with one's particular station in society.

> There I realize myself morally, so that not only what ought to be in the world is, but I am what I ought to be, and find so my contentment and satisfaction ... A man who does his work in the world is good, notwithstanding his faults, if his faults do not prevent him from fulfilling his station.[10]

Bradley's account provides a comprehensive answer to the questions with which this book is concerned. How should I live? What is the meaning or purpose of my life? Wherein lies its value? According to Bradley the answers lie in 'self-realization'; and self-realization means living in accordance with the 'self' defined by one's station in society. This does not mean that the purpose of my life is the purpose of something *other* than myself (i.e. society). The purpose is given by my station in society, but this means that it is my own, since *I* am what I am in virtue of that station. Hence the way to self-realization is that of 'my station and its duties'.

Bradley's claim that we 'identify ourselves and others with the station we fill'[11] is supported by some of the ways in which we refer to people. In traditional societies, people were actually named according to their trades or professions – a practice which is reflected in many surnames today (Smith, Baker, etc.). In some languages (Hebrew, Russian) a person's name included a reference to his father ('... the son of so-and-so'). And when we speak of 'the Prime Minister' or 'the prophet Jonah' we identify these individuals by their station. The question 'Who is he?' will often be a question about social relations. What does he do? Where does she work? Is she the friend (wife, daughter, etc.) of so-and-so?

This kind of identification is normative; it tells us what a person is supposed to do, what his duties are. It is also peculiar to man – the 'political animal'. In describing a blackbird we would describe its physical appearance and behaviour. But this has no normative implications; for we cannot distinguish between the actual behaviour and that prescribed by duty, in the case of a blackbird. (This is also true of 'social' animals, such as bees.) By contrast, the identification of a person by his social relations has implications about how he ought to behave.

Bradley's thesis is both logical and moral. The identity of human beings has a certain logical character, and from this follows a prescription of how we ought to conduct our lives. According to Bradley, the only question to ask is 'Am I fulfilling my appointed function or not?' But may I not also ask whether this function is the right or best one for me? In Bradley's time, this may have been an idle question as far as most people were concerned. They were expected to remain in the station into which they were born; and probably had no choice in the matter. But the same is true, to a large extent, also in our society. We are members of a given nation and imbibe its culture before we can even conceive of alternatives; we belong to a family whose members are related by a network of duties; and although we can choose our careers to some extent, the choice does not in practice present itself, to most people, as one of a great number of alternatives. And once I have committed myself to a given career or occupation, these will impose certain duties on me, and a certain identification of myself as a member of a larger organism.

Nevertheless, having recognized these facts, I may still ask myself whether my 'appointed function', whether imposed or self-chosen, is the best one for me; and it must be admitted that Bradley's prescription will not help me to deal with this question. But to what extent can such questions be asked? Of course, I can make comparisons between working for one firm and working for another, and so on. But what about more radical alternatives? Would I be happier leading the life of an airline pilot, a shop assistant, or a fashion designer, rather than the one I actually lead? Would I be happier as a citizen of another country, rather than that to which I belong? Bradley might say that under these conditions *I* would not be the same person; so that the comparison would not be between *myself* leading one kind of life and leading another. (This is similar to the difficulty about actual and potential desires, discussed in Chapter Nine, Section 2). What I would need to consider is not how a certain kind of life would appeal to me, being the person I am, but whether 'I' would wish to be the kind of person that I would become (or would have been), leading another kind of life. Yet, when these complications have been allowed for, it cannot be said that there is no sense in such questions. The person who makes (or perhaps suffers) a radical change in his or her way of life does not undergo a total change of personality. And when such changes take place, or are contemplated, in real life, the people concerned do in fact make comparisons, even though this may be difficult.

Again, those who cannot get a job may feel that they have *no* proper function, and that Bradley's prescription is not applicable to them. Now there is obviously more to life than paid employment – other functions, and other ways of self-realization. Even so, many unemployed people feel a lack of function, and it is not clear how Bradley's analysis could help them. Finally, some stations in life are, by any reasonable human standard, bad; and those who find themselves in such a position would be right to do all they can to improve their lot, regardless of Bradley's point about identity.

Bradley also held that good in general is defined by the values existing in a given society. However, he did not deny absolutely that these values might be questioned.[12] 'My station and its duties' cannot give us all the answers to questions of morality and the meaning of life. Sometimes the path of duty, and of self-realization, lies in questioning accepted values and in not being content with the station in which one is placed. Nevertheless, for many of us, and for much of our lives, the relationships in which we find ourselves, and the corresponding duties and obligations, determine both what we are and how we may find self-fulfilment.

2 'MAN MAKES HIMSELF'

Several of the previous chapters were about attempts to deduce conclusions about the good life, and the meaning of life, from claims about the essential nature of human beings. Man is a rational animal; man is a political animal; therefore the path of fulfilment must lie in the direction of reasoning or political activity. Man is essentially what he was in the 'state of nature', before the emergence of societies; hence he should return to that state and resume the life for which he was fitted. All men desire happiness; this is the goal for which we must strive. An individual is defined by his or her station in society; here lies the path to self-realization.

All of these views may be described as 'essentialist', being based on claims about the essential nature of man. Opposed to them all is the 'existentialism' of Jean-Paul Sartre and others. 'Existence', he declared, 'comes before essence'.[13] 'Man as the existentialist sees him is not definable ... there is no human nature.'[14] 'Man makes himself; he is not found ready-made.'[15]

In declaring that there is 'no human nature', Sartre does not mean to deny that human beings share certain mental and physical qualities by nature, nor that people have qualities which are natural to them as individuals. He is talking about the capacity that human beings have to detach themselves from these facts of nature, and to make choices independently of them. For example, a person may find in himself certain 'motivations' and 'drives', which may cause him to act accordingly; but he is also free to act otherwise. 'These drives', says Sartre, 'are realized with my consent . . . I lend them their efficacy by a perpetually renewed decision concerning their value.'[16] Similarly, 'when a man says, "I am not easy to please", he is entering into a free engagement with his ill temper'.[17]

Again, where Bradley sees self-realization in the performance of one's duty in the station in which one finds oneself, Sartre emphasizes our freedom as conscious human beings to stand apart from any such prescription. To conceal this freedom from ourselves is 'bad faith'. In a well-known example he describes a café waiter who gives himself up to an excessive extent to his role. 'He is playing *at being* a waiter in a café . . . [His] condition is wholly one of ceremony.'[18] He wants to persuade his clientele that he is a waiter and nothing but a waiter. Yet he cannot really be just a waiter, even if that is what he wants. An artefact, such as an inkwell, is wholly defined by its function, but this mode of being is not available for a human being, who can 'form reflective judgements . . . concerning his condition'.[19] Sartre describes how, when we form such judgements, there is a radical division of ourselves; the question 'Who am I?' has no single answer.

> It is precisely this person *who I have to be* (if I am the waiter in question) and who I am not. It is not that I do not wish to be this person or that I want this person to be different. But rather there is no common measure between his being and mine . . . If I represent myself to him, I am not he; I am separated from him as the object from the subject . . . I can not be he, I can only play *at being* him.[20]

Sartre's ethic is above all one of responsibility. Our actions are not dictated by an antecedent human or social or personal nature over which we have no control, but are up to us when the moment of choice arrives. 'Any man who takes refuge behind the excuse of his passions, by inventing some deterministic doctrine, is a self-deceiver.'[21] Sartre does not provide a refutation of determinism, but there is no need for him to do so. What matters is that human beings *are confronted* by alternative choices, that this is how life presents itself to us. Having noted that my character is such and such, and that I generally act in this and this way, it is still an open question for me whether I should do so now. I cannot resign my responsibility by pleading that my actions are predetermined by my essential nature or by my station in society. A person may act in a certain way because he has been 'conditioned' or 'indoctrinated' to that effect; and in commenting on his behaviour, we may explain it in such ways. This would be the same kind of explanation as that which we might give of any natural process, by reference to antecedent conditions and natural regularities. But for the person who tries to *justify* his or her action, this mode of explanation is insufficient. Asked to justify my intention to commit a theft, I cannot reply by talking about conditioning or indoctrination. Whatever may be said about determinism, there is no escape from the burden of responsibility which is part of the human condition.

Again, we cannot, according to Sartre, abdicate responsibility by taking orders from a supernatural source.

> If a voice speaks to me, it is still I myself who must decide whether the voice is or is not that of an angel. If I regard a certain course of action as good, it is only I who choose to say that it is good and not bad.[22]

He refers to the *Old Testament* story, in which an angel commands Abraham to sacrifice his only son on an altar. The story can be seen as illustrating Abraham's obedience – 'blind' obedience – to the word of God. But ought he to be blind – even when the word seems to come from an angel? 'Anyone in such a case', writes Sartre, 'would wonder . . . whether it was indeed an angel . . . Where are the proofs?'[23] It might be held that a being which gave such commands could not be an angel of God, and that no positive evidence could be strong enough to outweigh the negative evidence of the command itself. Or again, Abraham might have concluded that a God who issued such commands would not be worthy of his allegiance. But whatever he decided, the question was there to be faced; he could not, without self-deception, pretend that it did not exist.

There is, according to Sartre, no moral code that can prescribe to me how I should act, for a moral code is something that each one of us must create or invent for himself.[24] But if this is so, by what standard can one judge the behaviour of another? Is not every choice as good as every other?

> Whenever a man chooses his purpose and his commitments
> in all clearness and in all sincerity, whatever that purpose
> may be it is impossible to prefer another for him.[25]

There is, however, one single failing on which a person can be judged. 'One can judge a man by saying that he deceives himself.'[26] The self-deceiver is one who shuts his eyes to the all-embracing freedom that belongs to him as a human being.

How then should a person live according to Sartre? The positive counterpart of self-deception (or 'bad faith') is to be honest with oneself, or 'sincere'. 'To be sincere . . . is to be what one is.'[27] But – what is one? As we have seen, sincerity does not lie in acting according to one's nature or character. The person to whom I must be true, the choosing person that lies at the centre of existential man, is a thing of *no* character. 'As soon as we posit ourselves as a certain being' of such and such a character, 'then by that very positing we surpass this being – and that not toward another being but toward emptiness, toward *nothing*'.[28] 'The ideal of sincerity', he concludes, 'is in contradiction with the structure of my consciousness'.[29]

Existentialism is a philosophy of freedom, freedom from our own natures. A person is not a mere 'thing', subject to the blind determinism of laws of nature. The 'motivations' which I find in myself are realized, if they are, 'with my consent'. However, while freedom is often regarded as a desirable goal, the freedom of which Sartre speaks is an intolerable burden because it casts us loose from any standard or recipe by which we can live. We are, says Sartre, 'condemned to be free'. 'No limits to my freedom can be

found except freedom itself or, if you prefer . . . we are not
free to cease being free.'[30] It is, however, just this last
freedom – from freedom itself – that we may desire. Hence
we may prefer to believe that what we ought to do is laid
down for us by our nature, our station in society, or (rather
differently) by divine command or 'in a luminous realm of
values'.[31]

3   FREEDOM AND REASON

Someone who comes to Sartre's writings for the first time
may find them fascinating, challenging or bewildering. Is
this really what life is like? Do we not, sometimes, at least,
have reasons which prescribe how we should act? We
may agree with Sartre (and with Kant) that our moral
responsibility cannot be abdicated to a divine authority, and
that no prescription for living can be deduced from the
nature or essence of man, in the general or individual sense.
But does this cast us loose from reasons altogether?

Sartre's writings are full of vivid examples of people who
cannot find any reason for preferring one course of action
to another. There is the student who came to him during
the Second World War to ask whether he should join the
Resistance or stay to look after his elderly mother, only to
be told that there is no way of answering such questions.[32]
In Sartre's trilogy The Roads to Freedom, the philosophy
teacher Mathieu is invited by his friend Brunet to join the
Communist Party. 'The Party', he tells him, 'doesn't need
you . . . But you need the Party.'

> You have gone your own way . . . you are free . . . But what's
> the use of that same freedom, if not to join us? . . . You are
> an odd sort of creature, you know . . . You live in a void . . .
> you're an abstraction, a man who is not there. It can't be an
> amusing sort of life . . . You renounced everything in order
> to be free . . . Take one step further, renounce your own
> freedom . . .[33]

Mathieu knows that if he belonged to the Party his life
would have the kind of meaning that it now lacks; he would
have committed himself to principles and duties which

would fill his life with purposeful activity. But he cannot, without bad faith, decide to embrace these principles. 'Well, there it is. I can't join, I haven't enough reasons for doing so. I should be telling myself a lie.'

But such examples, interesting as they are, cannot support any radical conclusions about the impotence of reason in general. It needs no existentialist to point out that sometimes the reasons for and against an action are evenly balanced, so that we are left without any guide as to what we should do. Again, we can well understand the predicament of Mathieu, who would quite like to join the Party, but cannot find adequate reasons for doing so. In this case, it seems, he is obviously right not to join. However, the existentialist position is more radical and more challenging than this. What is at issue is whether we *ever* have adequate reasons for acting in one way or another, or for acting in any way at all. Mathieu, the philosopher who has thought the matter through, has arrived at an answer to these questions; it is 'no'. He has no adequate reasons for joining the Party – nor for doing anything else.

But to support such a view it is necessary to consider cases in which there seems to be no difficulty about reasons – simple, everyday cases, in which reason points only in one direction. Sartre's neglect of these may be compared with the argument of those who claim that morality is 'subjective', because moral questions can sometimes not be settled by reason. It is tempting to think that such questions take up the whole of morality, because they provoke much thought and discussion, are prominent in the newspapers, and so on. But this would be a mistake. Much of the moral reasoning which pervades our lives is straightforward and does not call for personal judgement or probings of conscience; and being straightforward, it hardly comes up for discussion and is thus easily overlooked. For example, if I have borrowed some money, then I ought to repay it, unless there are countervailing reasons. It is true that if there *are* such reasons, then it may be difficult or impossible to arrive at a conclusion as to what I should do. But in many cases there is none, and my obligation is clear and obvious. The same would have been true of Sartre's student if he had had only one obligation – say, that of looking after his mother. In that case, he would have known what he ought to do, and would not have needed to consult his teacher or anyone else.

According to Sartre, however, moral values are themselves a matter of individual choice. It is 'self-deception' to say that 'certain values are incumbent upon me; I am in contradiction if I will these values and at the same time say that they impose themselves upon me'.[34] Now it is true that I may deceive myself into thinking that something is 'incumbent upon me' when this would avoid an awkward choice; but the *existence* of values is not subject to my will. If I have borrowed some money, then it is incumbent on me to repay it. This 'value' is analytic to the concept of borrowing and not in any sense subject to my will.[35] Of course, I may choose not to repay the money, contrary to my obligation, because I want to keep it for myself. But to *fail* in one's obligation is not to deny that one has it; and while the first is a matter of personal choice, the second is not.

It is sometimes thought that morality needs the support of religion, so that in a secular age there is no longer any reason for behaving in a moral way. Such was the view of Dostoevsky, as quoted by Sartre: 'If God did not exist, everything would be permitted.' This, said Sartre, was the 'starting point' of existentialism. If God does not exist, then man is 'forlorn, for he cannot find anything to depend upon either within or outside himself'.[36] But this view is both false and dangerous. It is false because moral reasons exist independently of religion; and it is dangerous because if people have this view, then a decline of religious belief *may* lead to a decline of morality – in spite of the falseness of the view.

We must also consider reasons which are not of the moral kind. Much of our activity is motivated by natural human needs or inclinations and not by any moral code or principle. A man is hungry, he eats; another feels like fresh air, he goes for a walk; someone asks me a question, I reply. It is not clear how the existentialist rejection of reason can be applied to these simple cases. These considerations also affect Sartre's examples of 'bad faith', like that of the waiter.[37]

Immersing himself in that role, the waiter, according to Sartre, shuts his eyes to the alternatives which his freedom as a human being puts before him; forgetting that it is up to him to choose or not choose that role – 'as if it were not just in my power to confer their value and their urgency upon my duties ... as if it were not my free choice to get up each morning at five o'clock or to remain in bed, even though it meant getting fired'.[38] But what if he does get fired? Perhaps, if he cannot get another job, he will have to go hungry. It may be, then, that he sticks to his job because he wants to eat. But could he not choose to go hungry? Not in the sense in which one might choose one job rather than another, or choose to join the Communist Party (or some other). In making choices of this kind, one takes on a role or commits oneself to a set of values or duties; and here there is a certain loss of autonomy – as implied by the expression 'commit oneself' – a signing away of one's original freedom of choice. But in eating rather than going hungry one is not taking on a role or committing oneself to a particular set of values or duties. The need to eat is with us whether we are free or committed. It may be admitted that the waiter is playing a role, and perhaps he is also deceiving himself as to the necessity of this particular role. It may be that, if he took a proper view of himself, he would recognize other possibilities. But insofar as he plays this role because he wants to make a living, he is not playing a role, nor signing away his freedom as a self-conscious human being; for the desire for food and certain other things is part of his nature whatever he may do.

Here is an aspect of human nature which does not fit into the dispute between essentialists and existentialists. It is part of a human being's nature or essence to desire to eat; but one does not decide to eat because that is so, but because one is hungry. And we do all sorts of other things because we need to do them, feel like doing them, like doing them, etc. These cases stand in contrast to the kind of reasoning of which Aristotle is a paradigm, where we decide on a certain way of life because it is thought to follow from what we, personally or collectively, essentially are. Thus we may opt for such and such a life on the ground that 'man is a political animal'; or I may, personally, choose to be (or remain) a waiter because I hold that this accords with my identity as defined by my station and its duties. But no such reasoning is at work when one decides to eat, go for a walk, etc.

Let us suppose, however, that such reasoning is at work. Suppose that, after thinking carefully about the arguments of Aristotle, Rousseau or Bradley, I conclude that I should follow one or other of their prescriptions. Would the resulting action be lacking in freedom or sincerity? Now it may be that the reasoning in question is incorrect, and that essentialism, or that particular version of it, is false. But this would not matter. The freedom of an action is not contingent on the *correctness* of the reasons for which it is done, nor on its being the *right* action in the circumstances. We know only too well that many mistaken actions are freely done. Perhaps a defender of existentialism will say that the reasoning in this case – essentialism – is not merely incorrect, but based on self-deception which is a negation of one's freedom. But how could this be proved? There are no limits to mistakes of reasoning, and we can easily suppose that while essentialism, or a particular form of it, is false, the person concerned mistakes it – in all sincerity – for the truth. Such a person would be making a free choice in accordance with the truth as he or she sees it – mistakenly but without self-deception.

It may be thought, however, that reason and freedom are incompatible in a more general sense. We sometimes speak of reason as a kind of compulsion – as when one has 'compelling' or 'overwhelming' reasons to do X, or when, given certain reasons, one was 'bound' to choose X. Does freedom – true, ultimate freedom – lie in obedience to reason or in flouting its dictates? In Sartre's trilogy, the young pacifist, Philippe, thinks he must renounce reason in order to attain true freedom. It is 1938, and he has made up his mind to evade conscription by taking the train to Switzerland; he will not betray his freedom by doing what was expected of him. But can he be sure that the course he has embarked on will really be free? Will he not be acting merely in obedience to other reasons?

Seven minutes. Which would be the most revolutionary? he asked himself. To go or not to go? If I go, I revolt against others; if I don't go, I revolt against myself, and that is a nobler deed. Make every preparation, procure false papers . . . and then, at the last moment – pfftt! – I'm not going after all. Freedom in the second degree; freedom contesting freedom.[39]

He tosses a coin and it comes down 'heads'. 'Very well, I go! . . . Not because I hate the war, not because I hate my family, but by pure *chance* . . . I am at the extremest point of freedom.'[40]

Here we have a sublimation of the concept of freedom, of a kind that also occurs in other branches of philosophy. Can anyone really *know* that *p*? 'No', replies the philosopher. Knowledge requires absolute certainty, and this can never be achieved.[41] Can an action really be altruistic? 'No', is the reply; for if I do *X* to help my neighbour, then I must *want* to do *X*; and doing what I want is not altruistic. In these and other ways philosophers have eliminated descriptions and distinctions that we normally make and need to make. But in doing so, they appeal, implicitly or otherwise, to conditions that go beyond the normal usage of the words in question. For example, it is not part of the normal use of 'altruistic' that one must not in *any* sense want to do the action. Similarly, the existence of reasons (or compelling reasons) does not necessarily go against freedom of choice, as this expression is normally understood. Whether it does will depend on the nature of the case. If the compelling reason for handing over my money is that someone is holding a gun at my head, then this will not be a free act; if it is that someone in my family needs the money more than I do, then it will be. The argument of Philippe would have us eliminate this distinction; according to that argument, real freedom would only be attained by renouncing reason altogether. (Philippe does not really attain it, for his decision was, after all, the outcome of a process of reasoning, including obedience to the toss of the coin.) But the distinction between free and not free is not infringed by the effect of reason on what we do. What matters is not whether I do *X* for a reason, but *what* that reason is. Again, the question whether I act freely may need to be understood in a relative way. Is the waiter in Sartre's example free to stay in bed? In one sense he is, in another not. He must get up, since this is what his job requires. Yet in another sense he need not get up; he could stay in bed and accept the consequences.

4   BEING TRUE TO ONESELF

According to Sartre, as we have seen, the supreme and indeed only virtue is that of sincerity and avoidance of 'bad faith'. If a person chooses 'in all clearness and in all sincerity', then we cannot criticize him. This is the only value that is left, and through it we recognise that all other values are without foundation (other than arbitrary choice).

If we reject this view, how important is sincerity? To act sincerely is to be motivated in a certain manner. But in evaluating a person's actions, we need to take account of *what* he does, and not merely how he is motivated (whether sincerely or otherwise). If someone has chosen in all clearness and sincerity to become a brutal dictator, this would not mean that his behaviour is beyond criticism.

Again, consider the person who behaves well by nature, like the one in Kant's example (see Chapter Nine, Section 5). He would deserve praise for what he does (even if he is thought less deserving than the one who has to fight against his nature). But could he be accused of insincerity, in Sartre's sense, because he allows himself to act according to his nature? Here (as is often the case in philosophical issues) we find a disparity between the positive and negative (good and bad) cases; and both must be examined. The person who behaves badly, like Sartre's man who says 'I am not easy to please', may try to take shelter behind a false doctrine of essentialism or determinism – as if it were not up to him to decide whether to follow his nature or go against it. In this case sincerity – facing up to one's responsibility as a self-reflective human being – is what is needed. But there is no counterpart to this in the case of the person who behaves *well* by nature. In that case there is no need for excuses and no effort of sincerity is called for.[42]

There are other virtues besides sincerity, as we have seen. But that virtue itself is more complex than would appear from Sartre's account. In that account, it means taking a stand that is independent of one's own nature. But there is another virtue, also called sincerity, which consists in being *true* to one's nature. 'To thine own self be true, Thou canst not then be false to any man.' One way of following this precept is to avoid the kind of self-deception described by Sartre – by being true to the 'self' that stands apart from one's nature or character. But another way consists in being true to one's beliefs, principles or tastes; speaking and acting in accordance with them rather than following, say, the opinions or fashions of the majority. Such a person is 'not afraid to speak out'; nor does he pretend, to himself or to others, that his views and tastes – which make him what he is – coincide with the popular ones, when this is not really so.

This way of being true to oneself is different from Sartre's model; but it is not essentialism either, for the person concerned is not *deducing* a recipe for conduct from his essence or nature. He is merely 'doing what comes naturally' to him, and (provided this is not something vicious) we commend him for his sincerity in this sense.

There are also more subtle ways of being natural (and sincere in that sense), which have to do with the style of a person's conduct rather than with its content. Someone may be criticized for speaking or acting in an 'artificial' or 'affected' way, even though *what* he or she says and does is not under criticism. We are also offended by the person who speaks to us in clichés, jargon or vague abstractions, even if we understand perfectly well what he means. Such people hide themselves, their personal nature, behind a façade of impersonal language. These qualities are hard to define and their presence in a given case may be disputed. They do, however, play an important part in our evaluation of people – though receiving little attention in the standard moral theories.

Is the waiter in Sartre's example guilty of this kind of failing? Here is a man who suppresses his personal nature in order to act out a stereotyped role. Yet in this case we would not feel offended (unless he overdoes it). For, as Sartre rightly observes, the waiter's 'condition is wholly one of ceremony'. Here lies the difference beween him and the person who offends us with affected behaviour or stereotyped language. The waiter is being unnatural in a recognized context, in which such conduct is what we expect and want from him; it is part of the service we pay for. His role-playing is no more offensive than that of the person who carries out an official ceremony or the ballerina who dances according to a prescribed formula.

5   THE LIMITS OF REASON

Contrary to Sartre's view, the rejection of essentialism does not entail that we are left with only one virtue, that of 'sincerity', and without any reason for acting in any particular way. Nor is acting for a reason incompatible with acting freely. But if these points are granted, we may still be left with an 'anguish' about freedom, of the kind described by existentialists. For in many cases, and especially in the big decisions of life, reason may not take us very far. This is especially so if both essentialism and religious belief are rejected.

Dr Johnson, the eighteenth-century sage, was no existentialist. Yet even he could remark that 'to prefer one future mode of life to another, upon just reasons, requires faculties which it has not pleased our Creator to give us'. But scepticism about reason is more characteristic of our time. A number of developments have contributed to this outlook. First, the widespread questioning of religious beliefs has led to the opening up of questions which could previously be answered by appeal to authority. Now as I argued above (pp. 198–9), it is not true that 'if God does not exist, everything is permitted'; the fact that I ought to repay what I have borrowed is not contingent on the existence of God. Nevertheless there are certain questions, for example about sexual relations, which are more difficult than this, and which could previously have been answered, but can no longer be answered, by reasons drawn from religion or tradition. Secondly, society has become more fluid. When Dr Johnson made his remark, there was hardly any question, for the majority of people, of preferring one future mode of life to another. Their station in life was laid down for them by social circumstances, and only a relatively small number could think, in practical terms, of breaking out of this mould. Thirdly, there is the rise of modern technology and the mass production of all kinds of goods which are potential objects of human desire. In choosing among these we can no longer follow the straightforward dictates of human need, for the majority of them are far beyond the need of human beings as such (as distinct from the beings we may *become* under pressure of these goods). Finally, there is a general scepticism resulting from the evidence of what has actually happened as the result of human decision. This is especially so in the public arena. In democratic countries we see again and again that decisions which are taken on the available evidence and on the basis of democratic choice, have results that nobody would choose. Sometimes, no doubt, this is due to corruptions of the system and malpractices of various kinds. But in many cases the question to be decided is just too complicated to admit of a fully rational answer. This is not to deny that reasons are available and considered; but the reasons are nowhere near conclusive, and one cannot tell whether all relevant reasons have been taken into account. On the other hand, in countries ruled by a revolutionary ideology, we often find that a blueprint which promised greater justice and happiness leads to repression and misery.

The modern scepticism is also due to the rise of consequentialism – the view that actions are made right or wrong by their consequences (e.g. the promotion of happiness), and not by backward-looking considerations such as a promise, or a commandment of God. The backward-looking type of reason is more likely to yield a simple, straightforward prescription for action, since the field of reasoning may be restricted to one factor, or a small number of factors, which have already occurred. By contrast, in trying to evaluate an action by its likely consequences, we may need to engage in limitless speculations about the future.

There used to be a saying in the army about the need for being decisive. There are, so the saying went, three ways of responding when a decision is called for: do the right thing, do the wrong thing, and do nothing at all; the last being the worst of the three. In the army, as in other areas of life, we are often faced with a need for decision when the reasons are inconclusive, perhaps due to lack of time. Whether it *is* better to do the wrong thing than nothing at all will obviously depend on the case. But those who are able to make a decision, perhaps pretending to themselves that the case before them is simpler than it really is, will generally have a less troubled and more successful life – even if their decisions are quite often the wrong ones, and perhaps worse than if they had done nothing at all. 'It is not the clear-sighted who lead the world. Great achievements are accomplished in a blessed, warm mental fog.'[43] Existentialists, however, withdraw from decision-making. They are not prepared to pretend to themselves that such decisions are simpler than they really are. When Mathieu declines to join the Party, he 'hasn't enough reasons' for doing so. But could he ever have enough reasons for such a decision? Another person might, so to speak, shut his eyes and take the plunge. He would be 'committing' himself – entrusting his future self, and abdicating its freedom of choice, to the decision taken now (and, in this case, to another authority, the Party). If the existentialist is right, this is bad faith – a betrayal of the freedom which is ours; but the only alternative, it seems, is that of anguish and paralysis.

Through the ages people have regarded freedom as a great benefit – especially when the lack of it prevented them from living as they would wish. But it is possible to have too much freedom. Those who flee from the repression of communist countries to the free countries of the West have sometimes expressed consternation at the decision-making, in great and small matters, that is now thrust upon them. And those of us who live in free societies may be reluctant to face fully the range of choices that is open to us. Perhaps if we really did so, we would not know what to do. The waiter in Sartre's example may after all be deceiving himself in this way. As we saw, it is not certain that this is so, since he may believe, correctly, that this is the only way he has of making a living rather than going hungry. But for many people this is not so. They carry on with a way of life, not because it is the only viable one for them, but because they are reluctant to consider alternatives. Perhaps if they did so fully, they would find too many alternatives and too many imponderable complications to allow of any rational choice. Better to shut one's eyes to the problem, to pretend that one does not really have such a freedom of choice.

6   HOMO LUDENS

If we pretend that there is no freedom of choice, are we guilty of self-deception? Consider a person who has thought about the matter in the way described in the last section, and decides to stay where he is – carrying on with his 'station and its duties'. The person concerned might even be Mathieu, the philosophy teacher – or, for that matter, Sartre himself. Mathieu, as we saw, was told by his communist friend that he 'lives in a void'; he is 'an abstraction, a man who is not really there'. But no one lives in a void. As Bradley remarked, one is 'born not into a desert, but into a living world', 'a member of an individual social organism'. This is also true of Mathieu, however much he may consider his life from the existentialist standpoint. Mathieu, after all, *is* a philosophy teacher; that is the station in which he finds himself. What then should he do, having reached his sceptical conclusion? Should he abandon his role as a teacher of philosophy? (Should not Sartre have given up *his* role as a writer and philosopher after reaching this conclusion?) Why should he 'play at' being a teacher of philosophy, rather than, say, a waiter, a bus conductor or an Arctic explorer (supposing he had these choices)? Again, why choose to do something rather than nothing? Perhaps he reasoned as follows: 'people who are committed to a profession or set of duties generally get a sense of fulfilment from carrying these out and do not feel their lives to be meaningless. I have also experienced this

satisfaction – for example, when one of my students was
doing well as a result of my teaching. But given my existing
abilities, training, etc., I may as well stay in my present
position, and find my satisfaction there. I shall not get
this satisfaction, however, if I am constantly thinking of
alternatives and of the underlying sceptical questions. So I
shall put these things out of my mind and devote myself to
my job, playing the role that is expected of me and doing
it as well as possible.'

A similar point may be made about the role of *tradition* in
our lives. The station in which we find ourselves is not
merely a matter of having such and such work, and other
duties, to perform. There is also the fact that we are born
into a particular tradition in which certain things are
valued, and certain ways of behaving regarded as normal or
admirable. These things come naturally to us, not in the
pre-social sense, but because they are ingrained in the
tradition which, to some extent, makes us what we are.
'The basis of a moral community', writes John Kekes, is
not some 'fundamental principle' or 'overarching ideal'; it is
the 'largely spontaneous, unreflective, customary conduct,
the unarticulated feeling of ease in each other's company,
because there is much that need not be said'.[44] The radical
questioning of the existentialist would undermine this state
of affairs. It is not that he has arguments against these
patterns of conduct; but by his questioning he destroys our
unquestioning acceptance of them. With the decline of
tradition,

> people wonder about the meaning and purpose of their lives
> ... intimacy is increasingly based on joining forces to pursue
> self-interest ... incivility, rather than decency, prevails in
> impersonal social relationships ... People begin to question
> their moral tradition. Spontaneity disappears and self-con-
> sciousness takes it place.[45]

The alternative, again, is to put the sceptical questions out
of our minds, accepting the existing tradition and the
inculcation of it into our children. In this matter it is
important to strike the right balance, for we must not
assume, with certain relativists, that whatever is accepted

within a tradition cannot be criticized from an outside point of view. There are universal conditions of a satisfactory human life, and when these are lacking, the tradition in which this happens can and ought to be criticized. But within these basic constraints, there are many different ways in which life can be lived, and many traditional ways of behaving which we do well to follow unreflectively just because they belong to the tradition into which we are born.

Is it self-deception if we put such questions out of our minds? Of course the waiter (any waiter) would not be wholly unaware of the critical point of view. Perhaps when he is working he is so absorbed in his role that he almost forgets he is a free human being, and in that capacity transcends this or any other role. But he cannot wholly forget it. Suppose we take him aside to question him about his way of life. How does he like the work? What are its satisfactions and disadvantages? What other possibilities might be open to him? We may assume that he would immediately cease his 'ceremony' and adopt the standpoint of a critical spectator, viewing himself and his job 'from the outside'. And yet, when the interview is finished, he will be able to slip back into his role, immersing himself in it as if there were no more to life than being a waiter.

According to Sartre, the man is 'playing' at being a waiter. Now there is indeed a resemblance between him and an actor playing a role in the theatre. Richard Burton is playing Hamlet. He identifies himself with this character, abandons himself to the role, and so on. Is this a state of self-deception? It is akin to it. The audience too are in such a state. They follow the fortunes of the hero and heroine, feeling all sorts of emotions for them and on their behalf. Coleridge spoke of this condition as 'a willing suspension of disbelief'.[46] Are these people deceiving themselves? In a sense they are; they enter into the action of the play, feeling joy or sorrow, hope or fear, for fictional characters, forgetting their own identities and the fact that the whole thing is a show. Yet in another sense there is no deception. 'When the heroine falls into the clutches of the villain, he [the spectator] does not rush out of the theatre and ring up the police.'[47] And when the play is over, actor and spectator resume their normal personalities, and their responsibilities in the real world.

Would it be better if people did not, or could not, abandon themselves to a role or show in these ways? On the contrary, the best actors, the ones we praise and respect, are those who seem to give themselves utterly to their roles; and a good play or novel is one that absorbs us and makes us forget (though not really forget) who and what we are. Again, the actor himself may feel happier with his work, more satisfied and fulfilled, the more he can give himself up to his role, identifying himself with the character in the play. And the same may be true of the person who 'plays at' being a waiter, an auctioneer, or a teacher of philosophy. If this is self-deception, it is so in a benign sense, contributing to human fulfilment, and not a moral failing.

In previous chapters I have discussed a number of human characteristics in connection with the quest for self-realization. Man is a rational animal, a social being, an inquisitive, aesthetic, moral being, and so on. He also has the capacity of radical questioning, as stressed by existentialists. But another characteristic which might be regarded as definitive of man is that of play. *Homo ludens*, claimed J. Huizinga, is no less appropriate a name for the human species than *Homo sapiens*.[48] Moritz Schlick, as we saw in Chapter Two, recommended the life of play as an alternative to the modern obsession with means and ends – 'the curse of purposes'.[49] And according to Schiller, 'man plays only when he is in the full sense of the word a man, and *he is only wholly Man when he is playing*'.[50]

However, play may mean different things. Sartre regarded the play of the waiter as an example of self-deception or bad faith. Yet, in another part of *Being and Nothingness*, he identified play with freedom, *opposing* it to what he called 'the spirit of seriousness' – another example or aspect of bad faith.[51] The 'serious man', he said, is 'of the world'; he imagines that his actions are determined by requirements of 'the world', thereby hiding his freedom from himself.[52] By contrast, 'as soon as a man apprehends himself as free and wishes to use his freedom, his activity is play. The first principle of play is man himself; through it he escapes his natural nature.'[53]

In this passage, Sartre must have meant play as *opposed to* acting out one's professional role; for example, playing games, as opposed to playing the role of a waiter.[54] Now it is true that play in this sense is free as far as the demands of the world are concerned. One does not need to play games as one needs to eat, or to perform one's duties to others; and the consequences of *not* playing are not serious, as are those of not meeting the demands of the world. Yet in other ways play is not free. To say that through play man 'escapes his nature' is not correct, for the desire to play, in one sense or another, is part of human nature. Again, if by 'play' is meant playing a game, then one is constrained by the rules of the game. Now it may be said that the rules are themselves freely chosen (and not imposed by 'the world'). According to Sartre, 'man himself' sets the rules, and 'consents to play only according to the rules which he himself has established and defined'.[55] However, there is no such person as 'man himself'; and if I want to play a game, say of chess or football, then I must adhere to rules which were not established by me. In this respect playing a game is no more free than playing the role of a waiter or a role in the theatre.

When Schlick spoke of play, he must have meant something else again. He regarded youth as the time of play (see Chapter Two). 'Here', he wrote, 'we can learn from the *child*. Before he has yet been caught in the net of purposes ... [he] is capable of the purest joy.'[56] Now this may be plausible if we think of *childish* games – games of make-believe which are played without any set purpose or rules. In this case the child (as we say) 'uses his imagination' as he proceeds and is not 'caught in a net of purposes'. There is also a resemblance between this and the 'play' of the creative artist. But when we turn to games like chess or football, and competitive sports like athletics, we find a very different kind of play. In this case, purpose and the schema of means and end, are all-important. The purpose of the activity – winning – is defined by its rules, and so are the means by which this end is to be achieved. What appeals to us about this kind of play is not that it is free of constraint or not directed to an end, but, on the contrary, that the constraints and the end are *better defined* than those of ordinary life.

> Here we come across [a] very positive feature of play; it
> creates order, *is* order. Into an imperfect world and into the
> confusion of life it brings a temporary, a limited perfection.
> Play demands order absolute and supreme. The least deviation
> from it 'spoils the game', robs it of its character and makes
> it worthless.[57]

Now one way of bringing this order into the world is by
inventing systems of rules and purposes which correspond to
no human need – other than the craving for order itself; and
this is what we have in the case of games and sports. But
another way is to 'play reality', so to speak, as if it were a
game, treating our 'serious' concerns in the world in a spirit
of play. The prevalence of this kind of play in human affairs
was brought out by Huizinga. Ranging over activities such
as law, war, science, art and commerce, both past and
present, he was able to show that to a large extent these
activities resemble play, contain elements of play, or are
done in a spirit of play. The use of statistics in commerce,
for example, 'could not fail to introduce a sporting element
into economic life'.[58] He described how 'the great business
concerns deliberately instil the play-spirit into their workers
so as to step up production' and quoted from the speech of
'a captain of industry' who assured his audience that he had
never 'regarded the business as a task, but always as a
game'.[59] Now business is not merely a game, and the
stepping up of production is not done merely from motives
of sport. But anyone who has been involved in such activities
will know that 'the sporting side' is part of the motivation
and experience of them. This is also confirmed by the success
of business-like games, such as Monopoly.

A similar motivation is at work in the bestowing of tokens
of achievement in various walks of life. The player of a
game scores points or takes pieces, and gets a peculiar
satisfaction from this. Similarly, the soldier receives a medal,
the distinguished academic an honorary title, and the student
an examination grade or diploma. The power of such
incentives to students is well known, and it goes far beyond
mere utility in the 'real world'. This power is also evident

in the case of 'weight watchers', where the reduction of surplus weight is treated as a kind of game, with scores being kept and so on; in the success of 'sponsored walks'; and in various other cases.

The game-like quality of warfare (to take another example) has often been noticed. Throughout history wars have been fought in a spirit of play, not for the sake of real advantages, but for such artificial ends as honour.[60] Sometimes, again, the conduct of war has been governed by artificial rules, as when, in the fourteenth century, 'chivalry maintained that the combat must be personal and bodily; missiles that permitted combat at a distance were held in scorn'.[61] Such behaviour, as we might say, would not be 'playing the game'. On the other hand, in speaking of games in the primary sense, the terminology of warfare is often used. Thus, in a football match, there is attack and defence, victory, crushing defeat, and so on.

Finally, there is the playing of roles as distinct from games. In this sense, the play of the waiter is akin to that of the dramatic actor; and both are satisfying in their way.

The human propensity for playing, for finding meaning in play and for projecting the spirit of play into all kinds of activities, is a remedy for the existentialist's anguish, and for the lack of an ultimate purpose of life or prescription for living. If we can deduce such prescriptions neither from a natural nor from a supernatural source (neither from essentialism nor from a transcendental realm of value), we can still help ourselves through the spirit of play, finding fulfilment in the playing of a role or in regarding what we do as a kind of game. This is a kind of self-deception, but it is not irrational or morally wrong. We are, rather, taking advantage of certain propensities of man, of *Homo ludens*, which make life more satisfying than it would otherwise be.

NOTES

1   *The Politics*, p. 60.
2   *Ibid.*
3   *Ibid.*

4   *Ibid.*, pp. 60–1.
5   Bradley, F. H. (1962) 'My Station and its Duties', in *Ethical Studies*, Oxford University Press, p. 168.
6   *Ibid.*, p. 171.
7   *Ibid.*, p. 166.
8   *Ibid.*, p. 174.
9   *Ibid.*, p. 173.
10 *Ibid.*, p. 181.
11 *Ibid.*
12 *Ibid.*, p. 198.
13 Sartre, *op. cit.*, p. 26. *Existentialism and Humanism* is the text of a lecture given by Sartre in 1945, first published (in French) in 1946, and translated and reprinted many times. Although Sartre regretted its publication, it is more accessible to the reader than the formidable, though more authoritative, *Being and Nothingness*, which first appeared in 1943. In what follows, I draw freely on passages from both works, as well as from his novels. My intention is not to provide a complete account of Sartre's views, but to present certain lines of thought which are of special relevance to this book.

  Similarly, my discussion of Bradley is based only on one of his essays, and does not do justice to other aspects of his thought.
14 *Ibid.*, p. 28.
15 *Ibid.*, p.50.
16 Sartre, J.-P. (1958) *Being and Nothingness*, Methuen, p. 63.
17 *Ibid.*, p. 552.
18 *Ibid.*, p. 59.
19 *Ibid.*
20 *Ibid.*, p. 60. A similar state of mind is described in a novel by Saul Bellow:
    He exclaimed mentally, Marry me! Be my wife! End my troubles! – and was staggered by his rashness, his weakness and by the characteristic nature of such an outburst, for he saw how very neurotic and typical it was ... Ah, poor fellow! – and Herzog momentarily joined the objective world in looking down on himself. He too could smile at Herzog and despise him. But there still remained the fact. I am Herzog. I have to *be* that man.
    (Bellow, Saul (1969) *Herzog*, Penguin edn, pp. 72–3.)
21 *Existentialism and Humanism*, p. 51.
22 *Ibid.*, p. 31.
23 *Ibid.*
24 *Ibid.*, p. 49.
25 *Ibid.*, p. 50.

26 *Ibid.*
27 *Being and Nothingness*, p. 62.
28 *Ibid.*
29 *Ibid.*
30 *Ibid.*, p. 439.
31 *Existentialism and Humanism*, p. 34.
32 *Ibid.*, p. 35.
33 Sartre, J.-P. (1961) *The Age of Reason*, Penguin, p. 118.
34 *Existentialism and Humanism*, p. 51.
35 On the 'analytic' character of some moral obligations, see Hanfling, 'Promises, Games and Institutions', *ibid.*
36 *Existentialism and Humanism*, pp. 33–4.
37 *Ibid.*, p. 7.
38 *Being and Nothingness*, p. 60.
39 Sartre, J.-P. (1961) *The Reprieve*, Penguin.
40 In Hardy's *The Trumpet Major*, the toss of a coin is itself subjected to a similar critique. Bob Loveday, after considering whether he should go after a woman with whom he has had connections, resorts to the toss of a coin with positive result. But, having gone some distance in pursuit, a new thought occurs to him: 'I'll not be ruled by the toss of a coin.' With this expression of freedom he abandons the pursuit and returns home. Philippe's speech ('To go or not to go . . .') is presumably meant to throw an existentialist light on Hamlet's predicament.
41 The sublimation of the concept of knowledge is discussed in Hanfling, O. (1987) 'How is Scepticism Possible?', *Philosophy*.
42 Kant's example of the person who is not kind by nature, but acts kindly in spite of this, is closer to Sartre's ideal. However, Kant's view is also rejected by Sartre, because according to it there is a universal 'moral law' (the 'Categorical Imperative') to which all rational beings are subject.
43 Conrad, Joseph (1970 edn) *Victory*, Penguin Modern Classics.
44 Kekes, John (1985) 'Moral Tradition', *Philosophical Investigations*, 8, pp. 260–1.
45 *Ibid.*, p. 268.
46 See Price, H. H. (1969) *Belief*, Allen & Unwin, pp. 307 ff.; and Hanfling, O. (1983) 'Real Life, Art and the Grammar of Feelings', *Philosophy*, 58.
47 Price, *op. cit.*, p. 311.
48 Huizinga, J. (1970) *Homo Ludens*, Paladin, p. 17.
49 Schlick, *op. cit.*, p. 24.
50 Schiller, J. C. F. (1794–5) *Letters on the Aesthetic Education of Mankind*, Letter 15.

51 *Being and Nothingness*, p. 580.
52 *Ibid.*
53 *Ibid.*, pp. 580–1.
54 Sartre speaks of games in a parallel passage in the (1984) *War Diaries*, Verso Editions, p. 326.
55 *Being and Nothingness*, p. 581.
56 Schlick, *op. cit.*, p. 120.
57 *Homo Ludens*, p. 29.
58 *Ibid.*, p. 226.
59 *Ibid.*, p. 227.
60 Falstaff's denunciation of honour has not altered this (Shakespeare, *Henry IV*, Part I, V. 127 ff.).
61 Tuchman, B. (1979) *A Distant Mirror*, Macmillan, p. 86.

Index

Index by Justyn Balinski